Lyrical Strategies

Lyrical Strategies

The Poetics of the Twentieth-Century American Novel

✦

Katie Owens-Murphy

NORTHWESTERN UNIVERSITY PRESS
EVANSTON, ILLINOIS

Northwestern University Press
www.nupress.northwestern.edu

Printed in the United States of America

10 9 8 7 6 5 4 3 2 1

Library of Congress Cataloging-in-Publication Data

Names: Owens-Murphy, Katie, author.
Title: Lyrical strategies : the poetics of the twentieth-century American novel / Katie Owens-Murphy.
Description: Evanston, Illinois : Northwestern University Press, 2018. | Includes bibliographical references and index.
Identifiers: LCCN 2017028640 | ISBN 9780810136557 (cloth : alk. paper) | ISBN 9780810136540 (pbk. : alk. paper) | ISBN 9780810136564 (e-book)
Subjects: LCSH: American fiction—20th century—History and criticism. | Style, Literary.
Classification: LCC PS379 .O924 2018 | DDC 813.509—dc23
LC record available at https://lccn.loc.gov/2017028640

For my husband and daughter

CONTENTS

ACKNOWLEDGMENTS

I was fortunate to receive tremendous help and feedback on this project from its inception to its completion. Kit Hume and Robert Caserio deserve the first thanks for their tireless efforts to help me to conceive, shape, and reshape this manuscript; I am forever grateful to them for their direction, encouragement, and mentorship. Robin Schulze, Jack Selzer, and Kathy Grossman also made significant contributions to various chapters. Brian McHale and Jesse Matz helped me bolster my overarching argument and nuance my readings of individual texts. Heather Dubrow, Evan Brier, and David Hadar lent their time and expertise to help me to recalibrate chapter 6. The anonymous readers' reports solicited by Northwestern University Press provided excellent and sharp feedback on the project as a whole. Finally, Penn State's Center for American Literary Studies and Milton B. Dolinger Fellowship in the WWII Era, as well as the University of North Alabama's Laura Harrison Distinguished Professor of English Award, provided funding and course releases that also facilitated the development and completion of this project.

Sterling Brown's "Bitter Fruit of the Tree" is reprinted with the permission of Elizabeth A. Dennis from *The Collected Poems of Sterling A. Brown*, edited by Michael S. Harper, copyright © 1980. George Szirtes's "Piano" is reprinted with the permission of Bloodaxe Books from *New and Collected Poems*, copyright © 2008. Li-Young Lee's "Persimmons" is reprinted with the permission of The Permissions Company, Inc., on behalf of BOA Editions, Ltd., from *Rose*, copyright © 1986. Billy Collins's "Introduction to Poetry" is reprinted with the permission of the University of Arkansas Press from *The Apple That Astonished Paris*, copyright © 1988. Lucille Clifton's "good times" is reprinted with the permission of The Permissions Company, Inc., on behalf of BOA Editions, Ltd., from *The Collected Poems of Lucille Clifton,* copyright © 1987.

PREFACE

This study rests on the counterintuitive claim that novels should not necessarily be read as novels. In fact, it asks that we abandon our common-sense reading practices by reexamining canonical works of twentieth-century American fiction through the lens of lyric poetry. Why should we adopt this approach, given that lyric and narrative have often been defined in contradistinction to each other? Why take this approach, now that lyric poetry has lost so much of its cultural and institutional power, whereas the novel remains so pervasive that it has become a synecdoche for literature in general?

Such an undertaking, I argue, enables us to better navigate a type of novel that looks quite different from the novel in its earlier iterations. As a number of critics have noted, modern and contemporary novels are remarkably nonnarrative in both form and content, if we understand fiction as requiring a dynamic plot propelled by sequential (if not necessarily chronological) action.[1] Conspicuously lacking plot, external action, and logical temporal succession, many of our most acclaimed American novels from the last century contain ontological ambiguities that undermine the traditional staples of narrative fiction, though these same ambiguities lie at the heart of the lyric tradition. The lyric—a dynamic genre that has changed over time, and whose origins reach all the way back to the ancient world—has eluded many of the definitions critics have attempted to fasten to it, as chapter 1 demonstrates. Subsequently, I offer here a more conceptually flexible definition that helps us think productively about lyric and narrative in terms of their divergent ontological commitments, as demonstrated by a cluster of key tropes: repetition, polysyndeton, metaphor, dramatic personae, and exclusive address.

These tropes simultaneously showcase the lyric's detachment from, and narrative's entrenchment in, the ontological firmness that serves as the foundation for plot. Fundamentally, the lyric is a site of liminality: its reliance on repetition causes it to vacillate between movement and stasis, while its manipulation of syntax for heightened affective realism vacillates between mimesis and artifice; its extended metaphors hover between the literal and the figurative, just as the psychological unfolding of dramatic personae hovers between the real and the imagined; and its habitual use of the exclusive direct address positions its silent addressee (and silent reader) somewhere between presence and absence. Thus, lyric poetry routinely deploys tropes that toy with the reality and concreteness narrative fiction tends to adopt as its starting point.

While several of these strategies, such as repetition and figuration, are not necessarily exclusive to the lyric tradition because they occur in poetry more broadly, the relative brevity of the lyric poem intensifies these tropes, rendering them ever more pronounced in shorter forms. To some degree, of course, brevity is in the eye of the beholder: as poet-critic Elder Olson once playfully wrote, "Brief? How brief? An epigram is shorter" (1964, 1). Yet critics such as Alasdair Fowler and, more recently, Mark Jeffreys have convincingly argued for compactness as perhaps lyric poetry's primary defining feature precisely because of its association with the epigram in the sixteenth and seventeenth centuries: "As the epigram rose in favor, it not only influenced lyric, it became generically associated with lyric, in both theory and practice, through its merging with the primary Petrarchan lyric form, the sonnet" (1994, 122). Furthermore, they argue, the growing popularity of the epigram coincided with the rise of the anthology, both of which encouraged lyric poets to privilege efficiency over length (Fowler 1982, 222; Jeffreys 1994, 121). The result is succinctness, an extreme version of the "cognitive compression" that inheres in all language when we compress complex ideas into linguistic shorthand (Jeffreys 1994, 129).

Brevity—itself a quality that resists narrative structure—serves as a conceptual pressure cooker, working to compress and enhance poetic strategies such as repetition that are already deeply antinarrative in form as well as function. My readings of lyric poems in the following chapters demonstrate the relationship between brevity and lyricality in ways that also reveal the poems' resistance to narrative models of linear progression, eventfulness, and ontological firmness. What happens, however, when these tropes are extended over the length of a novel is another question this study seeks to explore. Consequently, a transgeneric framework enables us to investigate not only the outermost limits of narrative (how "lyrical" can a novel become before it ceases to be narrative?) but also the outermost limits of lyric (what happens to a lyric trope when it is swells to encompass two-hundred-plus pages of text?).

My purpose, however, is not to stake out definition claims about what constitutes lyric or narrative; I prefer to articulate generic difference in terms of degree rather than kind, as my discussion of narrativity and lyricality in chapter 1 will show. Instead, I hope to unsettle the rigidity that pervades our current and historical understandings of literary kinds. Prevailing notions of genre exaggerate differences among literary categories in ways that prevent us from seeing important areas of overlap. This project, therefore, is part of a growing body of work aimed at expanding the scope of narrative theory, which has largely neglected poetry, even narrative poetry, in favor of prose fiction.[2] Even more broadly, however, *Lyrical Strategies* represents an intervention in the field of literary studies that seeks to return our attention to lyrical tropes and their attendant reading practices. The study of lyricality is valuable not only for its own sake but also, I will argue, for a more complete understanding of the twentieth-century American novel.

Chapter 1, "Genres in Contest," situates this project within classical literary criticism's tripartite separation of literature into lyric, narrative, and dramatic forms, a division that has been generally upheld and reinforced by twentieth-century genre critics from Northrop Frye to Jonathan Culler. Despite its usefulness on a heuristic level, this model has not only obscured important kinships that cut across literary genres but effectively placed genres in competition for various forms of cultural and institutional power. Many twentieth-century American writers, however, seek to transgress the very generic boundaries scholars police, experimenting with elements of both lyricality and narrativity in their writing.

The rest of the study examines lyrical strategies at multiple levels and scales ranging from the word to the line to the work as a whole. Early chapters focus on smaller units of meaning—phrases and refrains, syntax and lineation—and their relationship to the larger works they constitute. Chapter 2, "Repetition and Insistence," explores the lyrical role of repetition in narrative texts by Gertrude Stein, Jean Toomer, John Dos Passos, and Kathy Acker. The repetition of sound patterns for dramatic, mnemonic, or aural effect is commonplace in poetry, which began as an auditory literary form, yet repetition is also a favorite device of experimental novelists, who replicate words, phrases, and in some cases, entire paragraphs in ways that disrupt the sequential progressions we expect from narrative fiction. As a result, these works foreground simultaneity over a narrative-oriented model that privileges a linear progression from beginnings toward endings. Chapter 3, "Rhythm and Insubordination," examines the role of polysyndeton, the deliberately repetitive use of coordinating conjunctions for dramatic rhetorical effect, in prose fiction. In the formally traditional poetry of earlier periods, polysyndetic coordinations are closely aligned with both meter and lineation, but this device creates a more flexible rhythm in the novelistic prose of Hemingway, Faulkner, Don DeLillo, and Cormac McCarthy. Because these coordinations grant equal significance to each term in the construction, polysyndeton also deliberately flattens the hierarchical arrangement of events and details that is typical of narrative fiction. The forms of repetition I trace in these chapters also reveal the lyric's complicated relationship to mimesis. Swinging between artifice and realism, these devices draw our attention to artistic form while seeking to depict reality with greater emotional intensity.

The remaining chapters discuss lyrical principles that govern novels on broader structural levels and with greater ontological ramifications. Chapter 4, "Metaphysical Conceit," examines the function of protracted metaphors in novels by Henry Miller, Zora Neale Hurston, Toni Morrison, and Russell Banks. While narrative fiction typically advances plot through literal, rather than metaphorical, action, this chapter considers novels that develop a single extended metaphor in a way that deliberately subordinates external events to the realm of figuration. Chapter 5, "Dramatic Personae," centers on novels by Henry James, Vladimir Nabokov, Bret Easton Ellis, and Chuck

Palahniuk that feature highly dramatized narrators. Twentieth-century fiction is known for its use of the unreliable narrator, but this device has an important ontological dimension that is highlighted by its generic precursor, the Victorian dramatic monologue. These works heighten characterization at the expense of plot, subordinating external events to the complex psychology of a dramatic speaker. Consequently, this device undermines plot in a radical way: has *American Psycho*'s Patrick Bateman committed *any* of the murders he reports? Chapter 6, "Exclusive Address," examines the other end of this equation—the addressee—by treating the use of the direct address in novels by Philip Roth, Louise Erdrich, Gloria Naylor, and Marilynne Robinson. These works feature first-person, character-bound narrators addressing a character-bound addressee who is *not* the reader. A number of novelists have used this device to frame intimate, even embarrassing narratives delivered by guarded narrators who place a premium on their privacy: in *Portnoy's Complaint*, for example, a patient addresses his therapist within the confines of their private counseling session together. The spectral presence of these silent addressees mirrors the spectral presence of readers: we are suspended somewhere between judgment and compassion as we awkwardly eavesdrop on a private confession not immediately intended for us.

Inevitably, these categories overlap. The treatment of repetition at the level of the word or phrase (chapter 1) bleeds into the treatment of repetition at the level of syntax (chapter 2). Novels that invoke the exclusive address (chapter 6) tend also to have dramatized, if not necessarily "unreliable," narrators (chapter 5). Some authors exhibit writing styles that might easily fall into more than one category, but I have tried to represent a broad range of novelists to better demonstrate the prevalence of lyrical techniques in American prose fiction. A number of the writers treated here are lyric poets as well as novelists, though they are much better known for their narrative fiction: Gertrude Stein, John Dos Passos, Vladimir Nabokov, Toni Morrison, Louise Erdrich, and Russell Banks, not to mention Faulkner and Hemingway, both of whom experimented (however unsuccessfully) with poetry in the early part of their careers. Nearly all of the authors I address have been labeled "poetic" or "lyrical" in one book review or another. This project provides one account of what, precisely, such labels might mean. To redress what I diagnose in chapter 1 as a disjunction between critics, who tend to separate genres, and writers, who tend to merge them, I also invoke theorists who are also poets and fiction writers—Pound, Eliot, Stein, Faulkner, Joan Retallack, Robert Pinsky, John Hollander, and Lyn Hejinian.

This project not only points to the permeability of generic borders; it offers fresh readings of canonical works of American fiction made possible by a more flexible approach to literary forms. Comparative studies of genre are rare, since our institutional partitioning of literature into genres produces specialists who focus on one area only: as Brian McHale puts it, "Some scholars specialize in narrative; others specialize in poetry; few specialize in both"

(2009, 12). Critics throughout the twentieth century have reinforced these divisions in their scholarship and course titles, but writers were very interested in breaking down the barriers that literary criticism since Plato has erected between literary forms. Just as twentieth-century poets were looking to reinvent lyric for a new era, so fiction writers were changing the face of narrative by experimenting with rhetorical strategies that erstwhile belonged to the realm of the lyric. By reversing our conventional reading practices, this project produces new readings of narrative texts by shifting our attention, paradoxically, to their nonnarrative components.

Lyrical Strategies

Chapter 1

✦

Genres in Contest

"We are living in the age of the Narrative Turn," writes James Phelan in the fortieth-anniversary edition of Scholes and Kellogg's *The Nature of Narrative*, "an era when narrative is widely celebrated and studied for its ubiquity and importance. Doctors, lawyers, psychologists, business men and women, politicians, and political pundits of all stripes are just a few of the groups who now regard narrative as the Queen of Discourse and an essential component of their work" (Phelan 2006, 285). Narrative is thriving and its significance uncontested, Phelan asserts; it has even broadened its scope to include a range of nonliterary discourses. As an example, he offers the 2004 U.S. presidential election: "Democratic politicians contended that their candidate John Kerry lost to George W. Bush because Kerry failed to articulate his vision for an improved America in a clear and persuasive narrative."

In response to the tyranny of the "Narrative Turn," critics have begun to lament the academy's neglect of lyric poetry, a genre that has traditionally been defined in contradistinction to narrative prose. Mutlu Blasing argues that our "current constructions of the 'discipline' of literary study, which emphasize the social, economic, or political determinants of literary production," have led to "the disciplinary censoring of poetry," since—unlike the novel—lyric poetry's focus on language does not translate easily into these larger cultural-political frameworks (2006, 4–5). Jonathan Culler has also objected to lyric poetry's marginalized status in literary studies, arguing that "narrative has become the norm of literature" at the expense of the lyric poem, which—when studied at all—"is frequently assimilated . . . to the model of narrative fiction" (2008, 201). While lyric thrives in the outside world of poetry readings and online publications, he argues, it has been relegated to the institutional margins of an academy in which "narrative is treated not as one possible literary form but as the very condition of experience." More recently, he has suggested another possibility: that we simply "lack an adequate theory of the lyric," which is too often and too simply defined against the novel, as my first chapter will also demonstrate (2015, 2).

Genres vie for cultural, commercial, and institutional power, and in the contest of genres, narrative has emerged the clear victor. At least, this is the way twenty-first-century criticism has articulated the relationship between lyric and narrative forms.[1] These state-of-the-field assessments rest on three assumptions this project seeks to overturn: a clear separation among generic forms, a relationship among forms that is essentially antagonistic, and the defeat of lyric poetry in the face of narrative's ascendancy. Pronouncements like these do not adequately account for the formal hybridity of twentieth-century literature or for the cross-generic projects upon which many modern and contemporary writers were explicitly embarking. From where have we inherited these positions about genre, which prevent us from seeing important interconnections among literary kinds?

The tripartite partitioning of literature into lyric, drama, and narrative (or "epic") and the subsequent rivalry among these genres has a long history in Western literary theory. In fact, our basic attitudes about genre can be traced back to the writings of Plato and Aristotle, both of whom created a tripartite division of literature that even today remains largely intact. Plato's *Republic* famously sorted literary kinds according to the degree of mimesis they achieve. For Plato's Socrates, literature's power to represent or "imitate" reality is dangerous, given its potential to seduce citizens of the ideal Republic away from the true realm of the Forms, which is accessed through philosophical inquiry alone. Narratives that are relayed through indirect discourse are the least deceitful of literary kinds, since they maintain the voice of a single speaker, unlike most epic poetry, which frequently disguises the narrator's voice through the direct dialogue of its characters; worse still is the dramatic form, in which the narrator furtively disappears altogether (Plato 1997, 393a–394c).[2] According to Socrates, poets are reckless imitators who appeal to the irrational part of the soul and create images "that are far removed from the truth" (605c). For this reason, he suggests, "lyric odes and songs" are the most dangerous of all genres. Consisting of "three elements—words, harmonic mode, and rhythm" (398d), the grace and beauty of the lyric make these imitations palatable, even downright pleasurable: "He speaks with meter, rhythm, and harmony, for if you strip a poet's works of their musical colorings and take them by themselves, I think you know what they look like" (601b). The poets represent such a threat to the realm of universal Forms that Socrates bans them altogether from his ideal society. They may reenter the Republic, Socrates judiciously offers, once they can rationally justify their art—naturally, in the dialectical style of philosophical discourse.

In the *Poetics*, Aristotle builds on Plato's diegetic/mimetic distinctions, creating a literary taxonomy based not only on modes of representation but also on unity, harmony, and scope. He concludes that tragedy is the highest literary form, superior to comedy as well as both epic and lyric poetry, since only tragedy possesses the proper degree of "magnitude" and "order," upon which beautiful art depends (1984, 1450b35). Whereas Plato's Socrates presents mimesis as a dangerous and misleading quality of art, Aristotle considers imitation to be a natural and healthy human tendency; consequently, while Socrates condemns drama for creating the illusion of reality, Aristotle praises it for this very reason: "Its reality of presentation is felt in the play as read, as well as in the play as acted" (1462b). Because Aristotle values mimetic art that is grounded in plot and action, he hardly dwells on lyric (here, specifically dithyrambic) poetry at all, spending most of his *Poetics* comparing and contrasting tragedy and epic in order to establish tragedy's superiority. The scope of epic poetry is too large and unwieldy, he decides, since it contains action that has "no fixed limit of time, whereas Tragedy endeavours to keep as far as possible within a single circuit of the sun, or something near that" (1449b10–15); and because Tragedy presents "an imitation of an action that is complete in itself" (1450b20–25), it is more unified and "comprehensible as a whole" (1451a10).

These formulations may appear outdated to the modern critic, but Plato and Aristotle established literary taxonomies that have persisted and set the tone for genre criticism in the Western tradition for over two millennia. Modern critics have maintained the classical separation of literature into lyric, narrative, and dramatic forms with emphasis on the distinctions among these groupings. They have also maintained the evaluative privileging of one genre over all others based on loaded and circular sets of criteria. While the uses and definitions of genres have undoubtedly changed over time, a brief survey of twentieth-century genre criticism demonstrates that the classical taxonomy endures.

Early twentieth-century genre critics not only reaffirm the classical taxonomy, but generally uphold Wordsworth's circumscribed notion of the lyric as the realm of private emotion—the "spontaneous overflow of powerful feelings" ([1805] 2007, 62)—in contradistinction to the more varied, textured, and dynamic storytelling functions of narrative. Bliss Perry, John Erskine, Charles Mills Gayley, and Benjamin Putnam Kurtz—modernist literary critics who were highly influential in their own time, though they have since faded into obscurity—all corroborate these distinctions in various essays and textbooks that attempt to dissect and classify literary forms.[3] Even more striking, however, than their validation of generic difference is their near-uniform condemnation of generic hybridity. Perry stakes out a definitive boundary between poetry and prose, arguing that the commingling of genres produces disastrous results: "At present nothing is to be gained, and much has evidently been lost, by confusing the territories of prose and verse, and producing, under the name of 'prose poetry' and the 'poetic short story,' a mass of nondescript gelatinous rhetoric which can be classified as neither flesh, fowl, nor good red herring" (1902, 44). In an essay on "the new poetry" of the emerging modernist writers, Erskine attributes the critical unpopularity of these new forms to their reliance on the techniques of prose fiction: "The main point is that the new poetry inherits its style from a prose ancestry and takes its methods and its subjects from the tradition of the novel; and we who like or dislike what we see are none the less witnessing one of those mutations by which from time to time literature re-invigorates itself, pouring old wine into new bottles or new wine into old bottles" (1920b, 109–10). Though Erskine here offers a defense of "the new poetry," he too casts these lyric-prose hybrids as aberrations or "mutations" that serve their purpose only insofar as they push genres to redefine themselves for a new era. The analogy he supplies also suggests that this redefinition is largely superficial—the same content in a new container, or else vice versa, an articulation that casts the blending of lyric and narrative as a predictable process in which form and content remain separate. Gayley and Kurtz likewise suggest that genres are natural kinds whose boundaries cannot be breached: "The authors can only say that they believe that types of a sort do exist, subject to gradual variation. By a constant factor are fixed the only possible moulds or channels of communication and, therefore, the primary types,—as for instance within the realm of poetry, the lyric, narrative, and dramatic" (1920, v). Genres are "fixed" by properties that remain "constant" across time and space—thus, Gayley and Kurtz appeal to the notions of transhistorical permanence and inflexibility that underpinned classical conceptions of genre.

Beyond the 1920s, literary critics have continued to restrict lyric poetry to the solipsistic realm of individual expression in contradistinction to the novel, whose scope becomes ever more expansive. Like Plato's Socrates, Mikhail Bakhtin formulates the distinction between lyric and narrative in diegetic terms in his essay "Discourse in the Novel" (1934–35), though he reverses Socrates's value judgments about the two genres. Whereas the lyric imposes an artificial unity by maintaining a single voice, that of the poet, the novel incorporates a robust variety of social discourses into its literary fabric:

> In the majority of poetic genres, the unity of the language system and the unity (and uniqueness) of the poet's individuality as reflected in his language and speech, which is directly realized in this unity, are indispensable prerequisites of poetic style. The novel, however, not only does not require these conditions but (as we have said) even makes of the internal stratification of language, of its social heteroglossia and the variety of individual voices in it, the prerequisite for authentic novelistic prose. (1981, 264)

The lyric expresses "the monologic utterance of the individual" (269); the novel, by contrast, is a socially democratic form that includes a range of dialects, languages, and other modes of discourse.

The final section of Northrop Frye's *Anatomy of Criticism* (1957), "Theory of Genres," further circumscribes lyric's capabilities by casting its speaker as not only individual but also completely private. Frye upholds John Stuart Mill's definition of lyric as "the utterance that is overheard" (249), even intensifying this point later in the essay: "The lyric is the genre in which the poet, like the ironic writer, turns his back on the audience" (271). Here, he articulates the relationship between the lyric poet and his audience in terms that suggest hostility and abandonment. Scholes and Kellogg's landmark work *The Nature of Narrative* (1966) reiterates this definition, creating sharp distinctions among narrative, drama, and lyric based on the position (or absence) of the "story-teller" in each genre: "By narrative we mean all those literary works which are distinguished by two characteristics: the presence of a story and a story-teller. A drama is a story without a story-teller. . . . A lyric, like a drama, is a direct presentation, in which a single actor, the poet or his surrogate, sings, or muses, or speaks for us to hear or overhear" (Scholes, Phelan, and Kellogg 2006, 4).

Contemporary theorists have continued to advance this definition of lyric as both private and emotional. In *The Pursuit of Signs* (1981), Jonathan Culler identifies Frye's conflation of genre (lyric) with a single rhetorical device (apostrophe) but insists that there is "good reason for it" (137). Here, Culler essentially reproduces Frye's conception of lyrics as invocations that "turn away from empirical listeners" and that "serve as intensifiers, as images of invested passion" (137–38), though more recently he has relaxed this Romantic conception by pointing to the lyric's historical relationship with forms of "social engagement" such as the epideictic lyric of ancient Greece (2015, 306). Similarly, W. R. Johnson's *The Idea of Lyric* (1982) argues that classical lyric discourse is distinguished by the "I/You" dynamic between speaker and audience; the "virtual disappearance of the lyric 'You' " in Romantic and modern poetry, however, marks the genre's shift away from rhetorical exchange toward a more solipsistic meditation (8). Helen Vendler also opposes lyric poetry to the so-called social genres of epic, fiction, and drama, which "make us look at the wide panorama of a social group—a nation, a village, a family" (2002, xlii). Though she does not agree that the lyric is "overheard," arguing instead that the lyric speaker always invites the reader to adopt his or her subject position, she does maintain, alongside Frye and Culler, that the lyric is "the genre of private life: it is what we say to ourselves when we are alone. There may be an addressee in lyric (God, or a beloved), but the addressee is always absent. . . . [T]he lyric represents a moment of inner meditation." Thus, even lyric poetry's defenders tend to align lyricality with solipsism, while narrative swells to include nearly all forms of "social" discourse from fiction to politics and law. More importantly, however, each critic uses his or her definition to accentuate and exacerbate differences among lyric forms. In both of his seminal works, Culler asserts that the apostrophe "works against narrative and its accompaniments: sequentiality, causality, time, teleological meaning" (1981, 149; 2015, 225); indeed, one of the reasons this device retains such significance for Culler is because it unearths what he takes to be a natural division between narrative fiction and lyric poetry.

Certainly, there is much value and utility to be found in these conceptual frameworks; critics are right to point out that lyric and narrative have divergent rhetorical aims and objectives. Yet genre critics continue to frame the differences between lyric and narrative in ways that not only portray them as mutually exclusive but also place them in direct competition—more often than not, at the expense of lyric and toward the exaltation of the novel. Anticipating the "Narrative Turn" celebrated by contemporary narrative theory, Bliss Perry argues that lyric may be the "finer art" but that narrative fiction is "the great modern art. By means of it we are brought into contact with modern ideas, with the tumultuous, insistent life of the present" (1920, 22). Perry's evaluation of the novel is echoed by Bakhtin, for whom the novel is the only form that bears on the contemporary moment: "The novel has become the leading hero in the drama of literary development in our time precisely because it best of all reflects the tendencies of a new world still in the making" (1981, 7). According to Bakhtin, the lyric is ideologically, as well as stylistically, problematic: whereas the heteroglossia of the novel is linked to a democratic poetics that allows for a variety of types of social discourse, the unity imposed by the lyric voice results in linguistic "enslavement" (271).

In fact, Bakhtin's analysis is part of a larger strain of Marxist literary criticism that famously privileges the novel over other forms, especially the lyric, because of the novel's distinctive capacity for registering social and economic inequalities. György Lukács has lauded the realist novel for its ability to counter, by "measuring them against social reality," the bourgeois "reactionary prejudices" that are produced and reproduced under capitalism ([1938] 2001, 1040); whereas the novel has the ability to "liberate from the bonds of sheer brutal materiality," he argues, poetic verse "can only weave a garland of freedom round something that has already been liberated from all fetters" (1971, 58). For Fredric Jameson, narrative is essential to the historiography upon which Marxism is premised, since only narrative can provide a coherent account of "political history, in the narrow sense of punctual event and a chroniclelike sequence of happenings in time; then of society, in the now already less diachronic and time-bound sense of a constitutive tension and struggle between social classes; and, ultimately, of history now conceived in its vastest sense of the sequence of modes of production and the succession and destiny of the various human social formations" (1981, 75). Such Marxist assessments often cast the novel as the more social, and socially responsible, of the two forms, a view that is bolstered—however inadvertently—by critics who cast the lyric as a distinctly solipsistic utterance.[4]

While genre criticism in the twentieth century has followed classical literary theory in fashioning lyric and narrative as rival genres without overlap, genre's practitioners did not conceive of these categories in such a fractured way. Many twentieth-century writers were interested in collapsing precisely this distinction, which they articulate as an artificial division between "poetry" and "prose." In "The Serious Artist," Ezra Pound addresses "the often asked question: What is the difference between poetry and prose?" by arguing that "the thing that counts is 'Good writing,'" since "both poetry and prose are but an extension of language. Man desires to communicate with his fellows" (2005, 242, 244). In her essay "Poetry and Grammar," Gertrude Stein argues quite simply that both forms emerge from a feeling that is articulated through carefully chosen diction: "Do you always have the same kind of feeling in relation to the sounds as the words come out of you or do you not. All this has so much to do with grammar and with poetry and with prose. Words have to do everything in poetry and prose" (1998, 313). Both writers focus on the confluence of lyric poetry and narrative prose, articulating a theory of genre that privileges kinship over difference and cross-fertilization over containment.[5]

The attitudes of Pound and Stein are echoed by a number of other writers, including William Carlos Williams, who experimented with both narrative and lyric forms in works such as *Spring and All* (1923), and who expresses his attitude toward genre in a letter to Horace Gregory: "Frankly I'm sick of the constant aping of the Stevens' dictum that I resort to the antipoetic as a heightening device. That's plain crap—and everyone copies it. Now Rodman. The truth is that there's an *identity* between verse and prose, not an antithesis" (1984, 265). Writing to his mother in 1925, William Faulkner boasts that his painstaking artistry has resulted in a concluding passage for his novel *Sanctuary* that approaches poetry: "I have just written such a beautiful thing that I am about to bust—2000 words about the Luxembourg gardens and death. It has a thin thread of plot, about a young woman, and it is poetry though written in prose form. I have worked on it for two whole days and every word is perfect. I havent slept hardly for two nights, thinking about it, comparing words, accepting and rejecting them, then changing again. . . . I have over 20,000 words on my novel, and I have written a poem so modern that I dont know myself what it means" (1977, 17). Charles Olson also argues for the fusion of lyric and narrative in a 1951 letter to Cid Corman: "Narrative writing is, at the moment, wholly waiting for the advance of verse. Only the poets now can pull the narrative writers ahead" (1969, 60). Joan Retallack has even framed this kind of formal innovation as a "conscious, strategic risk" that she calls "the poethetical wager" (2003, 21):

> Authentically innovative work is consciously poethetical. It vitally engages with the forms of life that create its contemporary context—the sciences, the arts, the politics, the sounds and textures of everyday life, the urgent questions and disruptions of the times. It's these factors that make it different from earlier work and for a time unrecognizable—to all but a few—as significant extension or transgression of existing genres. For the work to become poethetical it seems it must risk a period of invisibility, unintelligibility. (40)

The truly innovative writer necessarily risks "unintelligibility" in her violation of traditional generic boundaries—a wager that Retallack insists is a moral imperative for the serious artist. Thus, while critics were busy affirming—even policing—generic boundaries, these insights suggest that writers were, to the contrary, interested in pushing these lines of demarcation to their outer limits.

This project asks that we follow these writers in exploring alternative ways of articulating the relationship between lyric and narrative to the "contest of genres" that is perennially invoked by literary critics. In particular, I suggest that we take seriously Heather Dubrow's recommendation that we devote "proportionally less attention to conflicts between lyric and narrative in order to recognize the frequency and variety of their cooperative interaction" (2006, 264). Of course, one might take any number of approaches to such a dense and multidimensional interaction. Stephen Fredman's *Poet's Prose: The Crisis in American Verse* (1983) examines prose works written by lyric poets, including William Carlos Williams's *Kora in Hell: Improvisations* (1920), John Ashbery's *Three Poems* (1972), and Robert Creeley's *Presences: A Text for Marisol* (1976). Fredman's study is driven by an exegetical question about hybrid literary forms: "How are we to read a prose text that an American poet conceives of as poetry?" (1). One might extend Fredman's project by examining more widely read novels by lyric poets, of which there are many—e.e. cummings's *The Enormous Room* (1922), Robert Penn Warren's *All the King's Men* (1946), or Nathaniel Mackey's *Bedouin Hornbook* (1986), to name a few. I have chosen instead to work with novels that already receive our critical attention *as* novels, however, in order to demonstrate that our aesthetic judgments of narrative fiction are already indebted to the conventions of lyric poetry in ways that we take for granted. Critics may complain about the lyric's marginalized status in the university, but our canon of modern and contemporary fiction, largely made up of novels that lack discernible plotlines and other traditional hallmarks of narrative fiction, suggest otherwise.

Alternatively, one might also address what Wolfgang G. Müller has termed the "lyric insertion" or "the insertion of passages of lyric poetry in narrative and dramatic texts" (2005, 173). Examples of the lyric insertion range from book titles (Hemingway's *For Whom the Bell Tolls* [1940]) to epigraphs (such as Langston Hughes's poem, "Harlem," which opens Gloria Naylor's *The Women of Brewster Place* [1982]) to lyrics composed by the novelist for use in the plot: Ishmael Reed's *Flight to Canada* (1976), for instance, begins with a lyric poem composed by Raven Quickskill for his master, Arthur Swille, upon his escape from Swille's plantation. As Müller points out, however, these insertions effectively underscore, rather than undermine, generic distinctions: "If a novel or drama is equipped with lyric inserts, the difference between genres is highlighted. There would be no point in inserting a poem or a part of a poem into a non-lyric text if the specific generic status of the insertion were not perceptible" (2005, 173). Rather than choosing an approach that would replicate the divisions between lyric and narrative articulated by twentieth-century genre critics, I have opted instead for texts that deliberately blend literary kinds in ways that challenge, rather than reaffirm, classical models of generic classification.

Finally, one might also consider the interaction of narrative and poetic forms in longer verse poetry. Brian McHale's influential article "Beginning to Think about Narrative in Poetry" (2009) castigated narrative theorists for focusing almost exclusively on the novel and called for greater attention to verse forms. Critics have been quick to answer his call: Monique R. Morgan's contiguous study, *Narrative Means, Lyric Ends: Temporality in the Nineteenth-Century British Long Poem* (2009) and a May 2014 issue of the journal *Narrative* have devoted themselves to precisely this topic by addressing narrativity in a robust variety of poetic forms and, in Morgan's case, upending narratology's preference for narrative by placing it in service of the lyric. While these studies chiefly examine narrative strategies in poetic forms, however, my study seeks to uncover the poetic strategies that inhere in narrative fiction—strategies that ultimately elucidate the ontological uncertainties that underpin many twentieth-century American novels.

Our recognition of twentieth-century fiction's indebtedness to the lyric tradition has profound implications for our readings of modern and contemporary American novels and for our understanding of the nature of narrative, or what theorists increasingly refer to as "narrativity." The term *narrativity* boasts a number of advantages over hard-and-fast definitions of "narrative": it is more flexible, gauged on a sliding scale in terms of degree rather than kind, and it works to recast narrative as a property rather than a metaphysical category such that, rather than asking whether a text qualifies as narrative, we ask instead what degree of narrativity the text displays. This enables us to talk about narrative across a range of discursive sites, "from political speeches, legal briefs, or philosophical arguments to scientific proofs, psychoanalytic sessions, and L. L. Bean catalogues" (Prince 1999, 45). Of course, not all critics will agree on the "narrativity" of such disparate texts. In contradistinction to Mark Jeffreys's focus on the compactness of lyric poetry, Philip Sturgess reasonably ventures that extension or length constitutes one essential measure of narrativity (1992, 8)—one of the primary reasons I focus here on the novel rather than short fiction—but by and large, critics continue to dispute the criteria that ought to determine this property. As Porter Abbott explains, "There is no definitive test that can tell us to what degree narrativity is present. Do we, for example, need more than one event for there to be narrativity?" (2002, 22)

While the property-based approach lacks the precision of a concrete definition, its evocation of common sense and general consensus is one of its greatest strengths. This is especially true when reckoning with texts that deviate from the narrative tradition. Critics typically agree on works that exhibit what Gerald Prince has termed "low narrativity" (quoted in S. Friedman 2005, 194) and what Brian McHale has termed "weak narrativity"

(2001); that is, the idea that some texts—*Ulysses* (1992), *Gravity's Rainbow* (1973)—just don't feel very story-like, despite their encyclopedic length. More often than not, these works are avant-garde novels in the modernist or postmodernist tradition. Narrative theory is just beginning to develop a rich vocabulary and conceptual scaffolding for these texts, including the exciting work being done by Jan Alber in the pioneering subfield of "unnatural narratology" (2016), but narratologists have long grappled with the difficulties of building a comprehensive theory around novels that do not exhibit strong narrativity. After all, such works present an obvious and circular paradox: how can a novel be nonnarrative; and if a novel is nonnarrative, how can we really call it a novel?

This impasse reveals precisely what we stand to gain from a broader and more comprehensive understanding of genre. Understandably (if tautologically), narrative theorists continue to think of narrative as the default genre wherein novels that deviate from plotted eventfulness contain some deficiency of narrativity. Yet the novels examined here do not exhibit a dearth of narrative so much as they feature a surplus of lyricism, or what James Phelan has termed lyricality.[6] That is, they deliberately suppress important features of narrativity to facilitate a different set of reading practices that are rooted in the lyric tradition. Hence, linear sequence yields to repetition, and grammatical hierarchy to polysyndeton; action is subordinated to the realm of figuration, and eventfulness to the elaboration of a dramatic persona; and the inclusion of the reader in narrative texts gives way to the reader's exclusion or marginalization by way of the exclusive address. To this extent, my study necessarily reinscribes essential differences between lyricality and narrativity, but with a few key differences. Rather than arguing for a framework that establishes these genres as two separate, rival spheres that never touch, I argue that lyric and narrative can—and do—take on each other's qualities in a way that requires us to shift our reading habits accordingly. Moreover, the examination of lyricality in twentieth-century American fiction forces us to reckon with the limits and boundaries of narrativity in generically hybrid texts. What happens to novels when we infuse them with tropes and reading strategies that "belong" to a different genre?

This project does not deny the heuristic and practical utility of dividing literature into types or recognizing the rhetorical differences between genres. It does, however, insist that works of literature do not always fit neatly into these categories and that, in fact, literary texts often inhabit a variety of genres at once.[7] By analyzing novels alongside theories of lyric rather than theories of narrative, I hope to demonstrate the kind of work that can be done when we conceive of genres, or sets of textual properties, in terms of likeness and overlap rather than difference. After all, as Wai Chee Dimock reminds us, "genre is not just a theory of classification but, perhaps even more crucially, a theory of interconnection. *Kin* is every bit as important as *kind*. And, by kin, what I have in mind is not necessarily a genealogical relation, but just as often, a remote spectrum of affinities" (2006, 86). What productive comparisons might we draw between *Lolita* and Browning's dramatic monologues? What happens when we read Ernest Hemingway alongside Walt Whitman, or Toni Morrison with the seventeenth-century metaphysical poets? Or, more broadly, how might the study of lyricality illuminate the rhetorical structures of the twentieth-century American novel?

Chapter 2

✦

Repetition and Insistence

One of the most powerful passages from Kathy Acker's *Blood and Guts in High School* (1978) depicts Janey's last day with her father (also her lover) before he leaves her for another woman:

> A few hours later they woke up together and decided they would spend the whole day together since it was their last day. Janey would meet Johnny at the hotel where he worked when he got off from work.
>
> They ate raw fish and salad (*cerviche*) [*sic*] at a Lebanese joint and tea at a Northern Chinese place. They held hands. They didn't talk about Sally or anything heavy.
>
> Johnny left her, telling her he'd be home later. (21–25)

Nothing eventful happens here on the level of plot—the two meet up, eat a meal together, and part ways—but something is certainly happening at the level of form: the passage appears six times in a row, bringing Acker's bizarre though erstwhile linear story to a screeching halt. Acker is not the only author to deploy linguistic repetition in her narrative fiction, though she may be the most dramatic exemplar. Why should writers impede the progress of their narratives in such a way?

Because repetition violates conventions we hold to be essential to narrative fiction—sequence, progression, and a plot that develops over time—its pronounced presence in twentieth-century American fiction can create a significant roadblock for readers, who must adjust their reading practices when they encounter words, phrases, and even full paragraphs in duplicate. This chapter examines novels that make extensive use of repetition on linguistic, structural, and thematic levels in ways that disrupt the sequential progressions we typically find in narrative fiction, moving from a discussion of repetition's role(s) in the lyric tradition to its function in works by Gertrude Stein, Jean Toomer, John Dos Passos, and Kathy Acker. Because of their extreme reliance on repetition at the level of form as well as content, these novels demand reading strategies that are essentially lateral rather than linear. Lyrical repetition suspends readers between temporality and stasis, compelling us to read with an eye for wholeness and simultaneity and demanding that we read both backward and forward through echoes and reverberations that unsettle our notions not only of narrative progression but also of temporal and historical progression.

Repetition inheres in nearly all of poetry's traditional structural features, many of which derive from its oral (and hence, aural) roots. Rhyme, assonance, and alliteration are repeating units of sound; meter is a repeating pattern of stresses, syllables, or metric feet. Lyric forms such as the sestina and the villanelle rely on repetition to create intricate structural patterns based on words and refrains, respectively. Even the very etymology of poetry signals repetition, since, as Roman Jakobson reminds us, *verse* indicates a "return": "on every level of language," he argues, "the essence of poetic artifice consists in recurrent returns" (1987, 145). Repetition plays an important role in poetry on any number of formal planes—but to what effect?

Folk wisdom tells us that repetition contributes to the unity of a poem, a feature that becomes even more pronounced in the intensive economy of the lyric.[1] In lyrics that employ rhyme, the repetition of like sounds forges a phonic association among key terms that may have otherwise no natural connection to one another. John Donne's "The Flea" uses end rhyme, for example, to close the distance between the speaker and his resistant lover, emphasizing the carnal connection that already exists between them in the figure of the flea: "Though use make you apt to kill mee, / Let not to that, selfe murder added bee, / And sacrilege, three sinnes in killing three. / . . . Just so much honor, when thou yeeld'st to mee, / Will wast, as this flea's death tooke life from thee" (1985, 48). Indeed, one of the most pronounced features of this short lyric is its rhyme scheme, which effectively binds "thee," "me," and "three," reinforcing the unholy trinity invoked by the lyric speaker. If repetition forges rational connections between otherwise unrelated terms, it can certainly contribute to a poem's hermeneutical coherence, encouraging us to read each term in light of the other: to read the addressee, or "thee," of Donne's poem in relation to the trinity of "three" that includes the speaker and the flea. This is the poem's very gambit, since rhyme aids the speaker in closing the distance separating himself, the flea, and his lover. In this sense, repetition creates a synchronizing effect, often used, as Lyn Hejinian writes, "to unify a text or harmonize its parts, as if returning melody to the tonic" (2000, 44).

Yet repetition can be deeply disruptive, especially with regard to larger units of meaning such as the word or the line. In certain cases, the repetition of a term or phrase may work to unhinge, rather than fasten, its meaning by way of recontextualization. This is especially true of modernist lyric, which tends to enmesh repetition with irony in ways that disorient speaker and reader alike. Amy Lowell's "Patterns" (1916) exploits repetition in just such a way. The first appearances of *patterns* in the poem suggest opulence and beauty: "I walk down the patterned garden-paths / In my stiff, brocaded gown. / With my powdered hair and jeweled fan, / I too am a rare / Pattern" (2002, 58). As the poem progresses, however, these patterns become shackles, and the speaker fantasizes about throwing them off in an act of sexual liberation: "What is Summer in a fine brocaded gown! / I should like to see it lying in a heap upon the ground. / All the pink and silver crumpled on the ground" (59). Though together the speaker and her lover "would have broke[n] the pattern," they are deprived of the chance when he is killed in combat. As the poem concludes, she realizes that patterns also inhere in chaos, reflecting that her lover has given his life within "a pattern called a war" (61). Here, patterns take on a bitterly ironic meaning in a way that undercuts their auspicious deployment at the poem's beginning. The repetition of patterns in such a wide variety of contexts causes the speaker to question their very meaning in the poem's exasperated closing line: "Christ! What are patterns for?"

Similar examples of repetition's disruptive potential abound in short twentieth-century lyrics in which repetition swells to overtake the poem. Sterling Brown's "Bitter Fruit of the Tree" ([1939] 1980) opens with a command, "You are not to be bitter," directed at several generations of African Americans in the speaker's family. The imperative is repeated with mounting irony throughout the poem, reappearing after a litany of gross injustices: "When they sold her first-born and let the second die, / When they drove her husband till he took to the swamplands, / And brought him home bloody and beaten at last. / They told her, 'It is better you should not be bitter' " (200). The more the phrase is repeated, the less secure its meaning becomes, undermined as it is through its ironic juxtaposition to concrete and poignant instances of black suffering. Consider, too, a more contemporary example, such as Li-Young Lee's "Persimmons" (1986), which also exploits repetition's potential for irony and juxtaposition. The poem opens with the speaker's admonishment by his sixth-grade teacher for failing to recognize the difference between *persimmon* and *precision*; the remainder of the poem is a play on these terms, especially as the speaker explores all of the cultural and personal meanings persimmons ("Chinese apples") have held for him, from his mother's explanation that "every persimmon has a sun / inside, something golden, glowing, / warm as my face" to persimmons he has gifted to his father, who is going blind: "I gave him the persimmons / swelled, heavy as sadness, / and sweet as love" (18). The tactile qualities of the persimmons are so vivid for the speaker's father that he is able to paint them blind: "Some things never leave a person: / . . . the texture of persimmons, / in your palm, the ripe weight" (19). Indeed, the irony of this poem hinges on the teacher's overly technical—and punitive—handling of the term as it contrasts with the speaker's repetitive, deeply emotional experiences with persimmons, which are based instead on love, patience, and understanding.

Much twentieth-century lyric poetry is interested in repetition's potential to disrupt or undermine, rather than reinforce, a poem's hermeneutical coherence. In such cases, Lyn Hejinian continues, "the initial reading is adjusted; meaning is set in motion, emended and extended, and the rewriting that repetition becomes postpones the completion of the thought indefinitely" (2000, 44). Hejinian's account of repetition echoes that of one of her foremost influences, Gertrude Stein. In her famous essay, "Portraits and Repetition," Stein denies all possibility of repetition, arguing that words and phrases cannot possibly receive the same treatment each time they are used: "Is there repetition or is there insistence. I am inclined to believe there is no such thing as repetition. . . . [T]here can be no repetition because the essence of that expression is insistence, and if you insist you must each time use emphasis and if you use emphasis it is not possible while anybody is alive that they should use exactly the same emphasis" (1998, 288). Whatever Stein might mean here by "emphasis"—either the fleeting quality of the "continuous present," which, as soon as it is apprehended, is gone; or, more literally, changes in stress by either writer or reader—she is attuned to the dynamic potential of repetition in which recurring words and phrases are altered by the contexts that shift around them. By Stein's account, meaning is not fortified through repetition but delayed through a process of continuous alteration.[2]

If repetition has the power to dislocate meaning even in lyric poetry, consider its disruptive potential when used in narrative fiction, a genre that relies on progressive, if not necessarily chronological, plotlines that unfold through sequential action. Narrativity requires the representation of events in sequence—this is one of the oldest and most basic definitions, upon which a number of other definitions and distinctions essential to narrative theory are premised.[3] The classic story/plot distinction first articulated by the Russian formalists as fabula/suzjet hinges on a difference in sequence from the raw material of the story to the final artistry of the plot (Tomashevsky 1965, 67). A host of other common narrative devices also rely on sequence for their effect, including retroversions and anticipations—also known as flashbacks and foreshadowing—which deliberately deviate from chronology to construct an alternative sequence that is concentrated on causality.[4] Without a succession of events linked through causal and temporal relations, argued Boris Tomashevky, we may have a lyric or a travelogue, but we simply do not have a story (66).

Of course, we tolerate a certain amount of repetition in narrative forms, at least in the abstract. In his discussion of frequency, Gérard Genette (1983) argues that a single event may be narrated multiple times in a work of fiction, though his examples—*Rashomon* (1950), *The Sound and the Fury* (1929)—use repetition strategically to highlight differences in character perspective; that is, the event will not (indeed, must not) be narrated the same way each time. Repetition also occurs in other abstract forms: repeating images generate a motif, and motifs in turn cohere into larger themes.[5] We read narrative not just for story but for deeper meanings, and repetition often flags discrete images, symbols, or ideas that may connect to our overall understanding of a literary work.

The repetition of an event or theme, however, is distinct from the type of repetition that characterizes lyricality. Texts that repeat an event or motif can and do still exhibit strong narrativity by featuring plots that nevertheless hinge on chronology, sequence, and succession, however much filmmakers such as Akira Kurosawa and writers such as William Faulkner may manipulate these elements to foreground differences in point of view.[6] By contrast, lyrical repetition—which centers on concrete linguistic units rather than abstractions—defies chronology and sequence by returning our attention to the same sound, word, line, or phrase, deliberately obstructing the forward momentum and temporal logic on which narrativity hinges.

Certain avant-garde novelists in the twentieth century, however, demonstrate an investment in repetition as a device that offers a new way of reframing narrative fiction not as a coherent story that unfolds through a logical or chronological sequence but as a series of disordered and elliptical states or events that exist in a continuous state of revision and inter-referentiality. Such uses of repetition—of words and phrases, as in Stein's *Three Lives* ([1909] 2006); of whole lines and refrains, as in Toomer's *Cane* ([1923] 1975) and Dos Passos's *U.S.A.* trilogy ([1930] 2000; [1932] 2000; [1933] 2000); and of entire paragraphs, as in Kathy Acker's *Blood and Guts in High School* (1978)—encourage us to approach these narratives with a lyrical hermeneutic, what Peter Brooks calls a "simultaneity of meaning," in lieu of a narrative-oriented strategy that privileges progression from beginnings toward endings (1984, 20). Lyric poems, Brooks argues, demand to be read "backward as well as forward," since devices that are linked to repetition actively encourage us to read the separate parts of a poem against one another in a mutually reinforcing way that resists the traditionally sequential movement of plot. Beginnings and endings certainly exist in dynamic relationship to each other in narrative fiction, as Brooks demonstrates, but the lyric transforms this relationship into one of coherence and necessity: the first end-rhyme of a rhyming couplet simply does not make proper sense without the second, and vice versa. As Joseph Frank famously argued, such works tend to "spatialize" form in ways that resist temporal progressions, embedded as they are with "cross-references which relate to one another independently of the time-sequence of the narrative; and, before the book fits together into any meaningful pattern, these references must be connected by the reader and viewed as a whole" (2005, 62). Thus, they require active engagement and reconfiguration on the part of their readers, who must not only apprehend and make sense of these reprisals, but also reconcile the temporal nature of reading with the nonsequential nature of lyrical repetition.

The texts treated here are segmented into parts—volumes, sections, and subsections—that bear important heuristic relations to one another, much like the lines and stanzas that constitute the segments of a lyric poem. These novels resist sequential plotting through their unconventional stress on repetition, but they also resist sequential readings, divided as they are into discrete parts that interrupt, rather than forge, narrative continuity. Brian McHale, following Rachel Blau DuPlessis, recently deemed "segmentivity"—the division of a literary work into segmented units of meaning—a driving component in the meaning-making of poetry (McHale 2009, 14; DuPlessis 1996, 51). For DuPlessis, it is an essential part of what distinguishes poetry from prose: poetry is, she argues, "the kind of writing that is articulated in sequenced, gapped lines and whose meanings are created by occurring in bounded units precisely chosen. . . . [I]n short, all the meanings poetry makes are constructed by segmented units of a variety of sizes" (51). These units, she argues, are created by those spatial gaps—"line break, stanza break, page space"—that make up poetry's unique arrangement on the printed page.

While integral to lyric poetry, segmentivity is not necessarily unique to this genre. McHale points out that "prose fiction has its own formal segmentation into volumes, installments, books, chapters, sections, even paragraphs and sentences," although, he concedes, "its segmentivity is subordinated to its narrativity" (2009, 23). The novels of Stein, Toomer, Dos Passos, and Acker, however, foreground segmentivity over narrativity in a way that discourages the forward-propelled reading practice that suits most narrative fiction. Instead, they demand a lyric-based reading practice that frames these stories as complex networks of bounded parts that are interconnected even as they are self-contained. This heuristic is reinforced by each text's reliance on repetition, which deliberately stalls narrative progression through the reiteration of linguistic acts and events that have already appeared in the text. These repetitions, however, effectively bind together each novel's discrete segments through lexical and thematic recurrences that help us read these otherwise disjointed texts as coherent unities. As narratives, they are fragmented, but as lyrics, they are whole.

Reading these novels outside of sequence, however, does not mean that we must read them as static. Critics tend to stereotype lyric poetry as projecting a "gestalt in stasis," the atemporal expression of an idea or state of mind (S. Friedman 1989, 164). As the poetry of Lowell, Brown, and Lee demonstrate, however, repetition need not entail sameness or stasis at all. In fact, the changing contexts (or "insistences") that surround the deployment and redeployment of words and phrases include the reader's changing relationship to, and understanding of, these terms. Texts that make extensive use of repetition do exhibit dynamic movement, though not necessarily the sequential movement that we have come to expect in narrative fiction.

The difficult and repetitive styles of Stein, Toomer, Dos Passos, and Acker have garnered simultaneous admiration and frustration from critics who have struggled to make sense of their elliptical prose. "These stories . . . have a quite extraordinary vitality conveyed in a most eccentric and difficult form," writes an early reviewer of *Three Lives* (*The Nation*, January

20, 1910). "Whoever can adjust himself to the repetitions, false starts, and general circularity of the manner will find himself very near real people." This chapter explores in detail the "adjustments" to which Stein's reviewer refers, arguing that the adjustments we must make are from narrative to lyric expectations. Critics have largely circumvented the difficult prose styles of these writers by turning instead toward thematic or biographical analyses of their work. A formal analysis of repetition and its function in this fiction, however, sheds light not only on the content of the work but also, I argue, on our most basic assumptions about narrative form.

Like the novels it treats, this chapter deliberately deviates from traditional sequence, forgoing chronology for a trajectory that centers instead on the authors' variant understandings and manipulations of generic difference. We begin, therefore, not with Stein but with John Dos Passos, whose experimentations with genre in the pages of the epic *U.S.A.* trilogy supply an important framework through which we can better understand the other writers in this chapter, their relationships to traditional literary forms, and the role that repetition plays in their fiction.

The strikingly segmented form of Dos Passos's *U.S.A.* trilogy can be quite disorienting to first-time readers of this panoramic epic. The novels that compose the trilogy—*The 42nd Parallel* (1930), *1919* (1932), and *The Big Money* (1933)—are subdivided into four rotating sections: "newsreel" sections, which contain splices of historical newspaper headlines, article excerpts, and song lyrics; serial narrative sections that plot the lives of a number of fictional characters; historical biographies, which are brief and heavily editorialized versions of a historical figure's life and work; and "camera eye" sections, fragmented impressions that culminate in the burgeoning political consciousness of an unnamed speaker.[7] Critical work on the *U.S.A.* trilogy has typically treated one or another section in isolation from the rest, and not surprisingly, the majority of this work has focused on the narrative sections, which generally conform to our conventional expectations of the novel. The other sections, however, are not to be ignored, since all four work together and against one another in important ways that reveal their affinities and differences as variant modes of literary expression.

In fact, these sections exist on a generic sliding scale ranging from the dramatic to the narrative to the lyrical, if we measure these categories by the degree to which they are mediated by an organizing central consciousness. The newsreel sections unfold like a drama as headlines and song lyrics are deposited verbatim into these documentary-style sections without any discernible narrator. The fictional sections are mediated by an impersonal, extradiegetic narrator who operates mostly through free indirect discourse, giving voice to the thoughts and feelings of the trilogy's characters. The narrator of the historical biographies, by contrast, is deeply partisan in his depictions of real historical figures and their life events—a fusion of narrative sequence and lyrical subjectivity. Finally, the lyrical "camera eye" sections turn inward, recording impressions prompted by some external catalyst that ranges from the personal to the political. In the pages of Dos Passos's *U.S.A.*, then, is an assortment of generic possibilities that together represent the variety of approaches one might take to literary representation.

No one section or approach is privileged over the others in the *U.S.A.* novels, which feature all four modes at relatively even intervals, though they certainly have not received equal treatment in literary scholarship. In particular, critics have sidestepped the trilogy's lyrical component by virtually ignoring the "camera eye" sections. The subject matter of these passages is rendered oblique by their stream-of-consciousness style and by the lexical repetitions that appear and reappear at irregular intervals. Reviewers have panned these sections on aesthetic grounds: a write-up in the *New York Times* celebrating the trilogy's centenary called them "overripe and pretentious," the worst written of the four rotating sections (Gilman 1997). When excerpted sections appeared in *Esquire* in 1936, they were published alongside editor Arnold Gingrich's prescription for how to read them—which, ironically, instructs readers not to examine these sections with much scrutiny: "Do not insist upon making consecutive sense of every phrase and sentence as you go along. The effect is as cumulative as that of music or painting," he advises (1936, 51). Even Dos Passos himself has made dismissive comments about the camera eye segments, insisting that they were merely a "safety valve" for personal feelings from which he wished to spare the other sections: "It served a useful function . . . to distill my subjective feelings about the incidents and people described. . . . In the biographies, in the newsreels, and even in the narrative, I aimed at total objectivity by giving conflicting views—using the camera eye as a safety valve for my own subjective feelings. It made objectivity in the rest of the book much easier" (Sanders 1969). Despite even Dos Passos's pronouncements to the contrary, however, the camera eye sections—and the lexical repetitions they contain—are crucial to *U.S.A.* and are in fact the anchor for the trilogy's leftist politics.

The sections typically center on some formative event in the young speaker's political life: a presidential sighting, an overheard speech, a distasteful encounter with the wealthy elite. Sometimes, these sections culminate in epiphany; at other times, in a lingering rhetorical question. In most of the camera eye sections, however, repetitions are crucial rhetorical features that ground the passage in a fixed, politically charged image. In *The 42nd Parallel* ([1930] 2000), these images are often class markers or symbols that leave a strong impression on the child speaker. Mr. Pierce, for example—a wealthy family friend who once employed Dos Passos's father—fixes himself a toddy and tugs at his "dundrearies" four times in "The Camera Eye (15)." The term—which denotes long, full sideburns—derives from the 1858 British play *Our American Cousin*, which features a dim-witted aristocrat named Lord Dundreary famously played by Edward A. Sothern, who wore these bushy sideburns for the role. *Dundrearies* has since become a synecdoche or shorthand for this character type, and here, they absorb the speaker as a symbol for the vacuous superiority of the elite, recording the speaker's earliest impression of unmerited class distinction. The "fashionable lady" of "The Camera Eye (18)" marks his second such impression. Her penchant for "bullterriers" and for her "gentleman friend who was famous for his resemblance to King Edward" is repeated by the speaker with neurotic insistence, much as Mr. Pierce's dundrearies became a repetitive fixture in "The Camera Eye (15)." Accompanying her "on a fourinhand," the speaker is disturbed by her high regard for symbols of class distinction and her equally intense hatred for tradespeople ("The bullterriers bit the tradespeople. . . . No my dear they never bit nice people") and for children such as the speaker ("She loathed simply loathed most children"). The section ends with the speaker's renunciation of the fashionable lady and each of her class markers in turn, though he is left with an uncomfortable feeling of social displacement: "I didn't like her and I didn't like the bullterriers and I didn't like the fourinhand but I wished . . . I was home but I hadn't any home" (176).

Repetitions in other camera eye sections help to establish the novel's class and labor politics. "The Camera Eye (11)" depicts a trip to a Presbyterian church service in Pennsylvania with the influential Pennypacker family, but stalling the passage's development is the speaker's insistent yet apparently unrelated question, "Who were the Molly Maguires?"—a question that interrupts this section five times. The Molly Maguires, a secret Civil War–era Irish-American labor organization composed of anthracite coal miners from the Pennsylvania coal region, famously resorted to violent tactics in protesting their exploitation by the (largely Protestant) mine owners and supervisors. The church service takes place in the institution of the oppressors, one that will not allow the speaker to inquire about the labor union: "Who were the Molly Maguires? but it was too late you couldn't talk in church" (86). The question, despite its insistence, remains unanswered at the end of the section.

The Molly Maguires in "Camera Eye (11)" are also part of a larger repetition, only one example of the many labor unions that appear in the novel's other sections: the I.W.W., the A.F.L., the Western Federation of Miners, the Anarchist Union of Industry and Agriculture, all of whom, as Mac states, are "members of the same classconsciousness" (100).[8] Nearly every newsreel section highlights an advancement or setback in the labor movements of the century. "LABOR GREETS NEW CENTURY," declares "Newsreel I" (2). "GENERAL STRIKE NOW THREATENS," warns "Newsreel IV" (44). "Newreel VI" depicts an industrial accident caused by poor working conditions: "When the metal poured out of the furnace I saw the men running to a place of safety. To the right of the furnace I saw a party of men all of them running wildly and their clothes a mass of flames. Apparently some of them had been injured when the explosion occurred and several of them tripped and fell. The hot metal ran over the poor men in a moment" (63). "Newsreel VII" announces a "LABOR MENACE IN POLITICS" (67). These references to labor unions connect to still larger thematic repetitions in the novel that center on class warfare, from William Jennings Bryan's "Cross of Gold" speech—excerpted in his biography section (134–36)—to socialist movements all over the globe, including the Bolshevik and Mexican Revolutions.

The camera eye sections become less frequent in *1919* and *The Big Money*, though they function in much the same way. In *1919* ([1932] 2000), these repetitions are rooted in the horrors of the First World War, which supplies the overarching theme for this volume. Patrick Henry's legendary imperative regarding the righteousness of the Revolutionary War—"Give me liberty or give me death"—is reiterated in fragments in "The Camera Eye (30)": "*Give me liberty or give me Well they give us death. . . . Patrick Henry in khaki submits to shortarm inspection and puts all his pennies in a Liberty Loan or give me . . . or give me death*" (78–79). Here, Patrick Henry is satirized as submitting not only to inspection for venereal disease but to the wedding of capitalism and patriotism in the symbol of the Liberty Loan. The repetitive fragments also ensure that death, and not liberty, receives greater emphasis. Henry's imperative reappears in another ironic context in "Camera Eye (41)," as the speaker describes the French girl he meets at an "anarchist picnic": "I sat on the impériale of the third class car with the daughter of the Libertaire (that's Patrick Henry ours after all give me or death) a fine girl her father she said never let her go out alone never let her see any young men it was like being in a convent she wanted liberty fraternity equality and a young man to take her out" (335–36). The repetition enacted here displays the girl's perversion of the ideals of the American and French Revolutions, mobilized here to get her out of the house and on a date. The "anarchist picnic" itself, where "everybody wore black artist ties," is little more than a bourgeois façade: "C'est plutôt le geste proletaire," remarks a voice—"It is more like the *gesture* of the proletariat." In both camera eye sections, Patrick Henry's war cry is emptied of its original significance and rendered impotent against the realities of a purposeless war, on the one hand, and the weak political commitments of youth, on the other.

Repetition also performs much of the ideological work of *The Big Money* ([1933] 2000). The travesty of justice regarding the trial and execution of the Italian anarchists Nicola Sacco and Bartolomeo Vanzetti plays a major role in this volume and serves as the focus for "Camera Eye (49)" and "Camera Eye (50)." Dos Passos suggests that these immigrant anarchists—repeatedly tagged "haters of oppression"—are the ultimate patriots, even more American than those who are native born, effecting an ironic reversal of their criminal status in Massachusetts: "This fishpeddler you have in Charlestown Jail is one of your founders Massachusetts" (350). With this line, Dos Passos enacts yet another repetition in which the jailed fishpeddler is set up as a double for the founders of the Plymouth colony, depicted not only as "haters of oppression" but as pioneering freedom seekers. Repetition effectively repositions Sacco and Vanzetti as insiders rather than outsiders, heroes rather than convicts.

"Camera Eye (50)" transforms this repetition into an incisive question—or rather, accusation—that is posed to the nation: "Who are your oppressors America"; "Who are your betrayers America." Finally, these sections pit the first-person plural against the third-person plural, depicting a nation divided into them and us, the haves and have-nots: "How can I make them feel how our fathers our uncles haters of oppression came to this coast," asks "Camera Eye (49)"; "They have clubbed us off the streets they are stronger they are rich . . . there is nothing left to do we are beaten," concedes "Camera Eye (50)" (350, 371). These repetitions construct a powerful dichotomy—oppressor and oppressed, betrayer and betrayed—that culminates in the novel's most often-quoted line: "All right we are two nations" (371). This line, which depicts a country split based on class warfare, is *U.S.A.* writ large. The novels may span a variety of topics—labor unionization, communist revolutions, global imperialism, world war, the stock exchange, immigration, women's liberation—but the common denominator is a nation in which the wealthy and powerful wage civil war against the powerless.

These readings demonstrate Dos Passos's deeply political investment in the trope of repetition, a device that surfaces chiefly in camera eye sections that readers, critics, and even the author himself have tended to disavow. Repetitions work to focus these stream-of-consciousness fragments on a politically charged point or image that links up with larger thematic repetitions that course through the trilogy. They establish important connections between the local—represented here by the unnamed speaker's budding class consciousness, located in personal and even idiosyncratic connections to symbols such as Mr. Pierce's dundrearies—and national, even international, political movements toward socialism and anarchism. Repetition forges coherence in *U.S.A.*, and coherence has decidedly ideological stakes: we are meant to read Sacco and Vanzetti in terms of the nation's founders; the historical Patrick Henry against the Patrick Henry of "Camera Eye (41)" and "Camera Eye (30)"; and the industrial accident narrated in "Newreel VI" against the speaker's insistent question in "Camera Eye (11)," "Who were the Molly Maguires?" *U.S.A.*, after all, gains its momentum not from its stand-alone fragments but from the lexical and thematic repetitions that bind these fragments together. It is based on a heuristic of cross-association whereby each iteration of a phrase or fragment is necessarily read in light of the others. To read the trilogy or any of its volumes as a linear narrative progression is to distort the ambitions of this epic project, since, as Caren Irr has argued, *U.S.A.* rejects any "radically teleological view of national culture" reflected by nationalist historical narratives (1998, 45). For Dos Passos, in fact, quite the opposite is true—repetition, not teleology, signals real political headway, but we cannot make progress until we learn to read these repetitions in our own national history: to read Bartolomeo Vanzetti, "this fishpeddler you have in Charlestown Jail," as "one of your founders" (350).

The quartet of rotating sections that forms the trilogy celebrates four variant approaches to the historiographical project of *U.S.A.* in particular and to literary representation more broadly. Lyrical subjectivity, represented here by the camera eye sections, is granted a gravity and validity equal to the impersonal historical objectivity represented in the "newsreel" sections and also to the more familiar character-based narratives represented by the fictional biographies. The trilogy's form suggests that the intensely personal political consciousness of the lyric speaker is not only as powerful as those of the trilogy's fictional characters, many of whom come to identify with larger political movements in the course of their narratives, but also as powerful as the political consciousness of the nation itself, recorded through historic news headlines and article excerpts in the trilogy's "newsreel" sections.

The unique form of *U.S.A.*, manifested in its four rotating sections, demonstrates Dos Passos's awareness of generic difference, which he galvanizes here for political ends. The newsreel and historical biography sections may lend a wider scope and greater objectivity to the trilogy than what the lyrical sections afford, but the "camera eyes" lend repetition and insistence, forging political coherence among phrases, symbols, figures, and events that may otherwise seem politically irrelevant or, at the very least, disconnected. The form of *U.S.A.* also, however, demonstrates Dos Passos's willingness to simultaneously galvanize and undermine generic difference, performing in microcosm what twentieth-century American fiction performs on a broader level: the manipulation and, ultimately, rejection of the classical division between lyric and narrative.

Jean Toomer's tour de force, *Cane* ([1923] 1975), is another experimental, heavily segmented text that features all three major genres. It is divided into three main sections, the first and last of which take place in rural Georgia, the middle section taking place in Chicago and Washington, D.C. The first and middle segments are subdivided into titled segments I will call vignettes, many of which are further subdivided into numbered sections. In their discussions of *Cane*, scholars typically divide the text into discrete and self-contained lyric, narrative, and dramatic vignettes. Short fragments that appear in verse—"Reapers," "Cotton Song," "Georgia Dusk," and "Beehive," to name a few—are usually treated as lyric poems. Those longer prose vignettes that feature plot and character—"Karintha," "Blood-Burning Moon," "Box Seat," "Bona and Paul"—are considered narrative. "Kabnis," the long vignette that closes the novel, is cast as a drama.

This classical taxonomy, however, does not hold up under greater scrutiny. Though "Kabnis," for example, is invariably regarded as a play, the section also contains lyrical song refrains and long narrative sequences that are mediated by a central narrator and in which direct dialogue appears in quotation marks. Conversely, "Theater," "Box Seat," and "Bona and Paul"—three of *Cane*'s purportedly "narrative" sections—are partially narrated in dramatic form, complete with setting and stage directions. Lyrical refrains appear throughout the narrative sections of part 1, including "Karintha," "Becky," "Carma," and "Blood-Burning Moon"; part 2 is largely made up of prose poems, including "Seventh Street," "Rhobert," and "Calling Jesus." Like Dos Passos, Toomer has set up something that resembles a generic taxonomy only to merge these categories through deliberate instances of generic blending and amalgamation.

The trope that most consistently cuts through these various segments and genres is repetition. *Cane* contains a dizzying number of lexical repetitions that dominate the "lyric" sections but also figure prominently in the narrative and dramatic pieces by way of the refrain. Like Dos Passos's "camera eye," these refrains ground the vignettes in a fixed image that bears some heuristic relationship to the rest of the text. In the vignette titled "Becky," the phrase "the pines whisper to Jesus" appears six times; this refrain constructs nature as a witness to Becky's suffering and a mouthpiece that reports her suffering to the heavens. "Harvest Song" contains phrases—"I hunger," "my throat is dry"—that appear at least four times each, emphasizing the visceral toll that harvesting takes on the body. The phrase "Doris dances" appears eight times in the vignette "Theater," underscoring Doris's desperate efforts to communicate her hopes and desires to John through the movement of her body. The broken phrase, "Crimson Gardens. Hurrah! So one feels," opens three nearly consecutive paragraphs in the vignette "Bona and Paul" and is coupled with parataxis to convey the energy of the Chicago jazz club: "The drinks come. Four highballs. Art passes cigarettes" (76). These brief refrains provide the vignettes with a recurring point of focus, but their repetition also encourages us to read each instance in light of the others as they take on cumulative meaning. Doris's dancing, for instance, becomes increasingly hopeful with each repetition of the refrain, especially following her inner monologue, a heartfelt entreaty directed at John that she attempts to convey through her dancing alone: "O will you love me? And give me kids, and a home, and everything?" (52). Similarly, the whispering of the pines in "Becky" escalates from a repeated description ("The pines whisper to Jesus") to an apostrophe ("O pines, whisper to Jesus") to an imperative ("Pines shout to Jesus!") as the story reaches its climax with the collapse of Becky's house. The weight and momentum of these phrases increase with each iteration, making them exemplary cases of repetition as insistence.

The stanza-length refrains that appear throughout *Cane* also contribute to the work's segmentation, playing an essential role in framing and dividing *Cane*'s narrative sections. Sometimes, these refrains bookend a section by appearing at its beginning and ending, as in "Becky" and "Seventh Street." At other times, however, the refrains appear three times at even intervals that effectively divide the vignette into two or three discrete segments, depending on where they are placed. In these cases, repetition creates structure, and our readings of the vignettes are shaped by the structural divisions produced by repetition. The refrain in "Karintha," for instance—"Her skin is like dusk on the eastern horizon, / O cant you see it, O cant you see it, / Her skin is like dusk on the eastern horizon / . . . When the sun goes down"—not only establishes Karintha's paradoxical relationship to time, drawing our attention away from the setting sun on the western horizon to the earth's shadow in the east; it also divides the vignette in half by appearing and reppearing at the beginning, middle, and end. The first segment documents Karintha's childhood as she prematurely attracts the attention of older men from an early age: "Old men rode her hobby-horse upon their knees. Young men who danced with her at frolics when they should have been dancing with their grown-up girls. God grant us youth, secretly prayed the old men. The young fellows counted the time to pass before she would be old enough to mate with them" (1). The segment ends with Karintha's movement toward puberty and sexual awakening, indexed again by the reactions she draws from men of various ages: "Old men could no longer ride her hobby-horse upon their knees. But young men counted faster." The second section discloses Karintha's unhappy fate as a result of her sexuality, which has been hastened by these men. Not only has she "been married many times," but she delivers a child in the forest whom she abandons to a smoldering "pyramidal sawdust pile" (2). In this segment, we are told three times that "Karintha is a woman"—a repetition implying that her unhappiness is a consequence of her gender. In dividing the narrative in half, with Karintha's transition into puberty serving as the fulcrum, this vignette's segmentation suggests that Karintha's tragedy hinges on her sexuality, which has "ripened too soon" on account of her predatory suitors.

"Blood-Burning Moon" is divided into three numbered sections, each of which closes with the refrain, "Red nigger moon. Sinner! / Blood-burning moon. Sinner! / Come out that fact'ry door." The divisions created by the numbers and refrains construct the vignette as a three-part tragedy. In the first segment, we learn that Louisa is being courted by Bob Stone, her white employer's son, and also by Tom Burwell, a black sharecropper. In the second segment's rising action, Tom confronts Louisa when he learns about Bob, though she manages to smooth things over. In the third segment, however, Bob accosts Tom in a cane field and is killed; the town responds immediately by lynching Tom in the factory. The climactic action of the closing section echoes against each part of the refrain: the "ghost of a yell slipped through the flames and out the great door of a factory," a direct allusion to the refrain's imperative—"Come out that fact'ry door"—and Louisa's view of "the full moon, an evil thing, an omen" resonates against the ominous "blood-burning moon." The refrain, then, not only creates a tragic structure but also mirrors the violence of the vignette's climactic lynching scene, producing yet another layer of repetition.

As "Karintha" and "Blood-Burning Moon" demonstrate, the refrains in *Cane* not only help structure the vignettes into meaningful segments, but often bear important connections to the texts they are framing. Many of these repetitions center on the image of the lynched black body, as Susan Edmunds has argued (2003). This is certainly true for the refrain in "Kabnis"—"Whiteman's land. / Niggers, sing. / Burn, black children / Till poor rivers bring / Rest, and sweet glory / In Camp Ground"—which first appears as the whispering of the "night winds in Georgia," depicted here as "vagrant poets" (81). Kabnis hears their refrain as he drifts off to sleep in the beginning as well as the ending of the first section. The imperative in this refrain—"Burn, black children"—harkens back to the lynching tree depicted in "Song of the Son," to the burning corpse of Tom Burwell in "Blood-Burning Moon," and to the conceit established in the closing lines of the lyrical vignette "Portrait in Georgia": "And her slim body, white as the ash / of black flesh after flame" (27). It also, however, foreshadows the story's second section, in which Kabnis—a newcomer to the South—learns of the town's dark history with regard to lynching, the most poignant instance of which is the story of Mame Lamkins:

> She was in th family-way, Mame Lamkins was. They killed her in th street, an some white man seein th risin in her stomach as she lay there soppy in her blood like any cow, took an ripped her belly open, an th kid fell out. It was living; but a nigger baby aint supposed t live. So he jabbed his knife in it and stuck it t a tree. And they all went away. (90)

When the refrain appears a final time in section 5, it has become the "womb-song" of a "pregnant Negress," a clear allusion to the tragic lynching of Mame Lamkins (103). The refrain in "Kabnis" is a haunting reminder of southern lynch law, the ever-present threat of violence rendered legitimate through white supremacy.

Lexical and thematic repetitions travel frequently across *Cane*'s sections and subsections, binding together these otherwise disparate parts. The whispering pines that appear so frequently in "Becky" reappear in "Georgia Dusk" and "Kabnis," in which a sister's singing voice is likened to "the sound of evening winds that blow through pinecones" (90). The canebrake functions as a charged site of sexual ecstasy, jealousy, and violence in "Carma," "Fern," and "Blood-Burning Moon." Sunsets appear in nearly every sketch, save "Kabnis," which ends in daybreak. Repetitions also link these segments in ways that are unsettling, however. One cannot read the curling smoke that rises from the "pyramidal sawdust pile" in "Carma" and "Georgia Dusk," for instance, without remembering its original deployment as the site at which Karintha burns her unwanted child. Likewise, the conceit in "Face"—"Her channeled muscles / are cluster grapes of sorrow / purple in the evening sun / nearly ripe for worms" (8)—and that in "Song of the Son" ("O Negro slaves, dark purple ripened plums, / Squeezed, and bursting in the pine-wood air" [10]) also echo the fate of the unhappy Karintha, "a growing thing ripened too soon" (2). *Cane* may romanticize aspects of rural folk life, but it is also filled with haunting reverberations of lynching, infanticide, and sexual abuse—reverberations one is likely to miss if one is inattentive to the text's lexical repetitions.

Despite his reliance on fragmentation, Jean Toomer conceived the structure of *Cane* as a circle, as he describes to his publisher and friend Waldo Frank in a letter from December 12, 1922:

> From three angles, CANE's design is a circle. Aesthetically, from simple forms to complex ones, and back to simple forms. Regionally, from the South up into the North, and back into the South again. Or, from the North down into the South, and then a return North. From the point of view of the spiritual entity behind the work, the curve really starts with Bona and Paul (awakening), plunges into Kabnis, emerges in Karintha etc. swings upward into Theatre and Box Seat, and ends (pauses) in Harvest Song. . . . Between each of the three sections, a curve. These, to vaguely indicate the design. (Whalan 2006, 101)

Indeed, *Cane*'s sections are separated by three curved lines that may be combined to form a completed circle. One may begin reading from any number of places, Toomer suggests, and arrive at different and legitimate readings that are all validated by the novel's cyclical form. In essence, Toomer declares here that sequence is unimportant—or at the very least, it is arbitrary, since a sequence based on one starting point is just as valid as another. This point is missed by critics who argue that *Cane* should be read as a linear novel that chronicles the development of a poet-narrator in what amounts to a *künstlerroman*, "the quest of a modern black artist for sociopsychological wholeness and creative authority" (B. Bell 1989, 97). Such an approach demands that we read those first-person singular pronouns which occasionally appear in the vignettes and lyrics as a single, consistent narrator who develops over the course of *Cane*. This model, which is based a narrative-oriented reading practice, does enable us to read *Cane* as a coherent whole complete with character development and a narrative arc. The imposition of linearity onto *Cane*, however, not only suppresses those formal elements—namely segmentation and repetition—that have made it the avant-garde experiment for which it is so widely known and cited, but also distorts Toomer's own sense of the novel as one that may be picked up and completed at any number of different places.

If one takes seriously Toomer's pronouncements regarding *Cane*'s circularity, repetition can produce a variety of readings based on one's starting point. Reading *Cane* from start to finish, the novel's many references to dusk, which serves as a major conceit for skin coloration as well as the setting for nearly every sketch, are finally offset by "Kabnis," the closing lines of which herald a new day and possibly a new way of life: "Outside, the sun arises from its cradle in the tree-tops of the forest. Shadows of pines are dreams the sun shakes from its eyes. The sun arises. Gold-glowing child, it steps into the sky and sends a birth-song slanting down gray dust streets and sleepy windows of the southern town" (116). The "birth-song" of the sun's rays suggests a new beginning for African Americans who, until this point in the text, have endured extreme prejudice, violence, and back-breaking manual labor for wealthy white landowners under a new economy that scarcely differs from slavery. Read straight through, the novel ends on a note of hope and redemption rather than pessimism or defeat. If we begin reading with "Kabnis," however, and finish after the middle section, the novel begins at daybreak and remains suspended in dusk until finally concluding at nighttime, the setting for "Bona and Paul." This sketch, which closes *Cane*'s middle section, ends with Paul's hopeful declaration that "something beautiful is going to happen," after which he discovers that Bona has disappeared (78). Read this way, *Cane* begins with the hopefulness of sunrise, moves through scenes of violence and despair at dusk, and concludes at night with yet another instance of a hope aborted.

Toomer's awareness of the variant patterns of movement that his novel yields—from simple to complex forms, and complex to simple; south to north, and north to south; spiritual awakening to despair and back again—demonstrates repetition's resistance to a single linear sequence and its tendency toward a multidirectional movement that can sustain a multiplicity of readings. A novel like *Cane*, which demands to be read both forward and backward, showcases repetition's potential for both coherence and disruption within a single text. *Cane*'s fragments may cohere in the repetitions that build overarching themes and patterns through which we can read the novel as a whole, but the different contexts they supply for these phrases and images unsettles any stability of meaning we might be tempted to assign to them, just as the enigmatic image of the smoldering sawdust pile appears in contexts ranging from Karintha's infanticide to industry and labor in "Carma" and "Georgia Dusk," where it is coupled with the blowing of the sawmill whistle that signals the end of the workday. Repetition urges us to read each instance of a term or image against the others, but not without an eye for difference. After all, the variations and breaks in these patterns are often as important as the pattern itself, just as the closing lines of "Kabnis" signal a significant break from the theme of dusk, which may be interpreted in a variety of ways depending on where we begin reading.

Approaching *Cane* through a lyrical framework enables us to read the text as a relation of parts in a way that accounts for, rather than ignores, its cyclical thematic and lexical repetitions. In fact, a lyrical reading of *Cane* would bring together two divergent and conflicting strains of scholarship that argue for readings based on either fragmentation or unity. Critics such as John Reilly (1970) and Linda Wagner-Martin (1995) have insisted that *Cane* is a collection of fragments that never quite coheres into a unified whole, whereas others, including Catherine Innes (1972) and Patricia Watkins (1972), have argued that the text is united by certain overarching themes and symbols, such as "man's inability to communicate and interact with fellow humans; the inability to understand and therefore to love; the inability to quicken another human soul" (Watkins 1972, 305). If we read *Cane* the way we might read a lyric poem—as a series of interrelated parts that bear heuristic relations to one another through linguistic and thematic repetitions—we are able to account for both fragmentation and unity without contradiction.

Gertrude Stein is known for her use of repetition, and *Three Lives* ([1909] 2006) is no exception. The work, which presents three discrete but thematically connected fictional lives, appears to be predicated on the sequential progression that the biography mode demands, but each section is dominated instead by repetitions that suggest an elliptical, rather than linear, movement. The novel's repetitions at the level of language defy readers to track the changing meanings of these repeated terms, which become increasingly unstable with each new deployment. These linguistic repetitions are, however, brought to bear on the novel's content, as each "life" or section presents an implicit critique of traditional narrative form by presenting alternatives to worldviews premised on the logic of linear sequence. On the levels of both form and content, *Three Lives* suggests that lyrical repetition may provide a better account of our lived experience than the sequential progression that typically structures narrative fiction.

In contrast to Dos Passos and even Toomer, Stein uses repetition for purposes of dislocation rather than coherence. In particular, the epithets that supply the titles for two of the three stories—"The Good Anna" and "The Gentle Lena"—invite readers to judge and question precisely how "good" and "gentle," respectively, the titular characters might be. Homeric epithets in the epic tradition provided simple and memorable tags that, in part, managed reader response by "telling" rather than "showing" an audience how to feel about a character, but Stein deploys epithets in ways that almost immediately call these labels into question.

The opening lines of "The Good Anna," for example, which feature the first appearance of the titular epithet, center neither on the servant Anna nor on her goodness but on the merchants she has exasperated through her miserly bargaining tactics: "The tradesmen of Bridgepoint learned to dread the sound of 'Miss Mathilda,' for with that name the good Anna always conquered. The strictest of the one price stores found that they could give things for a little less, when the good Anna had fully said that 'Miss Mathilda" could not pay so much and that she could buy it cheaper 'by Lindheims' " (7). Subsequent appearances of the epithet corroborate this portrait of Anna as a manipulative micromanager. Anna brazenly dominates the employers she purports to serve, criticizing nearly every aspect of Miss Mathilda's lifestyle, from her clothes to her late night "country tramps" with friends to her finances and art collecting: "'And I slave and slave to save the money and you go out and spend it all on foolishness,' the good Anna would complain when her mistress, a large and careless woman, would come home with a bit of porcelain, a new etching and sometimes even an oil painting on her arm" (13–14). Powerless against the good Anna's stalwart personality, Miss Mathilda eventually relinquishes her decision making to her "good" yet officious servant: "Life was very easy for this large and lazy Miss Mathilda, with the good Anna to watch and care for her and all her clothes and goods" (14). In the early sections of the novel, the epithet is consistently placed in contexts that render it ironic, given Anna's stubborn need to control her environment. Equally domineering toward her friends and lovers, Anna becomes incensed when the widow Mrs. Lehntman—"the romance in Anna's life" (19)—adopts a child she cannot afford to maintain: "'My, Miss Annie is real mad now,' Julia said, as the house shook, as the good Anna shut the outside door with a concentrated shattering slam" (29). Anna is even authoritarian toward her dogs, constantly scolding them for bad behavior: "The good Anna," the narrator gently mocks her, "had high ideals for canine chastity and discipline" (8). The contexts in which "the good Anna" initially appears, then, seem to suggest that Anna's epithet is laden with sarcasm.

The good Anna does, however, exhibit a number of good qualities as the story unfolds, and the epithet is redeployed in ways that elicit greater sympathy for her character. She is disciplined and industrious, happiest when she feels needed and is able to fulfill her duty as a fiercely loyal—and nurturing—employee: "Taking care of Miss Mathilda were the happiest days of all the good Anna's strong hard working life" (40). She is also a caring friend and lover, though she is often exploited and betrayed by others, including Mrs. Lehntman, who abandons Anna and decides to pursue a heterosexual relationship with the new doctor in town: "This was most mysterious and unpleasant and very hard for our good Anna to endure" (36). Anna even becomes a generous philanthropist, despite her best efforts toward fiscal responsibility: "Save and you will have the money you saved, was all that she could know. Not that the good Anna had it so. She saved and saved and always saved, and then here and there, to this friend and that, to one in her trouble and the other in her joy . . . it always went, the hard earned money she had saved." In time, Anna's generosity extends beyond her friends to perfect strangers and animals: "So the good Anna gave her all to friends and strangers, to children, dogs and cats, to anything that asked or seemed to need her care" (42).

Yet Anna's compassionate generosity must be measured not only against her negative qualities but also against her hypocrisy, since her chief criticism of Mrs. Lehntman and her daughter, Julia, is their inability to manage their money wisely, whether through poorly financed philanthropic projects (in the case of Mrs. Lehntman) or selfish indulgences (in the case of Julia). Their irresponsible spending habits affect Anna so deeply that they darken her whole outlook: "The good Anna could not understand the careless and bad ways of all the world and always she grew bitter with it all. No, not one of them had any sense of what was the right way for them to do" (47). Anna, however, falls into the same spending pattern when she is nearly unable to maintain the boarding house she acquires because she charges so little in rent. Though her friends advise her to demand more money from her tenants, "the good Anna somehow could not do it" (50). As a result, Anna is forced to get rid of her hired help and effectively works herself into an early grave to stay afloat financially. Though the doctor pleads with her to rest, she stubbornly resists his advice, and following an operation, "the good Anna with her strong, strained, worn-out body died" (52). In these sections, Anna's epithet appears in contexts that are quite ambivalent: she is generous but perhaps unreasonably so, and certainly excessive in her criticisms of Mrs. Lehntman's inability to weigh her philanthropy against her finances; what is more, Anna's refusal to heed doctors' orders suggests that she might have something of a martyr complex, especially given the "strained" and "worn-out" condition of her overtaxed body at the time of her death.

"The good Anna," it turns out, is a complex character, not all good and yet not without redeeming qualities, stalwart and caring, though also stubborn, overly critical, and controlling. The epithet appears exactly sixty times throughout the story, and each instance must be weighed against the rest if readers are to develop a complete picture of the contradictory Anna. The first of Stein's "three lives," the good Anna moves between extreme states of being in a way that generates a paradoxical portrait, as she vacillates between service and authority, generosity and parsimoniousness. These epithets do not accrue cumulative meaning so much as they represent meaning that exists in a continuous state of alteration in which the "initial reading is adjusted" with each reiteration, as Lyn Hejinian suggests of repetition's role in avant-garde lyric poetry that rejects closure (2000). Stein too forgoes closure for a different kind of life-writing in *Three Lives*, one that refuses to contain its characters within the strictures of narrative biography.

In a similar vein, "The Gentle Lena" calls into question its titular epithet, since "gentle" appears in a wide variety of contexts that range from softness to stupidity to spinelessness. Though its initial deployment merely establishes Lena's pleasant demeanor—"Lena was patient, gentle, sweet and german"—the adjective quickly becomes an indication of weakness when it appears a second time as the servant Lena attempts to wake the children in her charge:

> Lena's german voice when she knocked and called the family in the morning was as awakening, as soothing, and as appealing, as a delicate soft breeze in midday, summer. She stood in the hallway every morning a long time in her unexpectant and unsuffering german patience calling to the young ones to get up. She would call and wait a long time and then call again, always even, gentle, patient, while the young ones fell back often into that precious, tense, last bit of sleeping. (149)

Though Lena's gentleness is again presented as pleasant and sweet, it is downright ineffectual, given her charge: her voice is so "soothing," so "delicate," that it fails to wake the children at all. Lena is increasingly linked to passivity and impotence as the story develops: "Lena, who was patient, sweet and quiet, had not self-control, nor any active courage" (154). In fact, it is her "gentleness" that makes her so pliable in the hands of others, especially in those of Mrs. Haydon, who manipulates Lena's penchant to follow orders because "she did not know that she could do anything different," bullying Lena into an early and unwanted marriage (156). Lena's husband-to-be, Herman, is also described as "gentle" in similar contexts: "He was gentle and a little fearful. . . . He was obedient to his mother and father" (157). Gentleness, it appears, has quickly become a euphemism for pusillanimity.

The term is also used to indicate Lena's lack of intelligence. Habitually described as "dull" and "simple" by Mr. Haydon (155), Lena is derided by the other girls in town for her stupidity: "The other girls . . . all liked the simple, gentle, german Lena very well. They all, too, liked very well to tease her, for it was so easy to make her mixed and troubled" (149). Lest this stir our sympathy for Lena, the narrator insists that Lena is too simple, her emotions too "gentle," to feel suitably hurt by their cruelty: "It was all a peaceful life for Lena, almost as peaceful as a pleasant leisure. The other girls, of course, did tease her, but then that only made a gentle stir within her" (150). Though this last line is repeated twice, we cannot take the narrator's declarations at face value, since neither the narrator nor the story's characters are very sympathetic toward Lena; as Marianne DeKoven points out, only two characters—the streetcar conductor and Mrs. Haydon's cook—express any compassion for Lena, and they are also the only characters to report that Lena has been crying (170n5). Lena's despair, as revealed by these characters, not only indicates the complexity of her emotions but also belies the narrator's insistence that, though Lena is continuously mistreated, she "never really knew that she was slighted" (155).

As Lena sinks into a profound depression at the end of the story, the adjectives *careless*, *dull*, and *lifeless* appear together to describe her new temperament on four separate narrative occasions. In effect, they replace, and are set in opposition to, the "gentleness" that defines Lena in the story's opening pages. Here, gentleness—in striking contrast to these new modifiers—is cast as some prelapsarian state of happiness that predates the births of her three children: "Sometimes Lena would wake up a little and get back into her face her old, gentle patient, and unsuffering sweetness," though, we are told, these occasions are increasingly rare (173). After Lena dies in childbirth, delivering a stillborn child who "was like its mother lifeless" (174), the cook chooses to remember Lena in her original state of gentleness: "She remembered how nice Lena had looked all the time she was in service with her, and how her voice had been so gentle and sweet-sounding" (174). Here, *gentle* is yoked to nostalgia, standing in for the simplicity and innocence of Lena's life before becoming a wife and a mother. Though the adjective has been associated with ineffectuality and stupidity, its evaluation changes again at the story's conclusion, preferred as it is to Lena's domestic misery.

Gentle takes on such a wide array of meanings that each instance must be weighed against the others for a full picture of Lena. Our readerly judgment of Lena and her circumstances hinges on our ability to chart the changing meaning of this elastic term, through which she is continuously defined. Beginning as a pleasant but meek servant girl, Lena is increasingly characterized as simple and dim-witted, though she regains our sympathy through her unhappiness and the complexity of emotions that her unhappiness betrays—all through the repetition of a single term. Despite the emphasis on biography and portraiture in *Three Lives*, Stein's characters remain elusive, in part because their epithets are too simple to be suitably descriptive or even accurate. Rather than cementing characterization, repetition suggests that we may never know these characters well enough to affix them with labels at all.

The violation of sequence in *Three Lives* also extends beyond the repetition of epithets. It is no accident that all three stories are domestic narratives that focus on home life and family structure. All feature unhappy women who must reconcile themselves to a heteronormative culture geared toward sexual reproduction, the ultimate manifestation of sequence and progress.[9] Not only does Anna resist translating her life into narrative terms through her failure to reproduce, but she is quite hostile to the children of her friends and employers, who tend to interfere with her relationships: Anna leaves the household of Miss Mary Wadsmith on account of her employer's daughter, Jane, and she is less than fond of Mrs. Lehntman's two children, becoming furious when Mrs. Lehntman expands her family by adopting another child without consulting Anna. Indeed, Anna's easiest and most felicitous relationship is her service to the single and childless Miss Mathilda. This relationship frames the story, which is structured not as a chronological sequence but through Anna's personal and professional ties. The most meaningful relationships in "The Good Anna" inhere not in vertical bloodlines but in lateral, elective alliances, suggesting the intrinsic value in what is nonsequential and nonreproductive. "The Gentle Lena" is likewise critical of domestic narratives premised on the familiar sequence of courtship, marriage, and children. Though she and Herman initially resist marriage, they succumb to pressure from Lena's aunt and Herman's parents. They follow a traditional sequence by having a child soon thereafter, and though "poor Lena was not feeling any joy to have a baby," she delivers two more before dying in childbirth with her fourth (172). In effect, sequence kills the gentle Lena, who cannot seem to find an alternative to reproduction in perpetuity.

These issues come to a head in "Melanctha: Each One as She May," the longest and most complex of the three lives, in which the repetition of Melanctha's "wandering" becomes Stein's alternative to narrative sequence. The very expression *wandering* suggests the kind of restless, antilinear movement inherent in repetition, and Melanctha's "wandering" implies everything from geographical exploration to introspective soul-searching to sexual experimentation. Primarily, though, Melanctha's "wandering" is connected to her quest for some primal form of knowledge and self-mastery: "She wandered, always seeking but never more than very dimly seeing wisdom" (60). *Wisdom*, another repeated term, is charged with sexual meaning and seems to be achieved through social and sexual deviance. Chided by townsfolk for her promiscuous "wanderings," Melanctha finally attains "wisdom" in her relationship with Jane Harden: "It was not from the men that Melanctha learned her wisdom. It was always Jane Harden herself who was making Melanctha begin to understand. . . . Melanctha began to really understand" (65–67).

Whole phrases are repeated throughout the story, with subtle changes in syntax and word order: Melanctha is "a little wandering and mysterious and uncertain in her ways" (56); Melanctha is "mysterious and uncertain and wandering in her ways" (57); and having found wisdom with Jane, Melanctha is no longer uncertain but is still "mysterious in her ways" (69). Melanctha, the only protagonist in the collection who is *not* tagged with an epithet, possesses a strong enigmatic quality that is absent from the other heroines of *Three Lives*. What's more, these phrases link Melanctha's mystery to her "wandering," forging a connection between psychological complexity and sexual self-discovery. Much of Melanctha's depth as a character is derived from her "mysterious" sexuality, which is never fully disclosed.

The local repetitions in "Melanctha" are replicated on a larger, structural level with the repetition of entire paragraphs that tie the end of the story back to its beginning, and vice versa: the paragraph that juxtaposes the "subtle, intelligent, attractive half white" Melanctha to the "coarse, decent, sullen, ordinary, black childish Rose," for instance—a juxtaposition that also, as a number of scholars have pointed out, reveals Stein's racism—reappears nearly word for word much later in the story (54, 131), as does the story's opening paragraph, which narrates the death of Rose's baby on account of Rose's inexplicable negligence (53, 140). In fact, the story begins and ends not with Melanctha at all but with Stein's portrait of Rose Johnson, whose simplicity and selfishness provide a marked contrast to the enigmatic yet kind-hearted Melanctha, who "always loved too hard and much too often" (56).

The lexical and grammatical repetitions in "Melanctha" may be fairly obvious—nouns (*wisdom*), verbs (*wandering*), adverbs (*certainly*), phrases, even paragraphs are repeated ad nauseum—but the story's content again works to reinforce these formal repetitions by forgoing linear progress for other kinds of movement and development. Melanctha's pursuit of knowledge through avenues that are elliptical and experiential, even carnal, suggests an alternative model of epistemology that is based on exploration and bodily feeling, as opposed to a narrative-based model premised on rational sequence and teleological progress.[10] Here, Jeff Campbell represents narrative, or the privileging of reason over feeling and progress over regress. After all, Jeff is wedded to quixotic ideas about racial progress that identify Melanctha's presentism as precisely the problem:

> I don't, no, never, believe in doing things just to get excited. You see Miss Melanctha, I mean the way so many of the colored people do it. Instead of just working hard and caring about their working and living regular with their families and saving up all their money, so they will have some to bring up their children better, instead of living regular and doing like that and getting all their new ways from just decent living, the colored people just keep running around and perhaps drinking and doing everything bad they can ever think of, and not just because they like all those bad things that they are always doing, but only just because they want to get excited. (76)

Melanctha counterassails by pointing to Jeff's cowardice as the real motivation behind his social philosophy: "You certainly are just too scared Dr. Campbell to really feel things way down in you" (77). Jeff's emotional life appears to corroborate Melanctha's insight, since Jeff is happiest when he yields to feeling and, subsequently, to "wandering": "It was sometimes pure joy Jeff would be talking to Melanctha, in these warm days he loved so much to wander with her. Sometimes Jeff would lose all himself in a strong feeling" (96). Only when he is apart from Melanctha does Jeff become mired in anxiety and self-doubt. He is overtaken by rationality, which, paradoxically, confuses rather than clarifies his position: "And Jeff tried to begin again with his thinking, and he could not make it come clear to himself, with all his thinking, and he felt everything all thick and heavy and bad, now inside him, everything that he could not understand right, with all the hard work he made, with his thinking" (106–7). Because he is ultimately unable to abandon himself to feeling, Jeff remains "uncertain" of himself and of his relationship with Melanctha (103); tethered equally to bourgeois conduct and rational analysis, Jeff never absorbs the "wisdom" that Melanctha tries to impart to him.

If we tease out the metafictional implications of "Melanctha," we might identify the story's tension between linearity and circumlocution as the dramatization of two contrasting literary modes: a narrative model premised on sequential development from beginning to ending and a lyrical model rooted in repetition and feeling. The structure—and content—of "Melanctha" leans much more heavily toward the latter than the former, which is criticized, even lampooned, in the depiction of Jeff Campbell, who refuses to admit elements of lyric into his worldview. In fact, we lose a great deal if we insist on reading this story as a sequential progression that charts Melanctha from her sexual awakening to her abandonment by Jane Harding, Jeff Campbell, and finally Rose Johnson, to her unremarkable death. Such movement, which traces a life in decline, may validate the view of the townsfolk, as well as that of Jeff Campbell, who believed that Melanctha "would never come to any good" on account of her wandering (69), and of Rose Johnson, who casts off Melanctha because she "never can have no kind of a way to act right, the way a decent girl has to do" (145). It fails, however, to capture Melanctha's heroism as a sexual iconoclast who achieves fulfillment through "wisdom"; it also fails to garner adequate sympathy for a character who falls short of happiness not because of her moral conduct but because of the anxieties and petty jealousies of others.

Reading "Melanctha" through a lyrical framework enables us to remain faithful not only to the story's organization but to Melanctha's achievement of sexual discovery and self-mastery. We are better positioned to see the structural connections between Melanctha and the story itself, reinforcing Melanctha as a sympathetic protagonist in spite of the negative commentary from other characters. Layers of repetition in the story cause the text itself to "wander" at various levels and scales, from the word to the paragraph to the story's overarching narrative structure. Accordingly, our attention also wanders—from the end of the story to its beginning and back again, from one linguistic unit of meaning to another, from Melanctha's relationship with Jane Harding to her relationships with Jeff Campbell, Rose Johnson, and Jem Richards. The text, like Melanctha, resists the imposition of sequence.

Like Toomer and Dos Passos, Stein experiments here with segmentivity, conceiving of her novel as an interrelation of parts to their whole. In an interview with Robert Haas in 1946, she described *Three Lives* as a narrative experiment akin to Cézanne's postimpressionism:

> Cézanne conceived the idea that in composition one thing was as important as another thing. Each part is as important as the whole, and that impressed me enormously, and it impressed me enormously, and it impressed me so much that I began to write *Three Lives* under this influence and this idea of composition and I was more interested in composition at that moment, this background of word-system, which had come to me from this reading I had done. I was obsessed by this idea of composition, and the Negro Story ["Melanctha"] was a quintessence of it. (Haas 1971, 15)

Stein suggests that the best way to navigate *Three Lives* is not through the narrative linearity represented by Jeff Campbell but through the lyrical structure represented by Melanctha's wandering. Such an approach better preserves the part-whole relationship that undergirds Stein's fractal project in which complex patterns of repetition occur at multiple levels and scales. Scholars typically treat one or another of these three lives in isolation from the others, but Stein's comments, coupled with the important formal and thematic connections among these stories—manifested primarily through repetition—suggest that they are best read together as stories that build an aesthetic as well as an ideological critique of narrative sequence.[11]

If Stein uses repetition for purposes of hermeneutic disruption, preventing characterization from ever crystallizing around her three protagonists, Kathy Acker takes repetition one step farther, turning it in the direction of satire. The punk/feminist/postmodernist writer's experimental novels flout social and narrative conventions alike, and *Blood and Guts in High School* (1978), Acker's best-known and most critically acclaimed work, has a plot so bizarre that it can hardly be summarized with any coherence. The novel loosely charts the story of Janey Smith, a precocious adolescent who is abandoned by her father, who is also her lover; subsequently, Janey enrolls in high school in New York City and joins a gang called "THE SCORPIONS," undergoes multiple abortions, is kidnapped and sexually abused by a Persian slave trader, and escapes to Tangiers, where she joins up with writer Jean Genet before dying of cancer at fourteen. Like Dos Passos's *U.S.A.* and Toomer's *Cane*, Acker's novel incorporates a variety of genres and modes into its textual fabric. Shifting unpredictably between narrative prose and dramatic dialogue, it is filled with crude drawings of genitals, lyrics lifted from other poets, a handwritten collection of "Persian poems" (a series of Persian phrases that Janey translates into English), a separate series of love poems Janey writes to her Persian captor, and a lengthy "book report" on *The Scarlet Letter*. The lyric sections in particular are filled with repetitions, some crude ("SUCK ME SUCK ME SUCK ME"), some rhetorical ("I like fire. / I like glory. / I like stars"), and some therapeutic, the articulation of words and feelings that Janie cannot seem to express to the men who routinely take advantage of her ("No No No No No No NO NO NO") (109–10).

Repetition also bleeds into Janey's main narrative, especially as it becomes a lexical and structural manifestation of her trauma.[12] One of Acker's most remarkable experiments with narrative form is her singular use of repetition on the scale of the paragraph, a device that quite literally stalls the progression of Janey's story for four entire pages. The passage in which Janey's father-lover spends the day with her before leaving her for somebody else, for example, appears no less than six times in a row. This "last day" is traumatic for Janey, who has anticipated this moment with mounting dread. In fact, she unwittingly seems to have willed it into being by way of repetition, insisting to her father, "You are going to leave me," seven times until it finally becomes a reality: "You said I was going to leave you before it even entered my mind," her father later reveals (23).

The day is brief and anticlimactic: they meet after work, they eat together, they avoid difficult topics, and they part ways. Nevertheless, the scene is replayed again and again as the narrator—who is closely aligned with Janey—desperately attempts to assign it some greater significance. The repetition of this passage is also, however, connected to Janey's psychological distress, which results not only from a father who treats her like a domineering wife, but also from his abandonment of her to a "totally fucked-up" world in which she can—and does—manage to fare much worse (66). As Suzette Henke has argued, the repetition in Janey's narrative reflects the symptoms of posttraumatic stress disorder listed in the DSM-IV: "Recurrent and intrusive recollections of the [traumatic] event, . . . 'psychic numbing' or 'emotional anesthesia,' and feelings of alienation characterized by a 'markedly reduced ability to feel emotions' " (quoted in Henke 2008, 94). Subsequently, she argues, "Janey Smith courts compulsive re-exposure to situations reminiscent of incest trauma and Oedipal abuse."

Indeed, repetition is built into the novel's very plot as Janey continuously seeks to replicate her bizarre and damaging relationship with her father in her relationships with other men. As Susan Hawkins points out, Janey is "doomed to reproduce her primal desire for Johnny within every heterosexual relationship she encounters. . . . Desire for her father recursively rules her life" (2004, 645). Janey is even comically self-aware of her psychosis: "This time when I run after a man who doesn't want me," she writes in her diary as she pursues the homosexual Genet, "I'm *really* going to run after him" (Acker 1978, 117). Cruelty and rejection, however, only seem to arouse desire in the broken Janey. Sexually abused by her captor Linker, she writes him a series of love poems: "Are you really crazy, doesn't my love mean anything to?" (105). When Genet tells her that she "stink[s] more than this gaol does. You lousy stinking pervert," she responds with another erotic lyric: "The night is opening up, / to our thighs, / like this cunt which I'm holding in my hand" (136). Janey has not only learned through repetition to cope with abuse, but she appears to crave it.

This constitutes the chief irony of Janey's narrative: though many events occur in sequence, nothing really changes as Janey compulsively recreates her unhealthy relationship with Johnny in all of the novel's major events, including her experiences with the gang, her kidnapping and enslavement by Linker, her romance with Jimmy Carter, and her adventures in North Africa with Genet. In this respect, the repetition of the passage that depicts her last day with Johnny stands in microcosmically for the narrative as a whole, which—even as it appears to move forward—is mired in repetition. Janey's life, not unlike Melanctha's, is characterized by a series of traumatic abandonments by abusive men—first her father, then Linker, then Carter, and finally Genet. The imposition of linear sequence onto *Blood and Guts* is not only difficult to effect, but it yields disappointing results, especially given the narrative's anticlimactic conclusion: "She dies" (140).

Blood and Guts has been called a "parodic Bildungsroman" (Hawkins 2004, 643), and certainly, part of the joke is Acker's deviation from the sequential progression that structures the traditional coming-of-age novel. *Blood and Guts* is divided and subdivided into sections with titles that misleadingly suggest growth and maturation, though these sections are filled with content that suggests otherwise. The major section titled "Inside high school," for example, follows Janey as she spends curiously little time inside high school at all, joining up instead with "THE SCORPIONS," who have other priorities: "Despite the restrictions of school, we did exactly what we wanted and it was good. We got drunk. We used drugs. We fucked. We hurt each other sexually as much as we could" (32). The segment "Janey becomes a woman" begins with Janey's description of her tenement slum—"All you hear is continuous noise, you smell garbage and piss which drips through the walls continually, and all the people you know live like you" (57)—and culminates in her beating and kidnapping as she is sold into "white slavery" (61). Womanhood for Janey is filled with poverty, violence, and sexual humiliation. Later in the novel, Janey complains that "Genet doesn't know how to be a woman. He thinks all he has to do to be a woman is to slobber. He has to do more. He has to get down on his knees and crawl mentally every minute of the day. . . . [Women] are whatever their men want them to be. They are made, created by men" (130).

Janey's maturation is not marked by the typical milestones that structure a bildungsroman, and despite the novel's title, school plays only a marginal role. As far as Janey is concerned, formal education is yet another tool of psycho-sexual exploitation in which "important men . . . train the child to suck their cocks. That's what's known as education" (94). Instead, Janey's life is measured by increasingly grim levels of abuse, not only by individual men but by the misogynistic institutions that concentrate their power, including the abortion clinic in which she finds herself: "The women in my line were handed long business forms: at the end of each form was a paragraph that stated she gave the doctor the right to do whatever he wanted and if she ended up dead, it wasn't his fault. We had given ourselves up to men before. That's why we were here. All of us signed everything. Then they took our money" (32). If there is any structure to our lived experience, Janey seems to suggest, it is based on a model of ruinous regress rather than progress. "In the beginning, on the desert island, the world was totally beautiful," she writes in the vein of Genesis. "Today in my room in New York City the world is horrible and disgusting. What the hell happened?" (69)

The tone of Janey's narrative, however, is remarkably far from tragic; Janey's mordant sense of humor and the levity with which she treats her own exploitation display instead the hallmarks of black comedy. By coupling tone with repetition, Acker effectively turns the lyric into a vehicle for satire. The object of satire, as in much postmodernist fiction, may remain obliquely "diffuse," to borrow the terminology of Kathryn Hume; *Blood and Guts* appears to target a number of deeply rooted social traditions and institutions ranging from patriarchy to education to sexual modesty. Yet Acker is also attacking the aesthetic tradition of narrative fiction by creating a novel that resists, even derides, sequential logic on linguistic, structural, and thematic levels.

By way of contrast, the most serious and earnest sections of *Blood and Guts* are Janey's dreams, which include nightmares as well as fantasies, drawn by hand in her "Map of my Dreams" (46–51). Her dreams resist narrative temporality altogether and are instead projected spatially, consisting of hand-drawn fragments, pictures, lines, and arrows that push readers to traverse the page from multiple directions and angles—up and down, left to right, right to left, diagonally. The mininarratives she creates within this dream map are in the present tense: "We run and run over the low rolling hills. I'm petting a lion as we run along," she narrates (46). Those elements that are missing from Janey's main narrative—childhood and love, as she has been deprived of both—are represented spatially here. In the space designated "THE CHILDHOOD LAND," Janey is able to access those standard childhood experiences she has missed as a result of her abuse: "Park of concrete where I play with other children. My mother watches. I scrape my knees to bloody pulp on the concrete" (47). She also justifies the blank spots on her map by spatializing what she most craves: "All the empty spaces are love," she explains (50).

These spatial maps deliberately frustrate narrative sequence, especially beginnings and endings.[13] Where does one begin reading on these maps, and where does one finish? It becomes impossible to tell. Even when the reader chooses an arbitrary starting point, there is no clear direction that leads from one picture or storyline to another. Instead, the map forces the reader's eyes to wander all over the page. Sometimes, text appears sidewise at a ninety-degree angle; sometimes it appears vertically as an acrostic. Arrows are aimless, pointing the reader in multiple and contradictory directions, a number of which simply lead to dead ends. A set of arrows that guides readers along with Janey through a series of parks, for instance, culminates in the following prompt: "There are no directions here. The river is a flood, rapids, huge waves. I love it" (50).

The pictorial and textual fragments displayed on the maps are disjointed, to say the least, but they provide a microcosmic and spatial representation of our experience of navigating the text as a whole. Spaces, lines, and arrows that should provide directional cues effectively frustrate our reading practices instead. Because linear reading strategies culminate in dead ends and cul-de-sacs, we are faced with the impossible task of trying to read everywhere at once. The dream map is one of many full-page diagrams, pictures, and poems that interrupt Acker's narrative; how, and at what point, do readers integrate these insertions into the main narrative? The structure and spatial arrangement of the text precludes any easy answer, forcing us to experience its pieces simultaneously in a way that quite deliberately evades the sequential logic of narrative fiction.

In part, these experiments with repetition are also experiments with reader response and cognition, as Kathy Acker has confessed: "How does the reader remember, or what does the reader remember when you repeat something over and over again? How do language and memory work even in the most well constructed, logical texts?" (E. Friedman 1989, 15). To be sure, repetitions present a special mnemonic challenge when placed within narrative fiction, since novels are much longer than lyric poems, and readers are forced to retain lines and images in their minds for far greater spans of time as repetitions are spread out among great expanses of narrative space. Ten pages separate Karintha's "pyramidal sawdust pile" from that in "Georgia Dusk" in *Cane*; 256 pages separate the first and second mentions of Patrick Henry in *1919*. The attentive reader finds herself flipping backward in these novels, wondering, haven't I read this before? where else did this appear? and, why does it appear again?

Repetition in narrative fiction, then, is an assault on our commonplace notions of genre, in which novels, unlike lyric poems, are to be read from start to finish without so much as a backward glance. "Narrative texts are usually fairly long, longer than most poems," argues Mieke Bal, "which is why one usually reads them straight through, not retracing one's steps as one tends to do in the case of poems" (1997, 82). Instead, the authors treated here have created novels premised on the structural logic of lyric poetry, in which segmentation, repetition, and interreferentiality are foregrounded over progress, sequence, and succession, forcing the reader to look backward nearly as often as she looks forward.

The repetitions I have traced through these novels have been marshaled for very different, albeit political, ends. Dos Passos fixes his "camera eye" sections with repeated phrases and images that crystallize the trilogy's leftist politics. Toomer's refrains and recurring images connect *Cane*'s disparate parts in a deliberately circular structure, with many of them linked to the reverberations of lynching and racial violence that course through the text. Stein deploys repetitive epithets and adjectives in changing contexts to unsettle any easy categorization we might place on her characters and to suggest modes of thinking and living that run counter to heteronormative notions of sequence. Finally, Acker repeats entire paragraphs and events for satirical effect to diagnose and critique the sexual trauma that is virtually omnipresent in Janey's experiences as a woman. Far from producing stasis, repetition enlivens these texts by calling for reader participation in sorting out these recurrences and determining their significance. It asks that we suspend our faith in sequence to read narrative fiction—and the world—in a different way, that we see the value in aesthetic, social, and political strategies that are nonlinear and nonteleological.

These repetitions are also fractal, operating at multiple levels and scales from micro-level units of language, including singular words and phrases, to macro-level structures that give shape to plot. At the macro level, repetition is thematized, becoming an integral part of the fictional world it orders. These levels work in concert to reinforce repetition as way of erasing or obscuring linear sequence. The following chapter extends this analysis by examining a particular brand of syntactical repetition that exhibits a similar fractal structure beginning at the level of the sentence. Together, these chapters demonstrate the grammatical lyricality of the twentieth-century American novel, which works against narrativity from the ground up.

Chapter 3

Rhythm and Insubordination

In the summer of 2001, B. R. Myers launched his controversial attack on what he diagnosed as "the growing pretentiousness of American literary prose" in the pages of the *Atlantic Monthly*.[1] He framed his article, "A Reader's Manifesto," as a rebellion against the literary establishment on behalf of readers yearning for accessible writing only to receive "affectation and obscurity" from our most celebrated contemporary authors. Among the high-profile targets of the polemic was Cormac McCarthy, whom Myers accused of amassing conjunctions in an effort to create a "stern biblical tone" unbefitting his quotidian subject matter (108). As an exemplar, Myers offers a line recounting a cowboy breakfast from *The Crossing*, the second installment of McCarthy's popular "Border Trilogy": "He ate the last of the eggs and wiped the plate with the tortilla and ate the tortilla and drank the last of the coffee and wiped his mouth and looked up and thanked her" (McCarthy 1994, 354; quoted in Myers 2001,108).

The critique of McCarthy's syntax is twofold. Not only does Myers chastise McCarthy for mixing genres with disastrous results—"It's really just bad poetry formatted to exploit the lenient standards of modern prose," he argues—but he also charges the writer with using this elevated syntax indiscriminately. Because it is applied to events of unequal importance, from a casual meal to a climactic knife fight, Myers argues that the results "can only be described as kitsch" (108). While we may or may not agree with Myers's dismissive evaluations—and I certainly do not—he isolates an important stylistic phenomenon in prose fiction rooted in lyricality. Polysyndeton, or the purposeful repetition of coordinating conjunctions, can be marshaled for a variety of dramatic rhetorical effects, including a patterned rhythm that reinforced and even came to supplant meter in verse forms. What is more, polysyndeton's deliberate exclusion of subordinating conjunctions (*if*, *since*, *because*, *although*, *unless*, even *when*) runs counter to the grammatical conventions of narrative fiction, which relies on subordination not only to establish cause and effect but also to organize narrative into a lucid hierarchy of details, some of which are necessarily more important than others. After all, as Gerald Prince has argued, "narrative is usually not a simple concatenation of events in time but a hierarchical one"; that is, narrative should focus our attention so that certain events and details seem significant while others do not (1982, 151–52).

This chapter explores the rhetorical construction that so offends Myers, which is used with remarkable frequency in twentieth-century American fiction. I address both prongs of Myers's critique, from polysyndeton's alignment with meter and lineation to the leveling or equalizing effect it creates in lyric and narrative structures alike. While Faulkner and Hemingway reserve this device for moments of narrative climax, Don DeLillo and Cormac McCarthy exploit polysyndeton with greater—and purposeful—frequency, ultimately using this syntax as the basis for fictional economies in which items of disparate value are rendered equal, even interchangeable. Why do so many stylists of the last century rely on this unusual syntax, and what effects does it produce in their fiction?

As Myers suggests, some of the oldest and best-known literary instances of polysyndeton appear in the authoritative English translations of the Hebrew Bible.[2] The opening chapter of Genesis, for instance, famously exploits this syntax in its depiction of God's creation and population of the earth: "And God made the beasts of the earth according to their kinds and the cattle according to their kinds, and everything that creeps upon the ground according to its kind. And God saw that it was good" (Gen. 1:24–25). The same syntax appears as God inventories all of the organisms over which man will have dominion in the great chain of being: "Then God said, 'Let us make man in our image, after our likeness; and let them have dominion over the fish of the sea, and over the birds of the air, and over the cattle, and over all the earth, and over every creeping thing that creeps upon the earth" (1:26–27). Passages like these showcase polysyndeton's chief rhetorical strengths, including the power of enumeration. When coupled with the catalog, polysyndeton effectively isolates and grants singular attention and importance to each item within the construction. This device also creates a cumulative or piling effect when and is the chosen coordinator. Each new item in the list is simply appended onto the last without provision. For this reason, polysyndetic sentences tend to build momentum, picking up energy with each new item or detail that is inventoried.

Polysyndeton also creates a democratic leveling effect by which each item is granted the same significance within the structure. Items that are granted equal weight in a syntactic sense are ipso facto granted equal weight in a narrative sense as well. Like its grammatical cousin, parataxis,[3] polysyndeton—by definition a coordinating construction—refuses to admit subordination into its structure. The democratic power of this construction has been famously exploited by Walt Whitman, whose *Leaves of Grass* (1855) couples this syntax with an equalizing message in which nature's smallest and most quotidian detail—a leaf of grass, a grain of sand—carries as much import as the happenings of the cosmos:

> I believe a leaf of grass is no less than the journeywork of the stars,
> And the pismire is equally perfect, and a grain of sand, and the egg of the wren,
> And the tree-toad is a chef-d'ouvre [*sic*] for the highest,
> And the running blackberry would adorn the parlors of heaven,
> And the narrowest hinge in my hand puts to scorn all machinery,
> And the cow crunching with depressed head surpasses any statue,
> And a mouse is miracle enough to stagger sextillions of infidels,
> And I could come every afternoon of my life to look at the farmer's girl boiling her iron tea-kettle and baking shortcake. (34)

Whitman is also aided here by hyperbole, though he may well resent such a term, since the content—and structure—of this passage work hard to link these items through relations of equivalence rather than through manipulations or distortions of scale. Polysyndeton deliberately flattens hierarchical relations by placing each item, or set of items, within the coordination on equal structural footing.

Because it resists narrative's urge to subordinate—and hence discriminate—among the things it depicts, polysyndeton is a difficult syntax to maintain in prose fiction. Narrative can compile items of equal significance only for so long before its forward movement grinds to a halt. This structure is therefore limited in the kind of action it can depict. The opening chapters of Genesis again supply an important example: "Thus the heavens and the earth were finished, and all the host of them. And on the seventh day God finished his work which he had done, and he rested on the seventh day from all his work which he had done" (2:1–3). As this passage demonstrates, repetitive *and*s may well imply temporal or logical succession, even if these causal links are supplied by the reader rather than the author. Seymour Chatman has argued that "our minds inveterately seek structure, and they will provide it if necessary. Unless otherwise instructed, readers will tend to assume that even 'The king died and the queen died' presents a causal link, that the king's death has something to do with the queen's" (1978, 45–46). Even when representing action, however, polysyndeton that relies solely on the conjunction *and* is difficult to sustain. How can the narrative introduce a contrasting idea, an exception, a consequence, or a turn in events? At the very least, a narrative would require alternative coordinating conjunctions to move things along. "The Lord God took the man and put him in the garden of Eden to till it and keep it," Genesis continues. "And the Lord God commanded the man, saying, 'You may freely eat of every tree of the garden; but of the tree of the knowledge of good and evil you shall not eat, for in the day that you eat of it you shall die" (2:15–17). At last, a complication is introduced: while these sentences are still expressed through polysyndeton, the conjunctions in this passage modify God's offer with a caveat ("but") and a potential consequence ("for"). As the plot develops, subordinating conjunctions are gradually admitted into the narrative's grammatical structure: "So when the woman saw that the tree was good for food, and that it was a delight to the eyes, and that the tree was to be desired to make one wise, she took of its fruit and ate; and she also gave some to her husband, and he ate. Then the eyes of both were opened, and they knew that they were naked" (3:6–7). The consequences of this transgression are also necessarily expressed through subordination: "And to Adam he said, 'Because you have listened to the voice of your wife, and have eaten of the tree . . . cursed is the ground because of you" (3:17). The relationships among these events would be obscured by polysyndeton; only subordination can introduce the kinds of causal and hierarchical relationships that traditional narrative demands.

Consequently, polysyndeton that limits itself to *and* constructions has played a much stronger role in the lyric than in the narrative tradition. These coordinations impede narrative development, blurring the contours of plot by obscuring distinctions of time, importance, and causality, but lyric poems typically offer something different from a temporally or causally plotted story: a rumination, a state of mind, a feeling, a desire. What is more, lyric poetry—unlike most prose fiction—is propelled by intricate types of formal movement, usually some combination or another of meter, rhyme, alliteration, and lineation. Together, these formal components contribute to a poem's rhythm, those patterned movements of repetition that establish some measure of structural regularity within a lyric poem.

Units of meaning are, of course, measured differently in poetry than in prose: poems are made up of lines as well as sentences, and as Robert Pinsky reminds us, "the line and the syntactical unit are not necessarily the same," a simple fact that generates many of the complexities that accompany the reading of a poem (1998, 30). In fact, he argues, whether or not they align helps to determine poetic rhythm and speed: "The run-over lines and pauses, the varying line lengths, the varying way the unit of syntax (that is, the grammatical phrases) coincides with the unit of rhythm (that is, the lines) or does not coincide—all of these create an expressive, flamboyant whole" (28). A syntactical unit that spills over the bounds of the line—otherwise known as enjambment—may be a case in which "the syntax is trying to speed up the line, and the line is trying to slow down the syntax," creating a push-and-pull dynamic that could alternately accelerate or decelerate our reading of the poem, depending on which unit—the line or the sentence—is granted priority. In either case, however, the line remains the central "unit of rhythm"; syntax may manipulate the speed of a poem, but lineation is the driving force behind its structural regularity.

In lyrical instances of polysyndeton, syntax exceeds lineation, but lineation aligns systematically with the structure's smaller syntactic units in a way that produces an even and steady rhythm, since the conjunctions in these coordinations typically signal the beginning of a new line. Take, for instance, the simple rhythm of Blake's "A Poison Tree" from *Songs of Experience* (1789):

I was angry with my friend:
I told my wrath, my wrath did end,
I was angry with my foe:
I told it not, my wrath did grow.

And I watered it in fears,
Night & morning with my tears;
And I sunnèd it with smiles,
And with soft deceitful wiles.

And it grew both day and night,
Till it bore an apple bright.
And my foe beheld it shine,
And he knew that it was mine,

And into my garden stole,
When the night had veild the pole;
In the morning glad I see
My foe outstretched beneath the tree. (2002, 78)

The poem is in trochaic tetrameter, and because it adheres closely to the form, its meter and lineation are regular, producing a steady and predictable pulse. In a poem like this, polysyndeton is aligned precisely with lineation, which occurs along the construction's syntactic fault lines: the repeated coordinating conjunction *and*. Polysyndeton overwhelms this short lyric, and while it does convey some degree of sequential action, its primary role here is to depict wrath's tendency to accumulate and overwhelm when it is left to fester; here it operates within the conceit of the "poison tree" that yields a lethal apple to be eaten by the speaker's "foe." The poem's lines, which consist of roughly even grammatical units, suggest further that wrath's accumulation occurs not all at once but in steady increments. Just as polysyndeton derives its rhetorical force from the cumulative effect of its otherwise simple grammatical parts, so wrath derives its power from a nearly imperceptible accretion through steady rumination.

In formally traditional poems like Blake's, polysyndeton is clearly tied to meter, but this construction continues to bear a strong relation to lineation and, hence, to rhythm in the free verse poetry of the late nineteenth and twentieth centuries. In fact, one might argue that this coordination is particularly integral to establishing prosody since, as Frances Mayes suggests, lines become our central cue for reading verse in the absence of meter and rhyme, "broken to punctuate how the poet wants us to hear perceptions, individual speech, or breath rhythms" (2001, 268). Even in poetry that features lines of variable lengths, polysyndeton continues to organize lineation around its repetitive coordinating conjunctions; as a result, this rhetorical structure often establishes greater metric regularity than is found in the rest of a free verse poem. Again, *Leaves of Grass* serves as an exemplar, since polysyndeton deftly orders Whitman's prose-like verse into a rhythmic incantation:

> I mind how we lay in June, such a transparent summer morning;
> You settled your head athwart my hips and gently turned over upon me,
> And parted the shirt from my bosom-bone, and plunged your tongue to my barestript heart,
> And reached till you felt my beard, and reached till you held my feet.
> Swiftly arose and spread around me the peace and knowledge that pass all the argument of the earth;
> And I know that the hand of God is the elderhand of my own,
> And I know that the spirit of God is the eldest brother of my own,
> And that all the men ever born are also my brothers . . . and the women my sisters and lovers,
> And that a keelson of the creation is love;
> And limitless are leaves stiff or drooping in the fields,
> And brown ants in the little wells beneath them,
> And mossy scabs of the wormfence, and heaped stones, and elder and mullen and pokeweed. (15–16)

Polysyndeton shifts almost seamlessly here from articulating the motion of the lovers—"And reached till you felt my beard, and reached till you held my feet"—to another democratic compendium in which the quotidian gains cosmological significance. Leaves of grass are as powerful here as the God that unites the speaker with the rest of humankind. All relations are leveled: distant strangers become intimate relations ("brothers" and "sisters"); the particular becomes universal (an orgasm representing "the peace and knowledge that pass all the argument of the earth"); the bounded item (a leaf of grass) becomes "limitless."

Polysyndeton deliberately forgoes traditional syntax for heightened dramatic effect—for repetition and rhythm, for the magnified importance granted to each item in the construction, for the accumulation of meaning and feeling that builds over the course of the sentence. It is a powerful device, therefore, for imbuing everyday moments with striking intensity, and Whitman is not the only poet to have exploited its syntax toward this end. Consider another example, D. H. Lawrence's "Snake" (1921), which manipulates polysyndeton to convey the grandeur of the snake's movements:

> He drank enough
> And lifted his head, dreamily, as one who has drunken,
> And flickered his tongue like a forked night on the air, so black,
> Seeming to lick his lips,
> And looked around like a god, unseeing, into the air,

And slowly turned his head,
And slowly, very slowly, as if thrice adream,
Proceeded to draw his slow length curving round
And climb again the broken bank of my wall-face. (1964, 350)

The cadence created by these successive conjunctions simulates the smooth and controlled motions of the snake's body. The long lines and uneven lineation of this passage—itself the lengthiest stanza in the poem—both retard and syncopate our reading, forcing us to slow down in order to account for the unpredictability of the poem's free form. Lineation also mimics the slow and unpredictable movement of the snake along the speaker's water trough, a movement that is mirrored in the poem's curvy visual presentation on the printed page. Suddenly ashamed of his reverence for the snake, the speaker shatters this harmony by launching a log at the creature as it disappears through a hole in the wall: ". . . that part of him that was left behind convulsed in undignified haste." The metrics of this line, which cause us to trip over *undignified*, break the patterned, albeit syncopated, spell of polysyndeton. On a formal level, it mimics the disruption enacted by the speaker, who—now ashamed of his irreverence—is left alone with his "pettiness."

As Lawrence's poem demonstrates, polysyndeton can turn the very ordinary into a thing of wonder. The boorishness of Lawrence's speaker—"How paltry, how vulgar, what a mean act!" he curses himself—creates an aesthetic as well as ethical failure, since the poem's majestic syntax aligns with the majesty of the snake. Yet the syntactical structure of polysyndeton is itself very simple, composed only of phrases and clauses linked through repeated coordinating conjunctions. The grammatical simplicity of this rhetorical construction is made explicit in the purposefully pared-down verse of Lucille Clifton, especially in her lyric "good times" (1970):

My Daddy has paid the rent
and the insurance man is gone
and the lights is back on
and my uncle Brud has hit
for one dollar straight
and they is good times
good times
good times

My Mama has made bread
and Grampaw has come
and everybody is drunk
and dancing in the kitchen
and singing in the kitchen
oh these is good times

good times
good times

oh children think about the
good times[4]

The good times consist of simple pleasures: settled bills, home-cooked food, the company of family. Accordingly, they are expressed in short lines, colloquial language, and seemingly artless syntax. This poem showcases the austere structure that undergirds polysyndeton, though, as we have seen by now, this structure can be harnessed for a variety of dynamic—and complex—rhetorical effects, from Clifton's minimalism to Whitman's exuberance, from the controlled meter of Blake's "A Poison Tree" to the loose syncopation of Lawrence's "Snake." In each case, however, polysyndeton accumulates rather than narrates details; also in each case, it generates a discernible rhythm, albeit one that is open and flexible.

Even in the absence of lineation—though probably, I suggest, because of its close alignment with lineation in the lyric tradition—polysyndeton continues to order language into rhythmic patterns in prose fiction. In fact, while Pinsky locates the line as the basic source of rhythm in free verse poetry, Paul Fussell points instead to patterns of language and syntax that do not necessarily require lineation for their effect: "Free-verse lines, deprived of pattern in one dimension, the metrical, tend to compensate by employing another kind of pattern, conspicuous repetition of phrases or syntactical forms" (1979, 79). Though he does not call these constructions by their rhetorical names, Fussell cites poems that make use of anaphora and polysyndeton as prime examples to support his claim. Polysyndeton's near-biblical repetition of the coordinator *and* creates rhythmic patterns in prose for special dramatic effect.

A number of prominent twentieth-century novelists have exploited polysyndeton's rhetorical strengths in their prose fiction. Generally regarded as master stylists on opposite ends of the stylistic spectrum, both Faulkner and Hemingway maximize polysyndeton's potential for generating rhythm during emotionally climactic moments of their prose, from tender instances of love and passion to intense violence and trauma. These passages provide stark contrasts to the rest of their prose, though for very different reasons: polysyndeton's reliance on coordination runs counter to Faulkner's proclivity for complicated layers of subordination, while the sheer length of these coordinations runs counter to Hemingway's preference for brief, compact sentences. DeLillo and McCarthy use polysyndeton with greater regularity, turning this device into a stylistic staple in ways that deliberately resist narrative's desire to sort details into hierarchies, much to the chagrin of B. R. Myers. These writers construct fictional worlds in which people and events are connected through neither causality nor purpose but rather coincidence and chance circumstance. Polysyndeton is an ideal syntactic structure for narratives like these, in which hierarchical distinctions are flattened in favor of lateral systems of interconnectivity. Each of these writers exploits a style of syntax that seems artificial, even unnatural, to achieve a greater degree of mimesis. Thus, they invite us to recalibrate our notions of artifice and reality, drawing our attention to literary structure that, even while announcing its presence, heightens our emotional engagement with the text.

Though it contains many of the themes, ambiguities, and exegetical difficulties of Faulkner's other works, *Go Down, Moses* (1942) is not generally regarded as one of his greatest literary achievements. Faulkner is admired for his experiments with structure and point of view in *The Sound and the Fury* (1929), *As I Lay Dying* (1930), and *Absalom, Absalom!* (1936), but somehow *Go Down, Moses* does not appeal to critics in the same way. To be sure, his reliance on lengthy polysyndetic catalogs in *Go Down, Moses* marks a departure from the hierarchical style of his more canonical works; this technique also further obscures the complicated value system that underpins his fictional Yoknapatawpha County. In what follows, I argue that polysyndeton gives expression to those themes to which Faulkner perennially returns—slavery, modernity, southern history, and all of the moral and political questions that are bundled with these topics—in a format that deliberately refuses to sort itself out.

One of the great difficulties of reading Faulkner's prose is his penchant for nested clauses and appositives, which cause his sentences to become so complex that their main clauses are buried under layers of subordination. Take, for instance, the following sentence from *Go Down, Moses* ([1942] 1990), which begins with a depiction of the black tenant farmer Lucas Beauchamp and his relationship to the McCaslin plantation, though it quickly sprawls in a variety of directions that become increasingly difficult to track:

> He had worked on it ever since he got big enough to hold a plow straight; he had hunted over every foot of it during his childhood and youth and his manhood too, up to the time when he stopped hunting, not because he could no longer walk a day's or a night's hunt, but because he felt that the pursuit of rabbits and 'possums for meat was no longer commensurate with his status as not only the oldest man but the oldest living person on the Edmonds plantation, the oldest McCaslin descendant even though in the world's eye he descended not from McCaslins but from McCaslin slaves almost as old as old Isaac McCaslin who lived in town, supported by what Roth Edmonds chose to give him, who would own the land and all on it if his just rights were only known, if people just knew how old Cass Edmonds, this one's grandfather, had beat him out of his patrimony, almost as old as old Isaac, almost, as old Isaac was, coeval with old Buck and Buddy McCaslin who had been alive when their father,

> Carothers McCaslin, got the land from the Indians back in the old time when men black and white were men. (36–37)

The main clause that begins the sentence—Lucas having worked the land since he was a small child—becomes submerged under the subordinate clause that depicts Lucas's age, which in turn becomes submerged under the clause detailing Lucas's genealogy, which in turn becomes submerged under the clause that traces the genealogy of the plantation itself. Sentences like these often require several rereadings, given the complexity of the grammatical hierarchies they establish.

Faulkner's reliance on a rhetorical device that deliberately resists hierarchical arrangement in key passages of *Go Down, Moses* may come as something of a surprise, since it marks a significant departure from an otherwise convoluted prose that strives for structural complexity. Then again, perhaps not, since—like *Absalom, Absalom!* before it—*Go Down, Moses* is deeply indebted to the Old Testament, one of Faulkner's most treasured literary inspirations. "The books I read are the ones I knew and loved when I was a young man and to which I return as you do to old friends: the Old Testament, Dickens, Conrad, Cervantes," he remarked during a 1956 interview with the *Paris Review* (J. Stein [1956] 2007, 51). Like the Old Testament, *Go Down, Moses* is structured as a family saga, tracking the complete history of the McCaslin family and its various branches over a hundred-year span. Traces of Faulkner's biblical influences course throughout the novel, but they are made most explicit at the level of textual and paratextual allusion, especially as Faulkner insists that we read the enslavement of African Americans in the antebellum South through the enslavement of the Israelites in Egypt. The novel's title derives from the black spiritual that depicts the events of Exodus, in which Moses leads the Israelites to freedom, and in the titular section that closes the novel, Mollie Beauchamp likens her grandson Samuel's eviction from the McCaslin plantation to his being sold into slavery: "Roth Edmonds sold my Benjamin. Sold him in Egypt. Pharoah got him" (353). Like the biblical Isaac, Ike McCaslin is born to older parents, and the Old Testament is even invoked by Ike himself during his lengthy debate with McCaslin Edmonds over his inheritance, the McCaslin plantation. Here, Ike rewrites Genesis—without introducing subordination—to articulate his belief that the South has broken its pact with God and humanity through the institution of slavery:

> Because He told in the Book how He created the earth, made it and looked at it and said it was all right, and then He made man. He made the earth first and peopled it with dumb creatures, and then He created man to be His overseer on the earth and to hold suzerainty over the earth and the animals on it in His name, not to hold for himself and his descendants inviolable title forever, generation after

> generation, to the oblongs and squares of the earth, but to hold the earth mutual and intact in the communal anonymity of brotherhood, and all the fee He asked was pity and humility and sufferance and endurance and the sweat of his face for bread. (246)

In replacing their own labor with the sweat of others, in violating the "communal anonymity of brotherhood" by creating a hierarchy instead, the plantation system violated the democratic configuration that, according to Ike, God had envisioned for mankind. Ike may adapt the content of the creation story to fit his narrative of the antebellum South, but he maintains the leveling syntax of the biblical passage in a way that underscores its inherent resistance to hierarchy, especially the brutal stratification established under slavery. Ultimately, Ike's belief in the illegitimacy of this hierarchy will lead him to repudiate his inheritance.

The imposition of hierarchy onto a democratic framework is the very kernel around which *Go Down, Moses* is organized, along with the question of how to restore some semblance of equality to a nation irreparably damaged by slavery. The manumission of the slaves on the McCaslin plantation by Buck and Buddy, the reparations they establish for the otherwise unacknowledged black lineage of the McCaslin family—the result of Old Carother McCaslin's affair with his slave Eunice and with their daughter, Tomasina—and Ike's refusal to inherit the land that was once the plantation all mark the McCaslins' attempts to redress sins in which they are all complicit. In a novel that struggles to correct the injustices of a hierarchy based on racism and brute power, perhaps it is not so surprising after all that Faulkner would rely heavily on a syntax that, like Ike's paraphrasing of Genesis, stresses equality.

One of the many uses to which polysyndeton is put in *Go Down, Moses* is the catalog, which has a strong metonymic function in the novel. Concrete objects often stand in for—or replace—abstract concepts, including the enigmatic bear, Old Ben, who serves as the object of the hunt in the long section "The Bear," which constitutes nearly a third of the novel. This is no ordinary bear but an instantiation of the wilderness itself and a piece of folklore that has reached mythic proportions: "It was of the wilderness, the big woods, bigger and older than any recorded document" (183). Until his appearance in the third subsection, Old Ben is depicted obliquely through catalogs of the damage he has left in his wake, which are as legendary as the bear itself: "The long legend of corn-cribs broken down and rifled, or shoats and grown pigs and even calves carried bodily into the woods and devoured and traps and deadfalls overthrown and dogs mangled and slain and shotgun and even rifle shots delivered at point-blank range yet with no more effect than so many peas blown through a tube by a child" (185). Like the biblical catalog in Genesis, the inventory that enumerates Old Ben's destruction picks up momentum through polysyndeton, amassing a rhythm that matches the accumulation of the bear's damage, which grows from ransacked corn patches to mangled animal corpses to Ben's imperviousness to shotgun slugs and rifle bullets alike.

Inventories also stand in metonymically for the competing value systems at stake in Faulkner's Yoknapatawpha County at the turn of the century. One of the novel's chief points of focus is the South's transition from agrarian to industrial economy, and the antebellum South is paradoxically depicted with deep nostalgia as Faulkner romanticizes the agrarian lifestyle that was buttressed by slavery. In the novel's climactic commissary scene, Ike traces this shift from agriculture to industry through the catalogs in his family's ledgers, which chronicle the "whole land in miniature . . . that slow trickle of molasses and meal and meat, of shoes and straw hats and overalls, of plowlines and collars and heel-bolts and buckheads and clevises, which returned each fall as cotton" (280–81). Ike also articulates this transition through yet another rewriting of Genesis adapted for the antebellum South, this time exploiting the original passage's focus on enumeration:

> Until one day He said . . . *This is enough* and looked about for one last time, for one time more since He had created them, upon this land this South for which He had done so much with woods for game and streams for fish and deep rich soil for seed and lush springs to sprout it and long summers to mature it and serene falls to harvest it and short mild winters for men and animals and saw no hope anywhere and looked beyond it where hope should have been. (271)

Here, the South is an agrarian cornucopia that competes with Eden in its beauty and bounty, though it is also devoid of hope because of its reliance on slavery. As in all of his novels, Faulkner's attitude toward the South is ambivalent in *Go Down, Moses*, and its agricultural economy is critiqued in some places, glamorized in others. The same passage, in fact, goes on to provide a cynical panorama of the rest of the country, depicted as a depraved medicine show against the quiet, natural beauty of the rural South:

> Where to East North and West lay illiminable that whole hopeful continent dedicated as a refuge and sanctuary of liberty and freedom from what you called the old world's worthless evening and saw the rich descendants of slavers, females of both sexes, to whom the black they shrieked of was another specimen another example like the Brazilian macaw brought home in a cage by a traveller, passing resolutions about horror and outrage in warm and air-proof halls: and the thundering cannonade of politicians earning votes and the medicine-shows of pulpiteers earning Chautauqua fees, to whom the outrage and the injustice were as much abstractions as Tariff or Silver or Immortality and who employed the very shackles of its servitude and the sorry rags of its regalia as they did the other beer and banners

> and mottoes redfire and brimstone and sleight-of-hand and musical handsaws: and the whirling wheels which manufactured for a profit the pristine replacements of the shackles and shoddy garments as they wore out and spun the cotton and made the gins which ginned it and the cars and ships which hauled it, and the men who ran the wheels for that profit and established and collected the taxes it was taxed with and the rates for hauling it and the commissions for selling it: and He could have repudiated them since they were his creation now and forever more throughout all their generations. (272)

Northern industrial business practices, these catalogs suggest, are not much of an improvement over the conditions of slavery. In fact, these polysyndetic coordinations suggest that they are more or less equivalent. The shackles of the plantation system have been replaced by the shackles of commercialism, a low-brow version of capitalism premised on sales gimmicks and peddled by charlatans. Unlike the world of agriculture, the business world does not even require a relationship with the land—unless, of course, the business is real estate, in which case the relationship is based solely on investment and profit:

> And the New England mechanics who didn't even own land and measured all things by the weight of water and the cost of turning wheels and the narrow fringe of traders and ship-owners still looking backward across the Atlantic and attached to the continent only by their counting-houses. And those who should have had the alertness to see: the wildcat manipulators of mythical wilderness townsites; and the astuteness to rationalize: the bankers who held the mortgages on the land which the first were only waiting to abandon and on the railroads and steamboats to carry them still further west, and on the factories and the wheels and the rented tenements those who ran them lived in. (275)

Hardly the bastion of "hope" it was intended to be, the North is represented in these catalogs as a dehumanizing wasteland, yet another system of profit and exploitation in which the planter has been replaced by the banker.

This schematic is reinforced by the catalogs depicting the fate of Major de Spain's hunting camp after he sells the land to a lumber company, which has begun to deforest the area that once served as the setting for the bear hunt. Years later, Ike returns to a scarcely recognizable camp that has been ravaged by the lumber and railroad industries:

> [Ike] looked about in shocked and grieved amazement even though he had had forewarning and had believed himself prepared: a new planing-mill already half completed which would cover two or three acres and what looked like miles and miles of stacked steel rails red

> with the light bright rust of newness and of piled crossties sharp with creosote, and wire corrals and feeding-troughs for two hundred mules at least and the tents for the men who drove them; so that he arranged for the care and stabling of his mare as rapidly as he could and did not look any more, mounted into the log-train caboose with his gun and climbed into the cupola and looked no more save toward the wall of wilderness ahead within which he would be able to hide himself from it once more anyway. (303–4)

The half-completed planing mill, the stacked steel rails, and the wire corrals and feeding trough for the mules that carry these materials of industry are cataloged here as metonyms for the larger process that is taking place, the erasure of the wilderness by the encroachment of industry.

From these nonnarrative catalogs emerge the novel's competing systems of economy and, subsequently, of value. The plantation carries aesthetic value but at the expense of the value of the human; business and industry apparently devalue both in favor of profit. Still, how Faulkner squares his critique of slavery with his disdain for its economic alternative remains unclear, since he presents these systems through lengthy polysyndetic inventories, the items of which are connected only through coordinating conjunctions. There is no hierarchy within or among these catalogs that would indicate what relationship the listed items bear to one another; instead, they contain only relations of equivalence, suggesting that northern business practices are modernity's counterpart to antebellum slavery.

Catalogs are only one of the many ways in which the apparently nonnarrative structure of polysyndeton becomes an important narrative mode in *Go Down, Moses*. In fact, polysyndeton becomes a formal strategy for articulating scenes of intense emotional climax. Faulkner is not noted for his tenderness; one of the great jokes in Faulkner studies is that the author reserves his most romantic and reciprocal love connection for Ike Snopes and Houston's cow in *The Hamlet* (1940).[5] There are moments in "The Bear," however, that approach this tenor, and they are depicted through the repetitive coordinations of polysyndeton, which produce an easy and flexible rhythm for these scenes of unusual softness. Ike's love and desire for his new wife—juxtaposed against her coldness—are narrated in this way:

> He wanted to see her naked because he loved her and he wanted to see her looking at him naked because he loved her but after that he never mentioned it again, even turning his face when she put the nightgown on over her dress to undress at night and putting the dress on over the gown to remove it in the morning and she would not let him get into bed beside her until the lamp was out and even in the heat of summer she would draw the sheet up over them both before she would let him turn to her. (299)

This polysyndetic passage also sets up Ike's betrayal at the hands of his young wife, who exploits Ike's desire for her to secure his promise that he will reclaim his inheritance. Gradually, she turns his refusals—"'No, I tell you. I wont. I cant. Never'" (300)—into consent muddled by passion: "Then he stopped thinking and even saying Yes, it was like nothing he had ever dreamed, let along heard in mere man-talking until after a no-time he returned and lay spent on the insatiate immemorial beach and again with a movement one time more older than man she turned and freed herself and on their wedding night she had cried and he thought she was crying now at first . . . [but she was] laughing and laughing" (300–301). The identity of Ike's young wife is left mysterious—she remains unnamed, and she dies young of undisclosed causes—but Ike's interactions with her, narrated via polysyndeton, constitute some of the most poignant scenes in the novel.

Other scenes of high emotional intensity are similarly propelled by coordinating conjunctions, including the hunting scenes that mark Ike's initiation into the wilderness by Major de Spain and General Compson. In a quasi-religious commemoration of Ike's first kill, Sam Fathers anoints Ike with the blood of his buck on one of their inaugural hunting trips together: "And Sam Fathers said, 'Now. Shoot quick and shoot slow': and the gun levelled rapidly without haste and crashed and he walked to the buck lying still intact and still in the shape of that magnificent speed and bled it with Sam's knife and Sam dipped his hands into the hot blood and marked his face forever while he stood trying not to tremble" (334). The long-anticipated killing of Old Ben is also narrated through polysyndeton, elevating the ritualistic hunt to an event of biblical proportions: "Then the bear surged erect, raising with it the man and the dog too, and turned and still carrying the man and the dog it took two or three steps toward the woods on its hind feet as a man would have walked and crashed down" (231). As in Lawrence's "Snake," polysyndeton delays narrative speed and appears to capture this scene in slow motion, protracting several seconds of action into multiple lines of prose.

The unusual syntax of polysyndeton is an ideal vehicle for articulating these lyrical moments of metonymic meaning and emotional intensity—and competing allegiances. Just as Faulkner struggles to balance the agrarian South with the sins of slavery, so Ike struggles to balance his rejection of slavery with his desire for his wife. In particular, polysyndeton is used here to articulate complicated instances of bonding: Ike's initiation into a primordial cult of masculinity and inheritance via Sam Fathers and his family patriarchs, and exploitation of this bond by Ike's wife, who initiates Ike into her own primordial rituals, "a movement one time more older than man" (301). Because Ike is confused about his own allegiances, polysyndeton, which grammatically as well as ideologically obscures these relationships and priorities, becomes an important vehicle for representing Ike's internal conflicts. Viewed this way, *Go Down, Moses* becomes one of Faulkner's most emotionally evocative works because it depicts these conflicts in lyrical rather than narrative terms.

Paradoxically, polysyndeton's disregard for complexity and conflict on a structural level also makes it an ideal syntax for representing those tensions and inconsistences that are not easily reconciled within character and author alike.

Faulkner and Hemingway are often positioned as stylistic contraries, and for good reason: unlike Faulkner, Hemingway is known for a prose style that is terse and laconic, described by Philip Young as "a colloquial and, apparently, a nonliterary prose, characterized by a conscientious simplicity of diction and sentence structure" (1966, 204). Hemingway is remembered as a pioneering minimalist, and it is this iconic prose style that effectively secured his position in our literary canon: when awarded the Nobel Prize in Literature in 1954, Hemingway was honored by the committee "for his mastery of the art of narrative, most recently demonstrated in *The Old Man and the Sea*, and for the influence he has exerted on contemporary style."

Like Faulkner, however, Hemingway was also deeply invested in polysyndeton, a rhetorical device that expands rather than contracts the sentence. Hemingway is so renowned for his economy of style that critics have not given sustained attention to his use of polysyndeton, though he frequently employed this construction for scenes of emotional intensity. In fact, the syntax of these polysyndetic coordinations is particularly striking against Hemingway's otherwise bare and minimalist prose, marking a dramatic departure from the concise, abrupt sentences that are usually associated with his style. Polysyndeton appears in nearly all of Hemingway's novels, but *A Farewell to Arms* (1929)—a work that spans life's extremities, from the horrors of war to the grandeur of love—contains some of its most poignant instances, which Hemingway used to articulate the outermost limits of pain and pleasure in the time of war.

Hemingway's reputation as a minimalist derives not only from his austerity with regard to language and syntax but also from his insistence on the power of narrative omission, now referred to as his famous "iceberg" principle: "If a writer of prose knows enough about what he is writing about he may omit things that he knows and the reader, if the writer is writing truly enough, will have a feeling of those things as strongly as though the writer has stated them. The dignity of movement of an ice-berg is due to only one-eighth of it being above water" ([1932] 1960, 154). The iceberg principle demands a mode of narration that is oblique rather than direct; consequently, it demands an active reader who is able to uncover those seven-eighths of the iceberg that remain submerged.

Polysyndeton contributes to Hemingway's iceberg principle by eliding those routine hierarchies—relationships of cause and effect or temporal succession, statements modified by caveats and exceptions—which typically order narrative fiction. The opening lines of *A Farewell to Arms* supply a beautiful example of polysyndeton's potential for obscuring relationships among items and events in a way that forces readers to piece them together:

> In the late summer of that year we lived in a house in a village that looked across the river and the plain to the mountains. In the bed of the river there were pebbles and boulders, dry and white in the sun, and the water was clear and swiftly moving and blue in the channels. Troops went by the house and down the road and the dust they raised powdered the leaves of the trees. The trunks of the trees too were dusty and the leaves fell early that year and we saw the troops marching along the road and the dust rising and leaves, stirred by the breeze, falling and the soldiers marching and afterward the road bare and white except for the leaves. ([1929] 1957, 3)

What appears to be an objective description of a neutral event—the movement of troops across a pastoral backdrop—is actually a subtle indictment of war, as James Phelan deftly demonstrates in his analysis of this opening scene. The troops are not only juxtaposed to the natural world; they are disrupting it, kicking up dust that causes the leaves on the trees to fall unseasonably early (1990, 55). Without those linking subordinators that would normally clarify the action of this passage, however, the antagonistic relationship between war and nature remains buried under a mound of conjunctions.

Hemingway, like Faulkner, also couples polysyndeton with the catalog when setting up scenes or items of metonymic importance, including the idyll of Frederic and Catherine's bucolic Swiss hideaway, their asylum from the war they have both just deserted. It is depicted in pieces through a polysyndetic inventory of the rustic track marks, structures, and terrains that make up the landscape. Time stands still as polysyndeton provides a spatial panoramic of the countryside:

> Outside, in front of the chalet a road went up the mountain. The wheel ruts and ridges were iron hard with the frost, and the road climbed steadily through the forest and up and around the mountain to where there were meadows, and barns and cabins in the meadows at the edge of the woods looking across the valley. . . . In front of the house where we lived the mountain went down steeply to the little plain along the lake and we sat on the porch of the house in the sun and saw the winding of the road down the mountain-side and the terraced vineyards on the side of the lower mountain, the vines all dead now for the winter and the fields, divided by stone walls, and below the vineyards the houses of the town on the narrow plain along the lake shore. (289–90)

Peppered with wheel ruts, cabins, and vineyards, their sanctuary is as removed from time and the ravages of modernity as it is from the war. The Italian province of Abruzzi—the home of Frederic's friend, the priest—receives a similar treatment as Frederic fantasizes about its rustic charm: "I had wanted to go to Abruzzi. I had gone to no place where the roads were frozen and hard as iron, where it was clear cold and dry and the snow was dry and powdery and hare-tracks in the snow and the peasants took off their hats and called you Lord and there was good hunting" (13). Here, the conjunctions not only contribute to Abruzzi's appeal but also convey Frederic's accrued regret over his failure to take his military leave in Abruzzi on the priest's recommendation: "I myself felt as badly as [the priest] did and could not understand why I had not gone. It was what I had wanted to do and I tried to explain how one thing had led to another and finally he saw it and understood that I had really wanted to go and it was almost all right. I had drunk much wine and afterward coffee and Strega and I explained, winefully, how we did not do the things we wanted to do; we never did such things." Both Switzerland and Abruzzi are figured as places of refuge untouched by war, though Frederic visits Abruzzi only in his imagination.

By replacing narration at key points in Hemingway's writing, polysyndeton underscores narrative's failure to articulate those moments that do not lend themselves to great lucidity. When Frederic attempts to articulate why he fails to visit Abruzzi, the result is a lengthy, rambling passage in which he reverts to polysyndeton because he "could not tell it":

> I had gone to no such place [Abruzzi] but to the smoke of cafés and nights when the room whirled and you needed to look at the wall to make it stop, nights in bed, drunk, when you knew that that was all there was, and the strange excitement of waking and not knowing who it was with you, and the world all unreal in the dark and so exciting that you must resume again unknowing and not caring in the night, sure that this was all and all and all and not caring. Suddenly to care very much and to sleep to wake with it sometimes morning and all that had been there gone and everything sharp and hard and clear and sometimes a dispute about the cost. Sometimes still pleasant and fond and warm and breakfast and lunch. Sometimes all niceness gone and glad to get out on the street but always another day starting and then another night. I tried to tell about the night and the difference between the night and the day and how the night was better unless the day was very clean and cold and I could not tell it; as I cannot tell it now. But if you have had it you know. (13)

Sentences are reduced to fragments as the subjects of Frederic's clauses disappear. Instead, his account of how he spent his leave is reduced to a series of sensations: "strange excitement," "not caring," "sharp and hard and clear," "pleasant and fond and warm." Narrative fails to articulate why we "did not do the things we wanted to do" or how "one thing had led to another" (13), though polysyndeton addresses the disorder and momentum behind the chain of events that prevents Frederic from realizing his good intentions.

In many ways, polysyndeton may be better suited to the reality of lived experience than are the traditional grammatical structures of narrative fiction. Hemingway strove to recreate the immediacy of lived experience in his writing, as he reveals in his personal letters while reflecting on his craft. Writing to his father, he explains, "You see I'm trying in all my stories to get the feeling of the actual life across—not to just depict life—or criticize it—but to actually make it alive. So that when you have read something by me you actually experience the thing" (Baker 1981, 153). Hemingway reiterates his sense that language can simulate experience in a letter to Everett Perry defending his use of profanity in *For Whom the Bell Tolls*: "I am trying, always, to convey to the reader a full and complete feeling of the thing I am dealing with; to make the person reading feel it has happened to them" (380). Hence, Hemingway labored and deliberated over language and its relationship to mimesis, understanding well that feeling may be conveyed more effectively through linguistic and structural artifice.

For Hemingway, love and war are as antithetical as Faulkner's North and South, and these extremes are depicted through the dramatic syntax of polysyndeton. When the fateful mortar shell that lands Frederic in the hospital explodes near his trench and sends shrapnel into his knees, Frederic articulates his pain and confusion through a string of coordinating conjunctions:

> Then there was a flash, as when a blast furnace door is swung open, and a roar that started white and went red and on and on in a rushing wind. I tried to breathe but my breath would not come and I felt myself rush bodily out of myself and out and out and out and all the time bodily in the wind. I went out swiftly, all of myself, and I knew I was dead and that it had all been a mistake to think you just died. . . . There was a great splashing and I saw the starshells go up and burst and float whitely and rockets going up and heard the bombs, all this in a moment. (54–55)

A single "moment" is protracted through polysyndeton to span nearly a paragraph of prose in this dramatic recreation of Frederic's fraught psychological state during the attack.

This same syntax, however, also depicts those quiet, tender, intimate moments between Frederic and Catherine that have made this novel one of the best-known love stories of the last century. Before he is injured, Frederic fantasizes about joining Catherine in Milan, where she has been transferred, and imagines their first romantic encounter in a hotel room:

> Maybe she would pretend that I was her boy that was killed and we would go in the front door and the porter would take off his cap and I would stop at the concierge's desk and ask for the key and she would stand by the elevator and then we would get in the elevator

> and it would go up very slowly clicking at all the floors and then our floor and the boy would open the door and stand there and she would step out and I would step on and we would walk down the hall and I would put the key in the door and open it and go in and then take down the telephone and ask them to send a bottle of capri bianca in a silver bucket full of ice and you would hear the ice against the pail coming down the corridor and the boy would knock and I would say leave it outside the door please. Because we would not wear any clothes because it was so hot and the window open and the swallows flying over the roofs of the houses and when it was dark afterward and you went to the window very small bats hunting over the houses and close down over the trees and we would drink the Capri and the door locked and it hot and only a sheet and the whole night and we would both love each other all night in the hot night in Milan. (38)

By the end of the passage, Frederic's narration is reduced again to sentence fragments—"and the door locked and it hot and only a sheet." The passage becomes a rhythmic incantation of images and sensations driven by sexual anticipation.

The smooth rhythm of polysyndeton also propels those passages depicting the illicit nights Catherine and Frederic spend together in the Milan hospital following his injury. Ministering to Frederic and the other injured soldiers during the day, Catherine pays special visits to Frederic during the night:

> Once in the night I went to sleep and when I woke she was not there but I heard her coming along the hall and the door opened and she came back to the bed and said it was all right she had been downstairs and they were all asleep. . . . She brought crackers and we ate them and drank some vermouth. . . . I went to sleep again in the morning when it was light and when I was awake I found she was gone again. She came in looking fresh and lovely and sat on the bed and the sun rose while I had the thermometer in my mouth and we smelled the dew on the roofs and then the coffee of the men at the gun on the next roof. (101–2)

This syntax appears again during one of the most sensuous passages in the novel, an iterative love scene in which the soft and controlled movements of the two lovers are channeled through the rolling conjunctions polysyndeton supplies:

> I loved to take her hair down and she sat on the bed and kept very still, except suddenly she would dip down to kiss me while I was doing it, and I would take out the pins and lay them on the sheet and it would be loose and I would watch her while she kept very still and

> then take out the last two pins and it would all come down and she would drop her head and we would both be inside of it, and it was the feeling of inside a tent or behind a falls. (114)

All of the rhetorical advantages of polysyndeton work together in this passage. Each motion is isolated and imbued with a solemn significance, from Catherine's kiss to Frederic's handling of her hair pins; the conjunctions convey the smooth continuity of their movements; and their repetition creates a steady, lyrical rhythm that contributes to the aesthetics of this climactic scene. Like the orgasm that generates "peace and knowledge" in Whitman's *Leaves of Grass*, the foreplay between Frederic and Catherine is a crucial palliative to the vulgar cruelty of war. In fact, one could easily translate this passage into a Whitmanian free-verse poem by inserting line breaks before each conjunction:

> I loved to take her hair down
> And she sat on the bed
> And kept very still
> Except suddenly she would dip down to kiss me while I was doing it
> And I would take out the pins
> And lay them on the sheet
> And it would be loose
> And I would watch her
> While she kept very still
> And then take out the last two pins
> And it would all come down
> And she would drop her head
> And we would both be inside of it
> And it was the feeling of inside a tent
> Or behind a falls. (114)[6]

Hemingway achieves rhythmic regularity by distributing these coordinating conjunctions more or less evenly throughout the passage, since—as the visual form of the free verse poem indicates—the length of the clauses separated by conjunctions is roughly equal. This moment of lyrical intensity is buttressed by a cadence that propels these nonnarrative passages through a formal rhythmic movement. The effect is soothing, especially compared to the jarring, syncopated rhythm that shapes Hemingway's war passages. Like the petty act of violence that causes Lawrence's speaker to break the patient spell of polysyndeton in "Snake," the war in *A Farewell to Arms* is "clumsy" and "vulgar" on a much greater scale, and the difference between love and war is registered in the very rhythms of Hemingway's sentences.

Hemingway reverts to the lyrical syntax of polysyndeton to articulate those feelings that narrative cannot always sort out: confusion and failure, pain and trauma, sensual pleasure. While this syntax captures a range of emotions, its rhythm is manipulated toward very different ends, exacerbating the conflict between love and war that plays out in the story's submerged plot. The syncopated placement of conjuctions in the passage depicting Frederic's injury creates a fractured rhythm that is juxtaposed to the smooth, steady rhythm of polysyndeton in the novel's love passages. Thus, polysyndeton becomes a vehicle for representing tension between opposites for both Faulkner and Hemingway, who generally reserve this syntax for moments of climax. By contrast, for DeLillo and McCarthy the device is a frequent fixture in their prose writing. These writers exploit polysyndeton's nonnarrative structure to build fictional worlds in which the traditional hierarchical arrangements of narrative—cause and consequence, degrees of importance and magnitude—no longer apply.

Hemingway's polysyndetic coordinations may be overlooked by critics, but they have not been lost on Don DeLillo. "The Hemingway sentence is what makes Hemingway," he once declared during an interview. "It's not the bullfights or the safaris or the wars. It's a clear, direct, and vigorous sentence. It's the simple connective—the word 'and' that strings together the segments of a long Hemingway sentence. The word 'and' is more important to Hemingway than Africa or Paris" (Nel 2008, 20–21). In another interview, DeLillo quotes the opening lines from *A Farewell to Arms*, paraphrasing the action but preserving the polysyndeton of the original passage as he recounts his formative reading experiences as a teenager in the Bronx: "And I'd look at a sentence in *Ulysses* or in *Moby-Dick* or in Hemingway—maybe I hadn't gotten to *Ulysses* at that point, it was *Portrait of the Artist*—but certainly Hemingway and the water that was clear and swiftly moving and the way the troops went marching down the road and raised dust that powdered the leaves of the trees. All this in a playground in the Bronx" (Begley 1993). The rhythm of Hemingway's sentences left an indelible impression on DeLillo, who states in the same interview that the sentence is the rhythmic kernel around which he builds his own prose:

> The basic work is built around the sentence. This is what I mean when I call myself a writer. I construct sentences. There's a rhythm I hear that drives me through a sentence. And the words typed on the white page have a sculptural quality. They form odd correspondences. They match up not just through meaning but through sound and look. The rhythm of a sentence will accommodate a certain number of syllables. One syllable too many, I look for another word. There's always another word that means nearly the same thing, and if it doesn't then I'll consider altering the meaning of a sentence to keep the rhythm, the syllable beat. I'm completely willing to let language press meaning upon me. Watching the way in which words match up, keeping the balance in a sentence—these are sensuous pleasures.

DeLillo discusses his prose as if it were syllabic verse. "One syllable too many," and the whole form threatens to collapse; rhythm takes precedence over content, which is malleable and subordinate to form. Readers of DeLillo may be surprised to learn of the careful attention to craft at sentence level the author articulates in these interviews. DeLillo is known as a postmodernist maximalist who forgoes craftsmanship for volume as well as "range and discursive multiplicity" in his effort to create narratives that are "encyclopedic" in length, scope, and allusiveness (O'Donnell 2008, 108). By the time he conducted this interview with the *Paris Review*, DeLillo had already published some of his most voluminous work to date, including *Ratner's Star* (1976, 448 pages) and *Libra* (1988, 480 pages). His next undertaking would be a mammoth expansion of his novella "Pafko at the Wall"—the critically acclaimed *Underworld* (1997), which weighs in at a staggering 827 pages. Ironically, DeLillo's longest novel most frequently employs "the Hemingway sentence."[7] Certain passages sound similar enough to *A Farewell to Arms* to qualify as rewrites, including the spontaneous love scene between Nick and Klara Sax, an older woman who is an installation artist, which takes place in her art studio: "She liked stopping and watching, or looking away actually, or guiding his hand, or going into the kitchen for a glass of water and coming back and pouring it partly on his chest, a body disproportionate to the bedding, and then handing him the glass and watching him drink and thinking there was nothing crazy going on that she should clearly locate except that she was naked in her workroom" (DeLillo 1997, 733). This iterative passage contains strong echoes of the (also iterative, also polysyndetic) free-verse love scene between Frederic and Catherine in the Milan hospital, in which Frederic reports that he "loved to take her hair down" while they made love (Hemingway [1929] 1957, 114).

Typically regarded as his magnum opus, *Underworld* (1997) is DeLillo's most ambitious project to date. The novel contains both fictional and historical characters, with cameo appearances by Frank Sinatra, Jackie Gleason, J. Edgar Hoover, and Lenny Bruce. *Underworld* also attempts to balance the global with the personal by chronicling the Cold War through the story of Nick Shay, who eventually becomes an executive for a nuclear waste management company. Nick's story is only one of the novel's many fractured plotlines, however. Another tracks the fate of the famous baseball that was hit by Bobby Thomson, causing the Giants to win the 1951 National League pennant. Another tracks the career of Klara Sax, who has become quite successful since her affair with Nick years ago. Another tracks subway graffiti artist Ismael Muñoz, whose artwork commemorates the dead in the down-and-out underworld of the Bronx. Still another chronicles Sister Edgar as she ministers to the Bronx's poor and homeless, taking special pains to save a young girl named Esmeralda who is eventually murdered. Unlike most of the other novels treated in this study, *Underworld* suffers from a surplus of plot, which splinters into a number of apparently unrelated strands.

In contradistinction to those bulky Victorian novels whose multiple plot strands eventually coincide in causally meaningful ways—the seemingly inconsequential escaped convict, for example, who frightens Pip at the beginning of Dickens's *Great Expectations* turns out to be Pip's secret benefactor as well as Estella's father—the characters and plotlines of DeLillo's *Underworld* only converge by happenstance. The novel is loosely organized around two major, though disparate, events of purportedly international significance: the home run that won the pennant for the Giants, dubbed "the shot heard round the world," and the explosion of a Soviet-engineered atomic bomb.[8] Hoover is in the stands of the pennant game when he is informed about the Soviet atomic testing, and the game-winning baseball changes hands many times until finally ending up with Nick Shay, but the two plotlines do not meet again until much later in the novel, when Klara's husband, Bronzini, picks up a newspaper as he sips his morning coffee:

> The front page astonished him, a pair of three-column headlines dominating. To his left the Giants capture the pennant, beating the Dodgers on a dramatic home run in the ninth inning. And to the right, symmetrically mated, same typeface, same-size type, same number of lines, the USSR explodes an atomic bomb—*kaboom*—details kept secret.
>
> He didn't understand why the Times would take a ball game off the sports page and juxtapose it with news of such ominous consequence. (668)[9]

Bronzini is mystified by the juxtaposition of these two unrelated events, one of which seems so insignificant on a global scale. "The Shot Heard Round the World? Is the rest of the world all that interested?" he asks his friend, the priest Father Paulus, who replies,

> "We may take it that the term applies to the suddenness of the struck blow and the corresponding speed at which news is transmitted these days. Our servicemen in Greenland and Japan surely heard the home-run call as it was made on Armed Forces Radio. You're right, of course. They're not talking about this in the coffeehouses of Budapest. Although in fact poor Ralph Branca happens to be half Hungarian. Sons of immigrants. Branca and Thomson both. Bobby himself born in Scotland, I believe. You see why our wins and losses tend to have impact well beyond our borders." (670)

Father Paulus effectively recalibrates Bronzini's conception of the global, shifting the terms from scope and importance to terms of interconnection. Americans across the globe can share in the same national event at the same time thanks to modern media technology. The players' status as second-generation immigrants also suggests the interconnectedness of nations by way of immigration. One of the great themes of *Underworld* is this vague relational quality that DeLillo identifies as interconnection. In fact, the novel ends not in the Bronx, nor in Phoenix where Nick currently lives, but in cyberspace, where even the novel's most disparate characters and plotlines become hyperlinked to one another: "The bulldog fed, J. Edgar Hoover, the Law's debased saint, hyperlinked at last to Sister Edgar—a single fluctuating impulse now, a piece of coded information. Everything is connected in the end" (826).

"Everything is connected"—a line borrowed from another encyclopedic novel, Thomas Pynchon's *Gravity's Rainbow* (1973)—is iterated and reiterated by waste manager Jesse Detwiler (289), Nick's brother Matt Shay (465), and the novel's intermittent third-person narrator (408, 825, 826). Indeed, many things in the novel are connected, on a rhetorical level, through polysyndeton. *Underworld* contains a number of lengthy nonnarrative passages in which items are connected ambiguously through lengthy strings of coordinating conjunctions. Given Nick Shay's fieldwork, many of these polysyndetic passages are naturally devoted to mounds of waste—trash dumps, atomic waste burial sites, and piles of garbage heaped on residential street corners: "The garbage was down there, stacked in identical black plastic bags, and she [Klara] walked home past a broad mound that covered a fire hydrant and part of a bus sign and she saw how everyone agreed together not to notice" (388). *Underworld* notices; as its title suggests, it compulsively unearths the waste that everyone else tries to bury. "We built pyramids of waste above and below the earth," Nick muses to himself. "The more hazardous the waste, the deeper we tried to sink it. The word plutonium comes from Pluto, god of the dead and ruler of the underworld" (106).

Nick's colleague, Brian Glassic, shares Nick's fascination with the waste that no one else ever "saw or thought about." For Brian, as for Nick, a trash heap is a "unique cultural deposit" that invites us to imagine, via metonymy, the lives of others through their discarded items:

> Specks and glints, ragtails of color appeared in the stratified mass of covering soil, fabric scraps from the garment center, stirred by the wind, or maybe that teal thing is a bikini brief that belonged to some secretary from Queens, and Brian found he could create a flash infatuation, she is dark-eyed and reads the tabloids and paints her nails and eats lunch out of molded styrofoam, and he gives her gifts and she gives him condoms, and it all ends up here, newsprint, emery boards, sexy underwear, coaxed into high relief by the rumbling dozers. (185)

Brian manages to spin an entire life portrait—complete with steamy relationship—around a bikini bottom through the mounting drama of polysyndeton as each new imagined detail is appended to the last.

Nick's depictions of waste tend toward romanticism, particularly in the novel's closing passages. Nick describes his pilgrimage to the local landfill with his granddaughter in the soft rhythm produced by polysyndeton:

> I drive out there sometimes and see grackles sparking across the landfill, down past the Indian tribe streets, and sometimes I take our granddaughter along when she is here on a visit and we see the sage gray truss of the waste facility and the planes in their landing patterns and the showy desert plants spilling over the pastel walls above the parking area. (805)

The passage, which depicts a wasteland—a waste facility amid a desert—very nearly approaches the pastoral. Birds and patterned airplanes alike flying overhead, plants "spilling" over pastel-colored walls. The sentence creates a strangely aesthetic aerial depiction of an unremarkable garbage dump. Once inside the recycling shed that stands across from the landfill, Nick even admits that he feels a certain "reverence for waste, for the redemptive qualities of the things we use and discard" (809). The public is mesmerized by the inner and outer workings of the plant, which are again depicted through the hypnotic rhythm of polysyndeton:

> The kids love the machines, the balers and hoppers and long conveyors, and the parents look out the windows through the methane mist and the planes come out of the mountains and align for their approach and the trucks are arrayed in two columns outside the shed, bringing in the unsorted slop, the gut squalor of our lives, and taking the baled and bound units out into the world again, the chunky product blocks, pristine, newsprint for newsprint, tin for tin, and we all feel better when we leave. (810)

Waste—its content, its many afterlives—is elevated to profound consequence when the novel's careful attention to trash is coupled with this lyrical syntax. The waste plants and recycling centers that recur in the novel also function, however, as an important conceit for the complex network of interconnections by which our waste, whether via decay, recycling, or radioactivity, inevitably returns to us in alternate forms.[10]

Garbage is only one of the many quotidian assortments of items to receive lyrical treatment in *Underworld*. Father Paulus once again raises an important metafictional insight into the novel while discussing the importance of the ordinary with his pupil, a young Nick Shay: "Everyday things represent the most overlooked knowledge. These names are vital to your progress. Quotidian things. If they weren't important, we wouldn't use such a gorgeous Latinate word. . . . An extraordinary word that suggests the depth and reach of the commonplace" (542). The "depth and reach of the commonplace," in fact, is quite emotional for a number of the novel's characters. When Nick Shay recalls his long-absent father, who left when Nick was eleven years old, he evokes his father's shaving routine:

> He used to shave with a towel draped over his shoulder, wearing his undershirt, his singlet, and the blade made a noise I liked to listen to, a sandpaper scrape on his heavy beard, and the brush in the shaving cup, the Gem blade and the draped towel and the hot water from the tap—heat and skill and cutting edge. (106–7)

Nick's distant memory of his father consists of the discrete parts of his father's shaving kit, isolated here through the syntax of polysyndeton. Though Nick never divulges his feelings toward the man who abandoned his family, the detail with which he recalls father's morning ritual betrays his pain.

Polysyndeton also sheds light on another vexed father-son relationship. Manx Martin prepares to forever mar an already strained relationship with his son, Cotter, by selling the pennant-winning baseball that Cotter caught in the stands while playing hooky from school. Suddenly, he is overwhelmed by the touching scene he encounters when he approaches the long line of people who are waiting to buy World Series tickets:

> He sees fathers and sons standing around the fires to warm themselves, masses of people if you could count them, and mounted police with horses breathing steam, and he feels a rare elation, a wanting-to-be-among-them, and he is pulled along a little slack-jawed because it's a great thing to see, and they're singing and roaring warring songs, they're back-and-forthing on the street with rough-and-tumble humor, all these ball fans striding toward the ticket lines at two or three in the morning or whatever the actual hour. (366)

The scene itself is unremarkable—a crowd waiting for baseball tickets—but the filial intimacy Manx witnesses between the other fathers and their sons produces in this otherwise aloof character a longing for connectedness: connectedness to his son, connectedness to this crowd and its spirit, connectedness to humanity. Manx's desire for these human connections is articulated through the coordinating connectors that link all of these people on a structural level, even those who root for opposing teams: "And they're all singing and roaring warring songs" (366).

Those passages in *Underworld* that strive most to represent connectivity rely on the syntax of polysyndeton. Artist Klara Sax has an epiphanic moment when she considers her preference for certain paints and materials in relation to her working-class background. She contemplates this connection through a polysyndetic inventory of the remarkably ordinary items that captured her imagination in childhood:

> For a while she used house paint, radiator paint. She liked rough surfaces, flaked paint on metal, she liked puttied window frames, all the gesso textures, the gluey chalks and linseeds that get mixed and smeared, that get *schmeered* onto a weathered length of wood. And it took her years to understand how this was connected to her life, to the working-class grain, the pocked sidewalks, beautiful blue slate in fact, cracked and granule at the corners, and the tar roofs, and the fire escapes of course, painted green and then black and how the flowoff of drips and trickles became elements of memory, and the aluminum paint on the whistling radiators, and the paint her father carried home to recoat the kitchen chairs, a chair upended on a newspaper page, and the spidery plash of white paint on the inked page, and the spattered page on the old linoleum. (471–72)

Klara realizes that her avant-garde painting style derives from her fascination with the nonartistic materials of her blue-collar background: cracked paint on a fire escape, aluminum paint on a radiator, the paint that her father accidentally slops on the floor as he coats the kitchen chairs. In the eyes of the artist, the ordinary is made extraordinary, a transmutation that is conveyed to the reader through these connecting coordinators.

Viewed one way, *Underworld* contains a surplus of plot; viewed another way, it is not really a plotted novel at all, but a novel about the relational quality of interconnection. These thin and fractured plotlines only seem to exist to intersect in ways that are coincidental: a ball game and a nuclear explosion appear side by side on the front page of the newspaper in the summer that Nick and Klara embark on their affair; long afterward, Nick purchases the winning baseball from a seller; Bronzini happens to be both Klara Sax's husband and chess teacher to Nick's younger brother, Matt; Sister Edgar shares a name with J. Edgar Hoover. Polysyndeton too plays an important structural role in forging connections and erasing difference. This syntax elevates the quotidian to the level of the profound in a way that erases the opposition between high and low culture, the hierarchy of orders of magnitude which suggests that the minute—a discarded bikini bottom, a father's shaving routine, a painted fire escape, or, in Bronzini's eyes, a pennant game—is less consequential than the detonation of an atomic test bomb.

The idea that "everything is connected in the end" has a number of obvious moral, social, and political implications, but *Underworld* seems more interested in exploring the aesthetic dimensions of this mantra. The middle of the novel features a lengthy digression as Klara and her artist friends attend a viewing of a lost film—titled *Unterwelt*, or *Underworld*—by legendary Soviet director Sergei Eisenstein, one of the first practitioners and theorists of montage. Montage is, in many ways, the visual equivalent of polysyndeton: images are conjoined in rapid succession for heightened emotional effect without any hierarchical connectors. As Klara watches the film, she admits to herself that "the plot was hard to follow. There was no plot" (430). In this sense, the film is a mise-en-abyme of *Underworld*: like DeLillo, Eisenstein abandons traditional narrative for new modes of expression that do not build stories based on hierarchical arrangements.

The anonymous young street artist Ismael Muñoz, known to the public only as Moonman 157—the signature he appends to his work—combines the experimental aesthetics of Klara Sax and Sergei Eisenstein by collapsing the distinction between high- and low-brow art and also in creating art that relies on the succession and juxtaposition of images. A graffiti artist in the Bronx who uses the sides of subway cars as his canvas, he becomes an international spectacle whose work is photographed by tourists and coveted by New York's finest art galleries. Much like Eisenstein's montage, Moonman's art necessarily appears in successive fragments, available to the observer only in fleeting glimpses as the subway blows past, a scene that is depicted, perhaps predictably, through polysyndeton:

> But you have to stand on a platform and see it coming or you can't know the feeling a writer gets, how the number 5 train comes roaring down the rat alleys and slams out of the tunnel, going whop-pop onto the high tracks, and suddenly there it is, Moonman riding the sky in the heart of the Bronx, over the whole burnt and rusted country, and this is the art of the backstreets talking, all the way from Bird, and you can't *not* see us anymore, you can't *not* know who we are, we got total notoriety now, Momzo Tops and Rimester and me, we're getting fame, we ain't ashame, and the train go rattling over the garbagy streets and past the dead-eye windows of all those empty tenements that have people living there even if you don't see them, but you have to see our tags and cartoon figures and bright and rhyming poems, this is the art that can't stand still, it climbs across your eyeballs night and day, the flicker jumping art of the slums and dumpsters, flashing those colors in your face—like I'm your movie, motherfucker. (440–41)

The passage itself is sandwiched between scenes of the *Unterwelt* screening in a juxtaposition that suggests connections with the Eisenstein passages. In effect, Moonman's subway car graffiti becomes the "underworld" equivalent of Eisenstein's montage.

Connections abound in this novel, but their meaning and significance are less certain.[11] Thanks largely to *Libra*, DeLillo's 1988 speculative novel in which Lee Harvey Oswald's assassination of John F. Kennedy is revealed to have been orchestrated by the CIA as part of an elaborate plot to lead the United States into war with Cuba, DeLillo is often classified alongside Pynchon as one of the great "paranoid" writers of postmodernism. Webs of interconnection among seemingly disparate characters and events are taken by critics to be paranoid projections on the part of author and characters alike.[12] To be sure, certain connections in the novel warrant this paranoid reading, not the least of which is the cause-and-effect relationship between nuclear testing and its human toll on the health of "downwinders," deliberately obscured by the U.S. government. "Nobody's supposed to know this. It's something more or less out in the open but at the same time. . . . Secret. Untalked about. Hushed up," Eric explains to Matt Shay, both of whom work for a government think tank that works on bomb components (405). Nor is the United States the only government that is keeping secrets: the Soviets have their own "downwinders" to whom this relation of cause and effect is vehemently denied. On a work trip to the Russian city of Semipalatinsk, Nick and Brian are taken by their host, Viktor, himself a detonator for underground nuclear testing, to a nearby radiation clinic: "Viktor has been here four times, he says . . . to prove to himself he is not blind to the consequences. . . . The clinic has disfigurations, leukemias, thyroid cancers, immune systems that do not function. . . . For many years the word radiation was banned" (800–801).

Other connections, however, are far less malignant, if no less unpleasant, than the case of nuclear fallout. Sister Edgar's grief for Esmeralda, the murdered homeless girl she desperately tried to rescue from the gutter, leads her toward a nihilistic view of the world as a random and purposeless series of accidents: "She believes she is falling into crisis, beginning to think it is possible that all creation is a spurt of blank matter that chances to make an emerald planet here, a dead star there, with random waste between" (817). Sister Edgar's worldview shifts yet again, however, at the novel's close when Esmeralda's face inexplicably appears on a billboard advertisement for orange juice: "She sees Esmerelda's face take shape under the rainbow of bounteous juice and above the little suburban lake and there is a sense of someone living in the image, an animating spirit—less than a tender second of life, less than half a second and the spot is dark again" (822). The vision is witnessed by a large crowd of elated onlookers. It is nothing short of a miracle—an effect without a natural cause.

DeLillo presents a fictional world that sits atop a "tunneled underworld" of complex interconnections (826). Most of these connections, however, are coincidental and nonhierarchical, not the type we typically expect in narrative fiction. Which plotline(s) most deserves our narrative attention? Which connections of plot and character are more meaningful than others? DeLillo's novel deliberately fails to supply answers to these questions. As a result, *Underworld* is a remarkably difficult novel to read, demanding that we direct our attention everywhere at once, but its lyrical syntax provides an important insight into the novel's rhizomatic structure and its stubborn refusal to allow events of even the greatest magnitude—the threat of a nuclear apocalypse—to dwarf the quotidian.

If DeLillo may be taken to be Hemingway's stylistic descendent, Cormac McCarthy is invariably taken to be Faulkner's, and for reason—the two writers even shared the same editor and publisher.[13] Orville Prescott (1965), Jonathan Yardley (1974), Caryn James (1985), Mark Royden Winchell (1990), Richard Woodward (1992), Harold Bloom (2001), and James Wood (2005) have all drawn comparisons between McCarthy and Faulkner, though Winchell provides one small but significant caveat: "Faulkner was at heart a moralist who believed in an irreducible core of human dignity. His works possess a moral center, either explicit or implicit, that judges the evil and depravity of the world. In McCarthy's universe that center either doesn't exist or cannot hold" (1990, 294). Reviewers and critics often suggest that McCarthy out-Faulkners Faulkner: his subject matter is darker, his diction more arcane and esoteric, his syntax more tortuous. *Blood Meridian*—the anti-Western that chronicles the bloody exploits of the historical Glanton gang—is widely regarded as his supra-Faulknerian magnum opus.

The novel's syntax, characteristic of McCarthy's style, is one of the reasons for this compulsory comparison to Faulkner. Critics such as Dana Phillips and Andrew Hoberek have frequently remarked on *Blood Meridian*'s "complex," even "convoluted" sentence structure, depictions that recall the dizzying layers of nested clauses in some of Faulkner's prose (Phillips 1996, 434; Hoberek 2011, 487). Perhaps the illusion of syntactic complexity is created by *Blood Meridian*'s recondite vocabulary, but in fact, the basic structure that underpins McCarthy's syntax is remarkably simple: like Faulkner, Hemingway, and DeLillo, McCarthy too relies heavily on polysyndeton, heightening drama at the expense of narrative coherence, as early reviewers of the novel complained.[14]

B. R. Myers shares in this complaint, arguing that "novels tolerate epic language only in moderation" and that strong narrative prose requires those hierarchical relations that are flattened by the "pseudo-Biblical" syntax of polysyndeton (2001, 111). What is more, he argues, McCarthy shows a lack of artistic discrimination in using the same dramatic syntax to depict events of unequal importance: "To record with the same somber majesty every aspect of a cowboy's life, from a knife fight to his lunchtime burrito, is to create what can only be described as kitsch," he maintains. "Here we learn that out west even a hangover is something special" (108). Of course, this is the point: McCarthy has taken pains in his border fiction to create fictional worlds that are devoid of the meaning, order, and hierarchical arrangement we ordinarily expect from narrative fiction, and he is quite explicit about this in the novel's more philosophical passages. McCarthy's universe is not structured around any moral—or narrative—order:

> The universe is no narrow thing and the order within it is not constrained by any latitude in its conception to repeat what exists in one part in any other part. Even in this world more exists without our knowledge than with it and the order in creation which you see is that which you see is that which you have put there, like a string in a

> maze, so that you shall not lose your way. For existence has its own order and that no man's mind can compass, that mind itself being but a fact among others. (1985, 245)

The universe dwarfs humanity, which—too limited to even comprehend its vastness—is merely "a fact among others." Passages like these have led some critics to read a good amount of nihilism into the novel,[15] but more than that, they participate in a strain of antihumanism that courses throughout McCarthy's fiction. As I have argued elsewhere, the human realm is at once diminished by and integrated into the forces of natural history in McCarthy's southern novels (Owens-Murphy 2011, 159). In *Blood Meridian*, the bleak landscape of the disputed border between Texas and Mexico plays as large a role in the novel as any of its characters, and no one detail is subordinated to any other. McCarthy is quite deliberate in his "optical democracy," as he calls it, enlisting polysyndeton to express the inherent parity of each feature on the landscape:

> In the neuter austerity of that terrain all phenomena were bequeathed a strange equality and no one thing nor spider nor stone nor blade of grass could put forth claim to precedence. The very clarity of these articles belied their familiarity, for the eye predicates the whole on some feature or part and here was nothing more luminous than another and nothing more enshadowed and in the optical democracy of such landscapes all preference is made whimsical and a man and a rock become endowed with unguessed kinships. (247)

This "strange equality" that underpins "unguessed kinships" resonates with *Underworld*'s insistence that "everything is connected"—and as in DeLillo's novel, these kinships, which remain mysterious, are necessarily nonhierarchical.

Polysyndeton flattens differences in value and import, effectively creating these "unguessed kinships" through its proliferation of coordinating conjunctions. The ordinary is rendered suddenly dramatic, especially when coupled with McCarthy's erudite vocabulary. Sunrises become theatrical, terrifying, and practically sentient:

> They rode on and the sun in the east flushed pale streaks of light and then a deeper run of color like blood seeping up in sudden reaches flaring planewise and where the earth drained up into the sky at the edge of creation the top of the sun rose out of nothing like the head of a great red phallus until it cleared the unseen rim and sat squat and pulsing and malevolent behind them. (44–45)

In this passage, order and hierarchy are deliberately reversed as "the earth drained up into the sky" rather than vice versa, with horizon demarcating the very "edge of creation." The sun itself is cast in earthly terms, positioned as an aggressive phallus, "pulsing and malevolent," an impending threat that hovers over the travelers. The mere movement of the wagons across the desert landscape receives similarly dramatic treatment:

> The wagons drew so dry they slouched from side to side like dogs and the sand was grinding them away. The wheels shrank and the spokes reeled in their hubs and clattered like loomshafts and at night they'd drive false spokes into the mortices and tie them down with strips of green hide and they'd drive wedges between the iron of the tires and the suncracked felloes. (45)

Hierarchy is reversed again as the sand "grinds away" at the wagons rather than vice versa: the desert erodes the travelers and their equipment, whose wheels seem to require continuous maintenance against the difficult terrain. The very landscape becomes a thing of wonder, even for the bloodthirsty Glanton—the leader of the scalp-hunting clan chronicled in the novel—who pauses to admire a single leaf as the snow finally gives way to spring: "The leaves shifted in a million spangles down the pale corridors and Glanton took one and turned it like a tiny fan by its stem and held it and let it fall and its perfection was not lost on him" (136). Here, Glanton becomes something of a stand-in for Whitman, a keen observer who can look at a single leaf with awe. Yet Glanton-the-poet stands in stark contrast to Glanton-the-murderer in ways that suggest madness if not outright travesty: how is it that Glanton can value nature without valuing life?

Such is the dark converse of McCarthy's optical democracy: the extraordinary necessarily sinks to the level of the ordinary. This is one of the most shocking aspects of *Blood Meridian*: its apparent disregard for human life, which receives as much—or as little—narrative attention as the leaf admired by Glanton in the previous passage. Before joining the Glanton gang, the kid travels with a group of American filibusters, a number of whom become ill and die en route to Sonora, the Mexican territory they are charged with seizing:

> On this day two men fell sick and one died before dark. In the morning there was another ill to take his place. The two of them were laid among sacks of beans and rice and coffee in the supply-wagon with blankets over them to keep them from the sun and they rode with the slamming and jarring of the wagon half shirring the meat from their bones so that they cried out to be left and then they died. (44)

One might easily fail to notice these deaths, as they are sandwiched among long descriptive passages depicting the journey to Sonora that rely on the same syntax: "The dust the party raised was quickly dispersed and lost in the immensity of that landscape and there was no dust other for the pale sutler who pursued them drives unseen and his lean horse and his lean cart leave no track upon such ground or any ground" (44). The stark, factual language surrounding death ("they died") matches those matter-of-fact descriptions of the landscape; it also matches the simplicity of the sentence structure, which works here to homogenize rather than individuate each fatality, given the anonymity and, hence, interchangeability of "the men" in this passage.

Because this syntax depicts a range of deaths—animals, nameless tertiary characters, and major characters alike—it suggests that no one loss is more or less dramatic than any other. Violence in *Blood Meridian*, after all, is disturbingly indiscriminate. Glanton demonstrates as much with his casually reckless target shooting:

> The pistol roared and one of the birds exploded in a cloud of feathers. . . . He fired again. A second bird spun and lay kicking. The others flared, piping thinly, and Glanton turned with the pistol and shot a small goat that was standing with its throat pressed to the wall in terror and it fell stone dead in the dust and he fired upon a clay garraffa [sic] that burst in a shower of potsherds and water and he raised the pistol and swung toward the house and rang the bell in its mud tower above the roof, a solemn tolling that hung on in the emptiness after the echoes of the gunfire had died away. (83)

A bird, a goat, a water carafe, a bell—all are equivalent in the bulls-eye of Glanton's pistol and in the democratizing syntax of polysyndeton. The targeted equation here of household items with animals suggests the targetless nature of his violence.

This system of equivalence undergirds the novel's thin but vicious plot. Governor Angel Trias hires the Glanton gang to protect the villagers of Chihuahua from Apache attacks. Under their contract with Trias, the gang may cash in Apache scalps for $200 a piece: that is, one life is the equivalent of $200. One scalp, however, looks like any other, and the gang soon realizes that they can trade in any scalp—Apache, Tigua, or Mexican—for bounty: that is, all lives are equivalent to $200. Before long, the Glanton gang is murdering the villagers it has been hired to protect, and the violence they wreak is consistently narrated through polysyndeton, the syntax of equivalence. Among Glanton's first casualties is an innocuous old woman: "A fistsized hole erupted out of the far side of the woman's head in a great vomit of gore and she pitched over and lay slain in her blood without remedy. . . . He took a skinning knife from his belt and stepped to where the old woman lay and took up her hair and twisted it about his wrist and passed the blade of the knife about her skull and ripped away the scalp" (98). Nor does the Glanton gang limit itself to defenseless villagers; it also attacks uniformed Mexican militia groups: "The Mexican captain was bleeding from a gunshot wound in the chest and he stood in the stirrups to receive the charge with his sabre. Glanton shot him through the head and shoved him from his horse with his foot and shot down in succession three men behind him" (182).

Of course, the Glanton gang members also slaughter a fair number of Apaches, though they are indiscriminate in their killing of men, women, children, and even those Mexicans who have been enslaved by the Apaches. Another polysyndetic passage depicts their gruesome raid on a refugee encampment:

> When Glanton and his chiefs swung back through the village people were running out under the horses' hooves and the horses were plunging and some of the men were moving on foot among the huts with torches and dragging the victims out, slathered and dripping with blood, hacking at the dying and decapitating those who knelt for mercy. There were in the camp a number of Mexican slaves and these ran forth calling out in spanish and were brained or shot and one of the Delawares emerged from the smoke with a naked infant dangling in each hand and squatted at a ring of midden stones and swung them by the heels each in turn and bashed their heads against the stones so that the brains burst forth through the fontanel in a bloody spew and humans on fire came shrieking forth like berserkers and the riders hacked them down with their enormous knives and a young woman ran up and embraced the bloodied forefeet of Glanton's warhorse. (156)

When they finally cash in their scalps at Chihuahua, they are greeted as heroes, though "within a week of their quitting the city there would be a price of eight thousand pesos posted for Glanton's head" (185).

The violence does not end there. The Glanton gang soon gains a foothold in a lucrative ferry business, displacing the doctor in charge and exacting outrageous prices from travelers. Though they had "come to terms with the Yumas in conspiring to seize the ferry" (256), the gang secures the ferry on its own and destroys the Yumas for good measure:

> On the floodplain below the fort a terrible destruction had passed and upward of a dozen of the Yumas lay dead or writhing in the sand. A great howl went up among them and Glanton and his riders defiled out of the wooded littoral upriver and rode upon them and they cried out in rage at their betrayal. Their horses began to mill and they pulled them about and loosed arrows at the approaching dragoons and were shot down in volleys of pistolfire and the debarkees at the crossing scrabbled up their arms from among the dunnage. . . . The horses of the Yumas reared and screamed and churned about in the loose sand with their hoopshaped nostrils and whited eyes and the

> survivors made for the willows from which they'd emerged leaving on the field the wounded and the dying and the dead. (261–62)

Here, polysyndeton merges with passive voice and with the ambiguous, shifting pronouns *they* and *them* to underscore the chaos of this violent scene; and though the gang can no longer cash in scalps for cash at Chihuahua, "they took the scalps" anyway (262). The Yumas exact their revenge, however, in a retaliative strike, killing Glanton, the doctor, and a number of others in an equally bloody and frenzied ambush:

> The savages built a bonfire on the hill and fueled it with the furnishings from the white men's quarters and they raised up Glanton's body and bore it aloft in the manner of a slain champion and hurled it onto the flames. . . . The doctor's torso was dragged up by the heels and raised and flung onto the pyre and the doctor's mastiff also was committed to the flames. . . . The other bodies eight in number were heaped onto the fire where they sizzled and stank and the thick smoke rolled out over the river. (275–76)

Violence in *Blood Meridian* may be brutal, but it is largely reciprocal. The counteroffensives launched by bands like the Yumas are as vicious and cruel as those offensives initiated by the Glanton gang—and this reciprocal equivalence is represented, once again, via polysyndeton.

The type of violence portrayed in *Blood Meridian*—ruthless, senseless, indiscriminate, and multidirectional—resists the hierarchical grammatical order of traditional narration, which would require a logic that is deliberately missing from the novel. Why does Judge Holden rescue an Apache child only to murder and scalp him several days later? Why does the Glanton gang continue to practice scalping after their contract with Trias has been cancelled? Why, in a novel that is often read in postcolonial terms, are the Apaches, Comanches, and Yumas as aggressively violent as the Glanton gang, the fraught emblem of Western civilization?[16] The lyrical syntax of polysyndeton foregrounds the visceral reality of violence over any rationale. After all, "it makes no difference what men think of war," as Judge Holden declares during one of his philosophical orations. "War endures. As well ask men what they think of stone. War was always here. Before man was, war waited for him. The ultimate trade awaiting its ultimate practitioner. That is the way it was and will be. That way and not some other way" (248).

War in *Blood Meridian* is not only ubiquitous; it is prosaic. As Winchell puts it, "McCarthy proves conclusively that it wasn't the Nazis who invented the banality of evil" (1990, 308). In large part, this effect is achieved through McCarthy's polysyndeton, which deliberately flattens traditional narrative hierarchies of order and value. Though B. R. Myers complains that McCarthy does not, in the manner of Faulkner and Hemingway, reserve this syntax for scenes of momentous climax, this is precisely the point. Natural landscapes, the seasons, life and death—all occupy the same order of magnitude in McCarthy's fictional world.

According to Myers, polysyndeton creates linguistic "obscurity," which amounts to "bad poetry" reformatted as prose (2001, 108). His assessment, however, reveals as much about his disdain for lyric as it does about his disdain for avant-garde narrative fiction. Literature, after all, does more than organize experience into neat hierarchies of magnitude and cause and effect: it also captures the messiness of felt experience in which these relations are not always clear, or even true; it aims for drama over logical coherence; and it takes a wide variety of forms and styles, each of which shapes our perception of its content in ways that are as meaningful and varied as they are deliberate. In these respects, polysyndeton carries a certain advantage over traditional prose syntax, equipped as it is to depict moments of intensity and networks of connection that can be difficult to narrate through the hierarchical structures of most prose fiction. Once again, artifice engenders mimesis.

Those rhythmic passages that are rendered dramatic through polysyndeton also tend to reveal the ideological and aesthetic stakes of these novels. Faulkner's syntax dramatizes the conflict between the competing systems of value and economy between the North and South, though it also dramatizes the inherent equality of all people—an idea that exists in tension with Faulkner's aggrandizement of the antebellum South. Hemingway too uses this syntax to explore all of the emotional contours in the vertical polarities of love and war. DeLillo tips this axis horizontally by exploring his philosophy of interconnection through the coordinating conjunctions of polysyndeton, which flatten hierarchies of value so that the quotidian becomes exalted; McCarthy unearths the darker aspects of this structural democracy through violence that is wreaked so frequently and so indiscriminately that life itself depreciates in value.

In examining the role of polysyndeton in twentieth-century American fiction, this chapter demonstrates significant overlap among writers that are generally taken to be stylistically disparate. In *The Program Era* (2009), for example, Mark McGurl asserts that "postwar American fiction has been driven by a strong polarity of minimalist and maximalist compositional impulses that might alternatively be called the Hemingway/Faulkner dialectic" (377). As we have seen, however, Hemingway is not always sparse, and Faulkner is not always tortuous. Both rely heavily on a lyrical syntax that is structurally simple—polysyndeton merely consists, after all, in the repetition of a single conjunction—but that produces an array of nuanced rhetorical effects, from rhythm and accumulation to the leveling or democratizing effect that is exploited by their literary descendants, DeLillo and McCarthy. Organizing these writers around a single rhetorical device not only uncovers their debt to the lyric tradition but also highlights dimensions of their writing that are too often overlooked when we insist on placing them within the same familiar schematic. Maximal in length but minimal in structural complexity, polysyndeton enables these writers to achieve a difficult balance between two extremities of prose composition. The result is a lyrical style that forges rhythm and erases subordination in ways that work against the hierarchical tendencies of conventional narrative fiction.

Chapter 4

✦

Metaphysical Conceits

A scientist, desperate to grasp the mystery of human life, inadvertently creates a monster. A young man murders his pregnant mistress so as not to jeopardize his romance with a wealthy socialite. Plots are rooted in concrete events that operate in time, and while the actions of both Victor Frankenstein and Clyde Griffiths may advance a number of abstract themes—including the moral dimensions of scientific and social advancement and the dangers of unbridled ambition—these abstractions are epiphenomenal, or secondary to the plots that produced them. As Peter Brooks puts it, "Plot is somehow prior to those elements discussed by most critics, since it is the very organizing line, the thread of design, that makes narrative possible because finite and comprehensible" (1984, 4). Thematic abstractions are available to us only once we've completed the novels and fully apprehended the trajectory of each story's events. Had things ended less unhappily for either protagonist, we might have generated an entirely different set of themes around these works, through which the mad scientist and the social climber might be vindicated rather than ruined. Plotted novels demand that we read their events in primarily literal and temporal terms, which is why we ask people not to tell us "what happens" if we haven't yet finished one. To be sure, we can and do read more deeply for those elements—like theme—that tend toward abstraction, but such ex post facto considerations are not necessarily a part of our immediate reading experience.

Unlike fiction, lyric poetry demands that we read primarily for abstraction, a tendency that can pose special challenges for readers. Billy Collins dramatizes and gently mocks some of these challenges in his self-reflexive lyric about the teaching of poetry: "I ask them to take a poem / and hold it up to the light / like a color slide / or press an ear against its hive . . . But all they want to do / is tie the poem to a chair with rope / and torture a confession out of it. / They begin beating it with a hose / to find out what it really means" (1998, 58). Taken to the extreme, Collins suggests, readers approach poems as coded mysteries that possess secret meanings, a hermeneutic that leads to much frustration and resentment when the poem refuses to make itself accessible. Yet Collins is also pointing out here that lyric poems rely more heavily than do other genres on tropes of figuration. Cleanth Brooks famously argued that “the essence of poetry is metaphor” (1947, 248), a point that has been echoed by many others, including poet-critic John Hollander: “Good verse of any sort is only half the story of good poetry, whose essential character is what Wallace Stevens called ‘fictive,’ and Robert Frost ‘ulterior,’ or ‘saying one thing and meaning another,’ or what we would simply call not being literal” (2000, x). As Seo-Young Chu has argued in her book, *Do Metaphors Dream of Literal Sleep? A Science-Fictional Theory of Representation* (2011), some concepts are so complex, so “cognitively estranging,” that they “elude representation” and are more successfully depicted through metaphor than through literal language (2–3). Lyric figures such as figuration and catachresis, she argues, are especially adept at transforming difficult concepts into referents that can be made “available for representation” and hence made “knowable” (75). Science fiction capitalizes on these strengths of lyrical figuration through what Chu calls “counterfigurative literalization,” or the translation of metaphor into “a perceptible world of literal facts” (68) such that the sublime becomes outer space, virtual reality becomes cyberspace, “imperceptible” realities become the fourth dimension, and so on (7). The tension Chu registers between the literal and the figural is not unique to science fiction, though she is right to point to its exacerbation in narrative forms, which—science fiction included—typically submerge metaphor under narrative action in the interests of plot.

This chapter examines lyrical figuration and its peculiar function in narrative fiction by focusing on perhaps its most estranging and radical form, the so-called metaphysical conceit made famous by T. S. Eliot in his 1921 essay, “The Metaphysical Poets.” Under the metaphysical conceit, metaphor swells to epic proportions, engulfing and often overwhelming the very object or relationship it is designed to elucidate. The conceit functions still more dramatically, however, in novels by Toni Morrison (1973), Zora Neale Hurston ([1937] 2006), Henry Miller ([1934] 1961), and Russell Banks (1985), where it foregrounds the elaboration of figures over the concrete action we typically expect from a plotted novel, demanding that we read plot in terms of metaphor rather than vice versa. This chapter examines metaphysical conceits that frame and even compete with plot in terms of primary importance in ways that deliberately blur our point of reference. Whereas fiction typically advances abstraction through themes and concepts that emerge from plot, these novels approach the meditative lyric by using plot as a vehicle for reflection rather than action. They suspend us somewhere between the concrete and the figurative as we attempt to read plot in terms of the extensive metaphors around which they are organized.

Metaphor, the dominant trope of figuration in poetry, has an elusive quality that underpins Hollander’s sense of poetry’s “saying one thing and meaning another.” Because it relies on concrete images for depicting abstract qualities or concepts, a metaphoric utterance never “means” precisely what it says. Max Black refers to this phenomenon as metaphor’s “mystery”: “That, *taken as literal*, a metaphorical statement appears to be perversely asserting something to be what it is plainly known not to be" (1979, 21). From this perspective, Black argues, metaphors are "plainly false and absurd. But such 'absurdity' and 'falsity' are of the essence: in their absence, we should have no metaphor but merely a literal utterance." Black's characterization of metaphor's "mystery" may position him as something of a Platonist—here, as in the *Republic*, poets are liars, at least in a sense—but it effectively demonstrates the necessity of shifting our reading practices to suit these complex modes of figuration.

At its most basic level, metaphor departs from literal uses of language by representing one thing in terms of another through the logic of analogy. This basic theory of transference by which a term is "transferred" to a new context was first fleshed out by Aristotle in the *Poetics*: "Metaphor consists in giving the thing a name that belongs to something else; the transference being . . . on the grounds of analogy" (1984, 1457b8–10). Evening depicted as the "old age of the day," or old age as the "evening" or "sunset of life," is a poetic condensation of the analogy "as old age is to life, so is evening to day" (1457b23–25). Metaphor dislodges terms from their literal usage by placing them in unusual contexts—a cognitive exercise that promotes a new understanding of the metaphor's referent, as Aristotle acknowledges in the *Rhetoric* (1410b10–15). In recent decades, critics such as George Lakoff and Mark Johnson have expanded on this point, arguing that metaphor is not simply linguistic but also conceptual in its function, and that it underpins our most fundamental cognitive activities: "The way we think, what we experience, and what we do every day is very much a matter of metaphor" (1980, 3). In fact, they argue, metaphor structures and conditions our experience in ways that we largely take for granted. Take, for instance, the act of arguing. "Your claims are *indefensible*" and "He *shot down* all of my arguments" are common figurative phrases that we use to recount arguments, and they indicate our understanding of argument primarily "in terms of war" to the exclusion of its other, more cooperative dimensions, such as "mutual understanding" (4, 10).

Some theories of metaphor, however, favor a more reciprocal relationship between the terms of a metaphor's implied analogy. Proponents of interactionist theories of metaphor, most notably Max Black, argue against the one-way relationship of transference articulated by Aristotle and, to some extent, by Lakoff and Johnson, maintaining instead that each term in a metaphor necessarily illuminates the other. A conceptual metaphor such as "argument is war," for example, shapes our understanding not only of argument but also of war, which, in this sense, is figured as a form of rational disagreement. According to interactionist theories, "The two subjects [of a metaphor] 'interact' in the following ways: (a) the presence of the primary subject incites the hearer to select some of the secondary subject's properties; and (b) invites him to construct a parallel implication-complex that can fit the primary subject; and (c) reciprocally induces parallel changes in the secondary subject" (Black 1979, 29). Our reading of one subject in terms of the other shapes our understanding of both. The result is a meaning that emerges from their interaction—a meaning that is not inherent in either subject in isolation.

Metaphor can help us see new dimensions of familiar concepts by placing them in unusual analogical pairings. While cognitive theorists such as Lakoff and Turner have demonstrated that metaphor is not necessarily unique to poetic language, relying on "conceptual schemas . . . that we use in comprehending our experience and in reasoning about it" on a daily basis, poets take metaphor one step farther, venturing "beyond the normal use of conventional metaphor to point out, and call into question, the boundaries of our everyday metaphorical understandings of important concepts. Indeed, the major poetic point being made can be the inadequacy of the conventional metaphor" (1989; 65, 69). Some metaphors become so "fixed and standardized" in language that they no longer stand out as metaphors at all, but poets who strive to develop new metaphors "breathe force and energy into discourse" through unexpected pairings of terms and concepts, prompting theorists like Paul Ricoeur to classify them under the rhetorical canon of "invention" (1977, 62, 63). Metaphors, after all—especially those "inventive" metaphors to which Ricoeur refers—do not simply reflect resemblance but create it. "Some metaphors enable us to see aspects of reality that the metaphor's production helps to constitute," Black argues (1979, 39). In other words, metaphors do more than articulate some "objectively given similarity" that exists "prior to the formation of the metaphor itself"; they forge similarity and communicate it to the reader through the vehicle of figuration (Kittay 1987, 17).

This anti-objectivist view, which stresses figuration's creative capacity, is not always held to be in metaphor's favor, however. It was on these grounds that Samuel Johnson famously condemned the seventeenth-century "metaphysical poets," as he disdainfully called them, through whom "the most heterogeneous ideas are yoked by violence together" (1971, 12). These poets, he argued, are overly concerned with wit and ingenuity at the expense of the emotions, bent as they are on "a voluntary deviation from nature in pursuit of something new and strange" (26). Yet this is precisely the literary significance and legacy of what we now know as the metaphysical conceit, the extension of metaphor to its outermost limits in terms of the disparity between the objects of comparison. Take, for instance, an example provided by Johnson himself, an excerpt from Donne's now widely anthologized "A Valediction: Forbidding Mourning," in which two lovers' souls are likened to the legs of a compass:

> If they be two, they are two so
> As stiffe twin compasses are two,
> Thy soule the fixt foot, makes no show
> To move, but doth, if the' other doe.

And though it in the center sit,
Yet when the other far doth rome,
It leanes, and hearkens after it,
And growes erect, as that comes home.

Such wilt thou be to me, who must
Like th' other foot, obliquely runne.
Thy firmnes makes my circle just,
And makes me end, where I begunne. (1985, 98)

Donne famously forges a connection between two unlikely subjects—romantic love and a mechanical drawing implement—by concentrating on the relationship between the compass's legs. Just as the central leg leans toward the leg that draws the circle, the poem claims, so the soul of one lover hearkens toward the other, regardless of the distance that separates them; and like the roaming leg, the departed lover will always return home. What's more, the shape created by his departure is a perfect circle that indicates the "firmnes" and the "just[ness]" of their spiritual bond even in the face of physical distance. The interaction between these two subjects produces a twofold result. Love's comparison to a compass in the poem characterizes it as steady, exact, and reliable; conversely, the personification of the compass invests this drawing tool with a surprising sentimental quality, transforming a mechanical metal leg into a pining lover. Such a metaphor is an exercise in intellect, since the cognitive labor required to read romantic love in terms of a compass is much greater than something like Burns's "O my luve's like a red, red rose," in which the objects of comparison are more obvious and more readily joined in our minds. Metaphor, especially in the case of the metaphysical conceit, resides chiefly in the reader's apprehension of similarity, since "we, the readers, are doing the elaborating and extending [of the metaphor] in ways that we take to be indicated or at least suggested by the poem" (Lakoff and Turner 1989, 67).

T. S. Eliot famously rescues the metaphysical poets from Johnson's rebuke in his review of Herbert Grierson's edited collection, *Metaphysical Lyrics and Poems of the Seventeenth Century: Donne to Butler* ([1921] 1975). Whereas Johnson accuses these poets of striving for wit at the expense of affective power, Eliot argues that, to the contrary, "they were, at best, engaged in the task of trying to find the verbal equivalent for states of mind and feeling" (65). So inarticulable are these moods and feelings, he suggests, that poets must reach for the unlikeliest of metaphors to approximate them in language. Eliot employs his own conceit in the opening lines of "The Love Song of J. Alfred Prufrock" (1915). The conceit establishes a sense of hope and deflation after which the rest of the poem is patterned. The first two lines are promising and dreamy—"Let us go then, you and I, / When the evening is spread out against the sky"—but are immediately undercut by the macabre conceit of a drugged patient lying "etherized upon a table" (1963, 3). So goes the rest of the poem, in which Prufrock makes a series of grandiose claims—"I have heard the mermaids singing, each to each"—only to retract them immediately: "I do not think that they will sing to me" (7). The conceit of the etherized patient articulates in material terms the feelings of paralysis and self-doubt that will plague the speaker throughout this meditative lyric.

To a certain degree, Eliot notes, the metaphysical poets simply render explicit the operations of metaphor that underpin all poetry, which are after all a "heterogeneity of material compelled into unity by the operation of the poet's mind" ([1921] 1975, 61). All metaphors cultivate similarity between items that are more or less dissimilar. Brief conceits like Eliot's rely on the "telescoping of images" in a "sudden contrast of associations" that is executed in a handful of lines (60). A number of metaphysical conceits, however, also rely on spatial extension for their effect, the "elaboration (contrasted with the condensation) of a figure of speech to the furthest stage to which the ingenuity can carry it" (60). It is this quality of elaboration, Eliot maintains, that chiefly distinguishes the conceit from other metaphors. Whereas Eliot's etherized patient, for example, only spans a single line, three of the nine stanzas of Donne's poems are devoted to the extension and development of the compass and its relationship to the geographically estranged lovers.

Eliot's essay heralded a return to the metaphysical conceit in twentieth-century American poetry, with a number of poets making use of the conceit and its capacity for elaboration to frame their poems. Langston Hughes's "Mother to Son" (1926) establishes a metaphor in its opening lines—"Well, son, I'll tell you: / Life for me ain't been no crystal stair"—which is developed and elaborated throughout the poem so that the speaker can convey the importance of firmness in the face of adversity (1994, 30). The speaker navigates a figurative staircase complete with "tacks," "splinters," and missing floorboards; each "landin" represents an occasion to either sit down or keep "turnin' corners." The same conceit functions not only as a testament to the speaker's hardships but also as a prescription for perseverance as she cautions her son against despair, depicted here as exhaustion: "Don't you set down on the steps . . . Don't you fall now" (30). In fact, the staircase becomes so vivid it seems concrete until we are reminded that it has no end: "I'se still climbin,' " the speaker finally asserts.

George Szirtes's "Piano" (2004) personifies the instrument's velocity sensitivity by comparing the body of a baby grand to that of a woman:

> It is a hybrid creature with only
> Three legs and a faint ephemeral grin,
>
> With feminine curves, a gorgeous womanly
> Voluptuousness. It seems almost indecent
> To be sitting beneath her, guilty and lonely,

Ignorant of the role she will play. The crescent
Of her one hip is a shelter and the gloss
Of her body temptation. Concupiscent

Discords swell into proper fifths, zealous
Arpeggios clamber over her. Learning
Her vast bourgeois temperament is the cross

A child must bear as she stands burning
In the summer sun. And Chopin and Bartok
Can be enticed from her with their strut and yearning.

You must woo her carefully with wealth and work,
Until one day, like the butterfly she is,
She shrugs and vanishes into the sudden dark

Of history and other shady business. (2008, 397)

The conceit, which draws out the responsiveness of the piano to the player's touch, constructs the instrument as a sensual but temperamental lover. The relationship between pianist and piano is a courtship, and the piano has all of the power, as their spatial positioning would indicate: "It seems almost indecent / To be sitting beneath her, guilty and lonely, / Ignorant of the role she will play." Her sound is unpredictable and can be coaxed from her only under precisely the right conditions: "And Chopin and Bartok / Can be enticed from her with their strut and yearning. / You must woo her with wealth and work." The pianist is in a position of complete subordination to the baby grand, an aspect of piano playing that is dramatized through the conceit of the fickle lover.

The poems of Donne, Hughes, and Szirtes are examples of short lyrics that are consumed by figuration. So integral are their conceits to an understanding of each poem's referent that one wonders which is the primary term—the pair of lovers or the compass? life's hardships or the staircase? the piano or the capricious lover? The metaphor rivals, even surmounts, the referent in terms of importance, though the metaphor and referent occupy very different realms of existence, since metaphors "exist" in a stylistic sense but not in an ontological one.[1] Under the operations of the metaphysical conceit, metaphor swells to new magnitudes, foregrounding what Roman Ingarden has termed metaphor's opalescence, its simultaneous existence and nonexistence within the world of the poem (Falk 1971, 142).[2] In a literal sense, there is no woman in Szirtes's lyric, though the figuration of the woman is what makes possible the depiction of the piano that serves as the poem's basis.

Certain novels employ the metaphysical conceit in ways that cause the text to hover between what Brian McHale calls "two frames of reference with different ontological statuses," that opalescence to which Ingarden refers (1987, 134). The pronounced role of figuration in these novels forces us to turn away from literal readings of narrative fiction in ways that may seem counterintuitive. In his discussion of narrativity, or the degree to which a text adheres to traditional narrative conventions, Gerald Prince argues that texts depicting concrete particulars are more "narrative" than those that depict abstract generalizations: "An event which is individualized will contribute more to narrativity than one which is not. Narrative shies away from abstraction and thrives on concreteness. It concentrates on the particular and not the general" (1982, 149). In diverting our attention from a narrative's concrete events to analogical frames based on abstraction, novels that rely heavily on metaphor do not exhibit much narrativity.

Metaphor also participates in description, the atemporal suspension of narrative action for the sake of illustrative elaboration, as Mieke Bal has argued. Descriptive passages are often considered antinarrative because they suspend time in order to dilate a given moment, the details of which are not sorted according to any particular hierarchy. "Theoretically, unbound by narrative sequentiality, the enumeration of the elements of the object in description is fundamentally arbitrary," Bal writes. "In contrast, the narration of events follows the chronology in which the events take place" (2006, 577). Metaphor, then, not only appears to violate narrative's commitment to literal action but also violates narrative's investment in temporal succession and hierarchical arrangement in a way that is reminiscent of those polysyndetic constructions treated in the previous chapter.

What is the function of such descriptive or metaphoric passages in narrative fiction? For Bal, they are important indicators of narrative perspective. "Description tends to follow the order of the object as it is commonly perceived," she writes (2006, 577). "In the same way as word order is regulated by syntax and narrative order by chronology, so descriptive order is guided by the double agency of the focalizer and the narrative this agent's gaze generates" (593–94). Description and metaphor are linked to focalization, or "the relation between the vision and that which is 'seen,' perceived" (Bal 1997, 142). Descriptive passages, in other words, align readers with the perspective of the "focalizer" or perceiver (typically a narrator, a character, or both). Consequently, they can provide important and revealing insights into a character's feelings, perceptions, and motivations.

This chapter treats novels by Toni Morrison, Zora Neale Hurston, Henry Miller, and Russell Banks that, in order of increasing insistence, rely on the metaphysical conceit as an important conceptual framework for understanding the narrative's story-events as well as its characters. While Morrison and Hurston develop conceits that supply interpretive frames for their plots, the novels of Miller and Banks are almost wholly devoted to elaborations on a single conceit, so that narrative action is effectively subordinated to figuration. In all four novels, plot and metaphor "interact" to produce new and reciprocal meanings by which figuration shapes the way we read each story's events—and vice versa.

For Toni Morrison, the stakes of metaphor are not only cognitive and creative but also ideological. Her widely cited 1992 study, *Playing in the Dark*, suggests that our cultural conceptions of race have been expressed and reified in American literature primarily through the trope of figuration. Beginning with an observation regarding "the pervasive use of black images and people in expressive prose" by white authors ranging from Willa Cather to Ernest Hemingway, Morrison goes on to identify what she calls an "Africanist presence" in the American literary canon that allowed these writers to "talk about themselves" through figurations of blackness (x, 17). Such figurations, she argues, are "Eurocentric" at best and racist at worst, consistently constructing blackness as an alien, taboo, or otherwise undesirable counterpoint to whiteness. For Morrison, metaphor's deployment in American literature has been inextricably tied to power and racial politics; she even goes so far as to argue that race itself "has become metaphorical—a way of referring to and disguising forces, events, classes, and expressions of social decay and economic division far more threatening to the body politic than biological 'race' ever was" (63)

As Morrison demonstrates, the question of who employs metaphor, for what audience, and to what end is important for uncovering metaphor's potentially ideological investments. Yet it is these contexts, and not the figure of metaphor itself, with which Morrison takes issue. Her solution is the thoughtful deployment of metaphor in fresh contexts that are not overburdened by clichés, including the prejudices of routine racism:

> The kind of work I have always wanted to do requires me to learn how to maneuver ways to free up the language from its sometimes sinister, frequently lazy, almost always predictable employment of racially informed and determined chains. . . . Both [writing and reading] require being mindful of the places where imagination sabotages itself, locks its own gates, pollutes its vision. Writing and reading mean being aware of the writer's notions of risk and safety, the serene achievement of, or sweaty fight for, meaning and response-ability. (xi)

Conventional metaphors are not only "sinister"; they are "lazy" and "predictable." In essence, they are used to perpetuate stereotypes. In calling for the liberation of metaphor from its more commonplace contexts and a renewed arousal of reader "response-ability," Morrison advocates an approach to figurative language that places her in the company of some strange bedfellows: Donne, Herbert, Crashaw, not to mention their twentieth-century champion and one of American modernism's worse offenders in terms of the racially charged figurations in his own poetry and prose, T. S. Eliot.[3]

In fact, however, metaphysical conceits appear in nearly all of Morrison's fiction, and more often than not, they depict poignant instances of black suffering—a deliberate reversal of those dehumanizing figurations of blackness Morrison has identified in *Playing in the Dark*. When the schoolboys harass Pecola for her skin color and her father's rumored tendency to sleep naked in *The Bluest Eye* ([1970] 2007)—"It was their contempt for their own blackness that gave the first insult its teeth"—they surround her "like a necklace of semiprecious stones" (65). A heartbroken Hagar, desperate for the lost attentions of Milkman, embarks on a futile cosmetic shopping spree in *Song of Solomon* ([1977] 2004), hoping that she can once again win his affections by assimilating to Western, consumer-driven standards of beauty: "Hagar breathed deeply the sweet air that hung over the glass counters. Like a smiling sleepwalker she circled. . . . Lipsticks in soft white hands darted out of their sheaths like the shiny red penises of puppies" (311). The scars on Sethe's back from the beatings she incurred as a slave in *Beloved* ([1987] 2004) are figured as a "chokecherry tree," the "wide roots and intricate branches" of which provide a corporeal mapping of her sorrows (17). Morrison frequently asks us to see images and events in new contexts, especially those that illustrate the humanity and anguish of the black characters who populate her fictional world.

Morrison's second novel, *Sula* (1973), is filled to the brim with conceits such as these, though figuration in *Sula* is concerned not only with anguish but also with its relief. Between these two poles lies a grieving process that permeates the novel and connects its wide cast of characters, all of whom suffer in different ways and from different ailments—war trauma, failed parenthood, lost friendship, lost love. So skilled, however, is Morrison at counterbalancing pain with pleasure and sorrow with humor that few critics have given attention to the novel's extended focus on suffering.[4] In what follows, I argue that *Sula* focuses not only on the felt experience of suffering and its corollary aesthetic representation but also on its resolution through the catharsis made possible by grief—all of which are conducted through the vehicle of the metaphysical conceit.

Following the exposition that provides a brief history of "the Bottoms," the fictional town that supplies the novel's setting, *Sula* opens with a scene of disturbing violent intensity witnessed by Shadrack during his service in the First World War:

> He turned his head a little to the right and saw the face of a soldier near him fly off. Before he could register shock, the rest of the soldier's head disappeared under the inverted soup bowl of his helmet. But stubbornly, taking no direction from the brain, the body of the headless soldier ran on, with energy and grace, ignoring altogether the drip and slide of brain tissue down its back. (8)

The conceit depicted here establishes an important pattern in the novel: the articulation of felt trauma through disparate terms in a strained and even discomfiting analogy.[5] Nothing, save maybe shape, would naturally link a soldier's helmet to a soup bowl beyond the single element the conceit is designed to emphasize: its contents. The soupy brain tissue that slides down the decimated soldier's back seeps from the helmet like soup from an upside-down bowl. The image evoked by this conceit unsettles not only because of its graphic violence but because the soldier's maimed body is depicted in terms of food. The metaphor not only shapes our conception of the soldier's brains in terms of soup, but also shapes our understanding of soup in terms of the soldier's brains.

Similar, if less gruesome, strained analogies are used by *Sula*'s third-person narrator to focalize Shadrack's residual war trauma. Strapped to a hospital bed in a psych ward, he struggles to make sense of his wartime experiences: "Laced and silent in his small bed, he tried to tie the loose cords in his mind" (10). Unlike the laces that hold him together, the thoughts in Shadrack's mind hang together tenuously, ready to fall apart at any moment. Upon his release, Shadrack finds it hard to connect to other people. They appear to him as "thin slips, like paper dolls floating down the walks. Some were seated in chairs with wheels, propelled by other paper figures from behind. . . . A good high wind would pull them up and away and they would land perhaps among the tops of trees" (11). Mistaken for a drunk, Shadrack is arrested for "vagrancy and intoxication" (13) and sinks at last into "a sleep deeper than the hospital drugs; deeper than the pits of plums; steadier than the condor's wing; more tranquil than the curve of eggs" (14). Psychological instability is figured as physical instability: slackness, weightlessness, hollowness. In struggling to articulate emotions that refuse to sort themselves out, the narrator, who takes on Shadrack's perspective, turns toward some unlikely metaphors—loose cords, paper dolls—as a way of approximating Shadrack's otherwise inexpressible felt experience.

Metaphor—sometimes articulated directly by *Sula*'s characters, and sometimes by the narrator on a character's behalf—becomes one of the few available avenues for understanding character motivation in the novel. One of the most puzzling and disturbing events in *Sula* is Eva's decision to murder her son, Plum, who is, like Shadrack, a shell-shocked veteran of the First World War. Upon Plum's return home, Eva could sense that "there was obviously something wrong" (45), and before long, he is discovered to be stealing money from his family, making mysterious trips to Cincinnati, and cooking heroin. He also appears to have retreated into childhood, as the contents of his bedroom suggest: "There in the corner was a half-eaten store-bought cherry pie. Balled-up candy wrappers and empty pop bottles peeped from under the dresser. On the floor by [Eva's] foot was a glass of strawberry crush and a *Liberty* magazine" (46). As Eva gathers him into her arms one night, he even begins to speak like a child: "Mamma, you so purty. You so purty, Mamma," he murmurs, half-asleep (47). Moments later and without warning, Eva douses him in kerosene and sets him on fire, leaving Plum to burn to death. A year later, when Eva's daughter Hannah gathers the courage to ask Eva about the awful incident—"What'd you kill Plum for, Mama?"—Eva's responds with a rambling attempt to construct a metaphysical conceit to explain her actions:

> It was such a carryin' on to get him born and to keep him alive. Just to keep his little heart beating and his little old lungs cleared and when he came back from that war he wanted to git back in. After all that carryin' on, just gettin' him out and keepin' him alive, he wanted to crawl back in my womb and well . . . I ain't got the room no more even if he could do it. There wasn't space for him in my womb. And he was crawlin' back. Being helpless and thinking baby thoughts and dreaming baby dreams and messing up his pants again and smiling all the time. I had room enough in my heart, but not in my womb, not no more. I birthed him once. I couldn't do it again. He was growed, a big old thing. Godhavemercy, I couldn't birth him twice. I'd be laying here at night and he be downstairs in that room, but when I closed my eyes I'd see him . . . six feet tall smilin' and crawlin' up the stairs quietlike so I wouldn't hear and opening the door soft so I wouldn't hear and he'd be creepin' to the bed trying to spread my legs trying to get back up in my womb. He was a man, girl, a big old growed-up man. I didn't have that much room. I kept on dreaming it. Dreaming it and I knowed it was true. One night it wouldn't be no dream. It'd be true and I would have done it, would have let him if I'd've had the room but a big man can't be a baby all wrapped up inside his mamma no more, he suffocate. I done everything I could to make him leave me and go on and live and be a man but he wouldn't and I had to keep him out so I just thought of a way he could die like a man not all scrunched up inside my womb, but like a man. (70–71)

In trying to articulate her sense of Plum's psychological regression, Eva reconstructs him as a helpless and needy infant. Eva's conceit oscillates between the literal and the figurative throughout this passage. While Plum is not actually attempting to crawl back into Eva's womb—and Eva more or less admits that this image is from a recurring "dream" that has figurative importance for her—the distinction that Eva draws between her heart and her womb is less clear.

"I had room enough in my heart, but not in my womb, not no more," she insists. In what figurative sense would the womb fail to align with the heart, especially since one appears to follow from the other, Eva's love for Plum (heart) deriving from her relationship to Plum as his mother (womb)? This portion of the conceit demands a literal reading: as a grown man, Plum cannot possibly fit "all scrunched up" inside Eva's womb (71). Such a literal understanding, however, returns us to the realm of figuration: a grown man cannot fit inside his mother's womb because he no longer belongs there.

This obscure conceit is the only window we have into Eva's rationale for murdering Plum. It is a complicated attempt to articulate complicated and conflicting feelings of love, contempt, sacrifice, and sorrow. The metaphor depicts Plum as staging an unnatural retreat from life back to the womb. While portions of the conceit are obscured by Eva's vacillation between literal and figurative realms, one thing is made clear: as a mother, Eva believes she is acting in Plum's best interests, even if the result is filicide. Having identified Plum's suffering, Eva sought to relieve it.

Figurations of suffering, grief, and relief from pain course throughout *Sula*, especially in those sections that center on the friendship between Sula and Nel. As Axel Nissen has argued, the novel is not only a celebration of friendship in early childhood but also an elegy for Chicken Little, whose death will haunt both girls and create a rift between them that widens as the years progress (1999, 272). Just prior to the tragedy, the girls are engaged in "grass play," a literal game that holds a great deal of figurative meaning for their relationship. "In concert, without ever meeting each other's eyes," Nel and Sula stroke grass leaves, strip twigs of their bark, and dig into the soil with their twigs "until the two holes were one and the same" (58). The two girls have achieved the same understanding of this arbitrary game, though "neither one had spoken a word" (59). The grass play scene demonstrates a unity and mutual understanding between these friends that is breached by two events, the first of which is the accidental drowning of Chicken Little.

Shortly after grass play, Nel and Sula are approached by the small neighborhood boy, whom Sula swings from a tree in jest, but who slips from her fingers and falls into the river, never to resurface. The panicked girls never confess to their role in the drowning, though their culpability drives a palpable wedge between them. They remain distant from one another at the funeral: "There was a space, a separateness, between them" (64). Guilt-stricken and afraid of retribution, they are unable to properly grieve for Chicken Little. Nel finds that her legs have "turned to granite," and Sula cries "soundlessly and with no heaving and gasping for breath" (65). In stark contrast, the local women in attendance are wildly expressive in their grief:

> As Reverend Deal moved into his sermon, the hands of the women unfolded like pairs of raven's wings and flew high above their hats into the air. . . . They spoke, for they were full and needed to say. They swayed, for the rivulets of grief or of ecstasy must be rocked. And when they thought of all that life and death locked into that little closed coffin they danced and screamed, not to protest God's will but to acknowledge it and confirm once more their conviction that the only way to avoid the Hand of God is to get in it. (65–66)

Grief is expressed through the body—swaying, dancing, screaming—and its suppression is figured, via Sula and Nel, as stoical silence. It will be many years, and many pages, before Nel finally learns how to grieve.

Many elements from this scene are recalled in the aftermath of a second traumatic event that drives Nel and Sula apart ten years later: Sula's affair with Nel's husband, Jude. The narrator focalizes the betrayal through Nel by constructing another elaborate conceit to articulate Nel's despair: "She waited for something to happen . . . inside. There was stirring, a movement of mud and dead leaves" (107). Her distress is vaguely identified as a "stirring," the thickness of her sorrow as mud. As Nel explores her sadness through the frame of this conceit, she recalls the mourners at Chicken Little's funeral:

> The women who shrieked over the bier and at the lip of the open grave. What she had regarded since as unbecoming behavior seemed fitting to her now; they were screaming at the neck of God, his giant nape, the vast back-of-the-head that he had turned on them in death. But it seemed to her now that it was not a fist-shaking grief they were keening but rather a simple obligation to say something, do something, feel something about the dead.

Yet even now, Nel finds herself incapable of grief:

> She waited. The mud shifted, the leaves stirred, the smell of overripe green things enveloped her and announced the beginnings of her very own howl.
>
> But it did not come.
>
> The odor evaporated; the leaves were still, the mud settled. And finally there was nothing, just a flake of something dry and nasty in her throat. (108)

Mourning is again figured through movement and its suppression through stillness. This earthy conceit in which sorrow is likened to mud also recalls the "grass play" game that signaled the strength of Nel and Sula's bond, which has been broken by Jude's—and Sula's—infidelity. Unsatisfied with this metaphor, however, the narrator shifts to a second, much lengthier and less coherent conceit, the ontological nature of which is more dubious than the first:

> She stood up frightened. There was something just to the right of her, in the air, just out of view. She could not see it, but she knew exactly what it looked like. A gray ball hovering just there. Just there. To the right. Quiet, gray, dirty. A ball of muddy strings, but without weight, fluffy but terrible in its malevolence. She knew she could not look, so she closed her eyes and crept past it out of the bathroom, shutting the

> door behind her. . . . She spent a whole summer with the gray ball, the little ball of fur and string and hair always floating in the light near her but which she did not see because she never looked. But that was the terrible part, the effort it took not to look. But it was there anyhow, just to the right of her head and maybe further down by her shoulder, so when the children went to a monster movie at the Elmira Theater and came home and said, "Mamma, can you sleep with us tonight?" she said all right and got into bed with her children and told herself each time that they might dream a dream about dragons and would need her to comfort them. It was so nice to think about their scary dreams and not about a ball of fur. She even hoped their dreams would rub off on her and give her the wonderful relief of a nightmare so she could stop going around scared to turn her head this way or that lest she see it. That was the scary part—seeing it. It was not coming at her; it never did that, or tried to pounce on her. It just floated there for the seeing, if she wanted to, and O my God for the touching if she wanted to. But she didn't want to see it, ever, for if she saw it, who could tell but what she might actually touch it, or want to, and then what would happen if she actually reached out her hand and touched it? Die probably, but no worse than that. Dying was OK because it was sleep and there wasn't no gray ball in death, was there? Was there? (109–10)

Here, Nel's betrayal is figured as a "gray ball" alternately described as "a ball of muddy strings," "a ball of fur," and a "little ball of fur and string and hair." Whatever its composition, the ball has an ethereal quality—light and floating, it is always in the margins of Nel's purview, too frightening to be confronted head-on. Like Shadrack's conception of psychological instability, Nel's sense of despair is figured as a mess of strings that hang together loosely. Unlike the conceits developed by Shadrack and Eva, however, Nel's has a decidedly material dimension. It startles her; it can be seen and touched; it is present in the way other material objects in the book are present. The gray ball hovers between the concrete storyworld and the realm of metaphor, providing a quasi-material formulation of the inexpressible sorrow that is haunting Nel. Ironically, however, this material conceit circles back around to the very object it aims to represent: "She would have to ask somebody about that [ball], somebody she could confide in and who knew a lot of things, like Sula" (110).

The narrator plays devil's advocate, alternately focalizing this betrayal through Sula, who fails to comprehend Nel's feelings. In fact, Sula justifies her affair with Jude through the very bond of friendship Nel believes to have been severed. After all, Sula reasons, the two girls "had always shared the affection of other people: compared how a boy kissed, what line he used with one and then the other. Marriage, apparently, had changed all that, but having had no intimate knowledge of marriage . . . she was ill prepared for the possessiveness of the one person she felt close to" (119). Sula, it turns out, feels an equal and opposite sense of betrayal by Nel, who no longer shares her understanding of the world. "Nel was the one person who had wanted nothing from her, who had accepted all aspects of her. . . . Now Nel was one of *them*" (119–20), she broods, grouping Nel with the townsfolk who judge Sula for her failure to conform to standards of social propriety. The narrator now constructs an elaborate conceit for Sula, who struggles to articulate her own sense of Nel's treachery:

> Now Nel was one of *them*. One of the spiders whose only thought was the next rung of the web, who dangled in dark dry places suspended by their own spittle, more terrified of the free fall than the snake's breath below. Their eyes so intent on the wayward stranger who trips into their net, they were blind to the cobalt on their own backs, the moonshine fighting to pierce their corners. If they were touched by the snake's breath, however fatal, they were merely victims and knew how to behave in that role (just as Nel knew how to behave as the wronged wife). But the free fall, oh no, that required—demanded—invention: a thing to do with the wings, a way of holding the legs and most of all a full surrender to the downward flight if they wished to taste their tongues or stay alive. But alive was what they, and now Nel, did not want to be. Too dangerous. Now Nel belonged to the town and all of its ways. She had given herself over to them, and the flick of their tongues would drive her back into her little dry corner where she would cling to her spittle high above the breath of the snake and the fall.
>
> It had surprised her a little and saddened her a good deal when Nel behaved the way the others would have. (120)

The people of the Bottoms are figured as the snake in this elaborate metaphor, their propensity for gossip signaled by the "flick of their tongues." Like the snake, they are predatory, and they use fear to police the behavior of potential nonconformists. Nel is the spider whose only concern is constructing a web to keep itself beyond the reach of the snake, more afraid of the "free fall"—or freedom—than of the snake itself. Though Nel "behave[s] as the wronged wife," Sula is the victim in this scenario. Now the spider, as well as the snake, has turned against her; all alone, Sula must navigate the free fall that will allow her to "stay alive" apart from the snares of spider and snake alike.

That Sula and Nel each feel equally betrayed, and that we as readers are invited to understand both positions through metaphor and focalization, emphasizes the difficulty of moral judgment in *Sula* and the importance of the conceit in framing their respective points of view.[6] Though critics have tended toward moralizing readings that are allied with Nel's perspective,[7] the sympathetic attention given to both Sula and Nel's interiority, accessed through metaphor, suggests that Morrison is cautioning us against joining the flickering tongues in the snake pit. Both Sula and Nel are suffering the loss of their friendship, which has been damaged by a lack of consensus regarding the extent to which their lives can be shared. Though Sula's return to the Bottoms after a ten-year absence had been welcomed by Nel as being "like getting the use of an eye back, having a cataract removed" (95), the two women soon find that what was an easy and simple friendship in childhood becomes more complicated in adulthood.

Nel's conceit returns in the last pages of the novel after Sula has passed away from an unstipulated illness. Visiting Sula's gravesite, Nel observes what could be a literal shift in wind patterns, but a reader attuned to lyrical conventions will recognize a figurative shift in Nel's emotions, the continuation of an earlier conceit: "Leaves stirred; mud shifted; there was the smell of overripe green things. A soft ball of fur broke and scattered like dandelion spores in the breeze" (174). The mysterious ball of fur that has been haunting Nel finally disappears, and the reappearance of the earthy odor and the movement of leaves and mud recall the metaphor's original deployment, in which "the odor evaporated; the leaves were still, the mud settled" (108). The resolution of the conceit at the novel's close is important, since it signals the consummation of Nel's grieving process, which had been stymied earlier in the novel. This time, Nel indulges her feelings of loss and finally recognizes the true purpose behind her suffering: "All that time, all that time, I thought I was missing Jude," she discovers. Like the grieving women at Chicken Little's funeral, she allows herself to cry out: "It was a fine cry—loud and long—but it had no bottom and it had no top, just circles and circles of sorrow" (174).

Sula is not so much a novel of plotted events as it is a novel of feelings, the most difficult of which are expressed through the metaphysical conceit. How does one begin to grieve for something that is irretrievably lost? The responses to this question that are offered in *Sula* are consistently framed in terms of metaphor, which becomes a complicated lyrical proxy for felt experience.

Like Morrison after her, Zora Neale Hurston pairs metaphor with focalization as a way of articulating her characters' feelings of loss and disenchantment in *Their Eyes Were Watching God* ([1937] 2006). Overwhelmed by her failing marriage, Janie "was a rut in the road. Plenty of life beneath the surface but it was kept beaten down by the wheels" (76); and though Janie knows her own worth, her husband takes her for granted: "She had found a jewel down inside herself and she had wanted to walk where people could see her and gleam it around. But she had been set in the market-place to sell" (90). Unlike *Sula*, however, *Their Eyes Were Watching God* is anchored by a single conceit to which the novel repeatedly returns. It is used to articulate the moment when Janie's "conscious life had commenced," her first kiss with Johnny Taylor:

> It was a spring afternoon in West Florida. Janie had spent most of the day under a blossoming pear tree in the back-yard. She had been spending every minute that she could steal from her chores under that tree for the last three days. That was to say, ever since the first tiny bloom had opened. It had called her to come and gaze on a mystery. From barren brown stems to glistening leaf-buds; from the leaf-buds to snowy virginity of bloom. It stirred her tremendously. How? Why? It was like a flute song forgotten in another existence and remembered again. What? How? Why? This singing she heard that had nothing to do with her ears. The rose of the world was breathing out smell. It followed her through all her waking moments and caressed her in her sleep. It connected itself with other vaguely felt matters that had struck her outside observation and buried themselves in her flesh. Now they emerged and quested about her consciousness. . . . Oh to be a pear tree—*any* tree in bloom! With kissing bees singing of the beginning of the world! She was sixteen. She had glossy leaves and bursting buds and she wanted to struggle with life but it seemed to elude her. Where were the singing bees for her? . . . Through pollinated air she saw a glorious being coming up the road. In her former blindness she had known him as shiftless Johnny Taylor, tall and lean. That was before the golden dust of pollen had beglamored his rags and her eyes. (10–12)

The "golden dust of pollen" does magical things to Janie's perception, transforming Johnny Taylor from a shiftless nobody into a "glorious being" (12). The sustained attention to the blossoming pear tree, the pollen it produces, and the bees that fertilize the blossoms in this passage not only suggests Janie's sexual awakening but also establishes these images as important recurring figurations for Janie's expectations of love and marriage. Though she anticipates a life of charmed romance, one that is "beglamored" by "the golden dust of pollen," she is continuously confronted by a reality that falls significantly short of her expectations.

A number of critics have pointed to the pear tree as a crucial image that marks a turning point for Janie. Mary Helen Washington points out that "Hurston uses two images from nature to symbolize Janie's quest: the horizon and the blossoming pear tree" (1979, 15). Others have made similar observations. Matthew Wynn Sivils argues for a regionalist reading of the novel in which the pear tree "marks [Janie's] first and most powerful connection with the natural world of the South," thereby "inscrib[ing] Janie's environment upon her [sexualized] body" (2006, 95–96). Glenda B. Weathers offers a religious, typological reading of the pear tree as a stand-in for the tree of knowledge, where Janie plays the role of Eve (2005, 202). These critics tend toward unidirectional allegorical readings by depicting Janie's sexuality as instantiated by the pear tree, which, in turn, functions metonymically for some larger concept—for the rural South, in Sivils's case, or for knowledge of good and evil, in Weathers's. These allegorical readings are illuminating, but they fail to address the complex and multidirectional interplay between Janie's sexuality and the cluster of images that make up the pear tree conceit, which is sustained throughout the novel as Janie moves through relationships with three very different men.

How does the pear tree frame marriage, and how does marriage frame the pear tree? This passage is filled with enchantment—"with kissing bees singing of the beginning of the world"—and Janie has been faulted by critics for adhering to an unrealistic picture of marriage (Clarke 2001, 605). A closer look at the pear tree, however, reveals a more balanced and nuanced picture of marriage than what critics have recognized. A solid relationship is poised here as a work in progress, a fertile plant that is only beginning to approach full bloom; and though it eventually morphs into something beautiful, it develops quite unevenly. Just as the parts of the pear tree range "from barren brown stems to glistening leaf-buds; from the leaf-buds to snowy virginity of bloom," so every marriage contains its rough patches, as Janie will learn soon enough (10). The most successful marriage, the narrator suggests through this conceit, is as natural as this spring scene, one that is given the chance to bloom without being hampered or stunted by artificial constraints.

Janie's first two marriages fail precisely because of the constraints that are imposed on her by self-centered and insecure husbands. The prospect of the much older Logan Killicks is foisted on Janie by her grandmother in the immediate aftermath of her kiss with Johnny Taylor. "Yeah, Janie, youse got yo' womanhood on yuh," her grandmother remarks. "So Ah mout ez well tell yuh what Ah been savin' up for uh spell. Ah wants to see you married right away" (12). Janie tries to shirk the suggestion, which runs counter to her own desires, now embodied in the blossoming pear tree: "The vision of Logan Killicks," she ruminates unhappily, "was desecrating the pear tree" (14). Janie dutifully obeys her grandmother and marries Killicks, but she frequently returns to the pear tree in the days leading up to her marriage: "Janie asked inside of herself and out. She was back and forth to the pear tree continuously wondering and thinking" (21). A monument to Janie's sexual awakening, the pear tree has now become a site of contemplation and a source of power. It has also, however, become an ideal to which her marriage fails to measure up. "Ah wants things sweet wid mah marriage lak when you sit under a pear tree and think," she cries to her grandmother a mere three days after the wedding, to which her grandmother replies, "Wait awhile, baby. Yo' mind will change" (24).

Janie's mind does not change, however; despite her grandmother's counsel, she adheres to a vision inspired by the initial image of the pear tree. While all of Nanny's advice to Janie stems from a single axiom derived from her own hardships—that "de nigger woman is de mule uh de world so fur as Ah can see" (14)—the natural world offers something much more promising. Disenchanted with her marriage to Killicks within a matter of days, Janie "waited a bloom time, and a green time and an orange time. But when the pollen again gilded the sun and sifted down on the world she began to stand around the gate and expect things" (25). Janie discovers that the natural world has its own epistemology, a kind of knowledge that she begins to intuit as she becomes increasingly attuned to its inner workings: "She knew things that nobody else had told her. For instance, the words of the trees and the wind. . . . She knew the world was a stallion rolling in the blue pasture of ether. She knew that God tore down the old world every evening and built a new one by sun-up. It was wonderful to see it take form with the sun and emerge from the gray dust of its making." The world is full of wonder, but it is also balanced: what is torn down is built up again as night gives way to day. Janie seeks to replicate both the marvel and balance of the cosmos in her relationships. When the scales tip, she becomes restless, and the pear tree imagery reappears.

Initially on his best behavior, Killicks shows his true colors "long before the year was up," demanding that Janie perform double duty in the kitchen and the fields (26). In a reversal of the sultry pear tree moment, Killicks forces Janie into a less ideal relationship with nature through a life of perpetual hard labor. She plows the fields and shovels manure, and she is threatened with violence when she voices her unhappiness: "Ah'll take holt uh dat ax and come in dere and kill yuh!" Killicks warns her (31). When Janie finally musters the courage to abandon the cranky Killicks and begin a new life with Jody Starks, who promises her a life of pleasure, the imagery of the pear tree returns again: "From now on until death she was going to have flower dust and springtime sprinkled over everything. A bee for her bloom" (32).

Almost immediately, however, Starks—like Killicks before him—begins to take Janie for granted. He becomes totally immersed in his new political and industrial ventures as mayor and lumber tycoon of Eatonville. Left behind to do the cooking and cleaning, Janie feels lonely and isolated. "Naw, Jody, it jus'looks lak it keeps us in some way we ain't natural wid one 'nother. You'se always off talkin' and fixin' things, and Ah feels lak Ah'm jus' markin' time" (46). Worse still, Starks begins to impose severe restrictions on Janie's freedom, forcing her to cover her beautiful hair with a rag and preventing her from participating in public forums and group discussions. Though Starks makes good on his promise to rescue Janie from a life of forced manual labor, his alternative is equally imprisoning, since he decides that "her place is in de home" and in the store that she operates for him—and nowhere else (43). The gradual deterioration of Janie's relationship with Starks is articulated again through a reversal of the pear tree imagery that represented Janie's expectations of marriage. Starks "took the bloom off of things" by refusing to allow Janie to speak in public (43). After he becomes physically abusive,

Janie finds that she is unable to be "petal-open anymore with him," a remark with decidedly sexual overtones (71). She no longer finds "blossomy openings dusting pollen over her man, neither any glistening young fruit where the petals used to be" (72). These extensions of the pear tree conceit reveal a relationship that is in a premature state of decay.

After twenty years of unhappiness, the marriage ends when Starks dies of kidney failure, and following a six-month mourning period, Janie meets Tea Cake, the last of her three husbands. In a paraphrase of her expectations regarding Jody Starks—that she was finally going to have "a bee for her bloom" (32)—Janie allows her hopes to rise once again with regard to Tea Cake: "He could be a bee to a blossom—a pear tree blossom in the spring. He seemed to be crushing scent out of the world with his footsteps. Crushing aromatic herbs with every step he took. Spices hung about him. He was a glance from God" (106).

Janie's marriage to Tea Cake is the closest she will come to the marital bliss depicted in the pear tree conceit. Their relationship achieves a balance that was not reached during Janie's first two marriages. Tea Cake teaches Janie how to drive and how to shoot. The two play checkers and other games together. Unlike Jody Starks, Tea Cake appreciates Janie's hair, even combing it for her; and unlike Starks, Tea Cake encourages Janie to spend time with their mutual friends and to "tell big stories" alongside everyone else (134). They also choose to work side by side in the fields. They manage to balance leisure and labor in a way that works for them. Certainly, their marriage is not without flaws, especially from a twenty-first-century perspective. Shawn E. Miller has drawn out some of these undesirable aspects of their relationship, aligning Tea Cake with Killicks and Starks in terms of his occasional machismo, possessiveness, and "sexual jealousy" (2004, 79). On one occasion, Tea Cake even hits Janie to "show he was boss" (147).

Despite these flaws, Janie does appear to achieve with Tea Cake the happiness that she envisioned in her grandmother's pear tree, as evidenced by the role that fertile plant life plays in their marriage. Tea Cake routinely "mak[es] flower beds in Janie's yard and seed[s] the garden for her," and following his untimely death in the aftermath of the hurricane, Janie gives away "everything in their little house except a package of garden seed that Tea Cake had bought to plant. The planting never got done because he had been waiting for the right time of the moon when his sickness overtook him. The seeds reminded Janie of Tea Cake more than anything else because he was always planting things. . . . [S]he meant to plant them for remembrance" (110, 191). In contrast to the decaying blossoms that characterized her marriage to Starks, Janie's marriage to Tea Cake is represented by the seed: a symbol of promise, growth, and perpetuity.

Recent scholarship runs counter to earlier readings of the novel by positioning Tea Cake as yet another oppressive patriarch and Janie as a woman who only manages to "master conventional marriage" rather than "escape from it" (Miller 2004, 76). This is certainly not how Janie would view her own story, though, and the narrator's perspective is continuously tied to Janie's by focalization. By tracing the pear tree conceit and its extension throughout the novel, we can see that Janie's final marriage is actually a felicitous realization of the expectations Janie has harbored since her first kiss with Johnny Taylor. For Janie, there is no one formula for a successful marriage; rather, every relationship has its own tone and tenor: "Love ain't somethin' lak uh grindstone dat's de same thing everywhere and do de same thing tuh everything it touch," she explains. "Love is lak de sea. It's uh movin' thing, but still and all, it takes its shape from de shore it meets, and it's different with every shore" (191). Certainly, not all relationships are equal, or even equally healthy, as Janie herself came to realize, but each is unique and cannot be measured against an ideal that attempts to standardize relationships for all people. With Tea Cake, Janie manages to find a natural balance through which she is finally able to blossom as an independent woman, without sacrificing her bloom.

Thus, Hurston's novel is an elaboration and exploration of the pear tree conceit, a crucial meditation on the nature of relationships that serves as a key to all three of Janie's marriages. None is ideal, though her marriage to Tea Cake closely approximates the fertility and balance depicted in the figure of the pear tree. Readers may struggle to understand Janie's motivations in the same way they struggle to understand those of Eva and Sula, but we are once again aided by metaphor, which supplies the logic that is missing at the level of plot.

Like Hurston, Henry Miller relies heavily on figuration as a means of linking sexuality to health and fertility. Most people are familiar with *Tropic of Cancer* through the highly publicized obscenity trials that followed its U.S. publication in 1961 by Grove Press. The novel then reached new generations of Americans through its appearance on a 1991 episode of *Seinfeld* in which the sitcom's characters recall having passed around a copy of the book on account of its steamy content when they were in high school. *Tropic of Cancer* has become so well known for its sexually explicit content that its aesthetic strategies largely remain overlooked, though it is precisely the novel's lyrical aims that rescued it from charges of prurience.[8] Miller's metaphysical conceit links sexuality to physical, emotional, and psychological vigor and links its repression to sickness, weakness, and death. Sexuality is deeply connected to Miller's aesthetic agenda, which seeks to rescue art from the overly intellectualized ennui of modern culture, or what Miller diagnoses as "a cancer eating itself away" ([1934] 1961, 2). By using sexuality to revitalize art, Miller restores art to its primal function as a generative and life-affirming act of creativity.

"This is not a book," warns *Tropic*'s narrator, also named Henry Miller. "This is libel, slander, defamation of character . . . this is a prolonged insult, a gob of spit in the face of Art, a kick in the pants to God, Man, Destiny, Time, Love, Beauty . . . this is a song. I am singing" (2). Thus, Miller explicitly aligns *Tropic* with the realm of the lyric in the novel's opening lines. Few events of significance occur; most of the novel is an apostrophic song of praise delivered to the female body. Miller's admonition to readers anticipates, however, his novel's reception, moving from the point of view of the novel's detractors—"this is a prolonged insult, a gob of spit in the face of Art"—to his own sense of the novel's aesthetic, indeed lyrical, achievements: "This is a song. I am singing." This discrepancy between the tastes and values of the world and those of the serious artist is a theme that is developed throughout *Tropic of Cancer*, in which Miller the artist is a visionary and a doctor who can identify, diagnose, and treat those illnesses to which the rest of civilization falls pray: sexual repression, social conformity, and the tendency to retreat from life before one can truly experience it.

The metaphysical conceit, so often used for lyrical meditation, is a vexed vehicle for Miller, for whom contemplation is a profoundly disgraceful "retreat" from the world of the senses. "[Man] will debauch himself with ideas," Miller writes. "He will reduce himself to a shadow if for only one second of his life he can close his eyes to the hideousness of reality" (96). Intellectual deliberation is consistently figured through illness, and even characters of a contemplative nature are marked by an embodied sickness, such as Sylvester, "the sick dramatist" (29): "The dramatist is sick and from above his scalp looks more scabrous than ever. His hair is made of straw. His ideas are straw" (27). Too much thought yields sterility, a point that Miller expresses in any number of ways: "In Europe one gets used to doing nothing," he complains. "You sit on your ass and whine all day. You get contaminated. You rot" (49). "Ideas have to be wedded to action," he maintains in another argumentative passage. "If there is no sex, no vitality in them, there is no action. Ideas cannot exist alone in the vacuum of the mind" (242).

Instead, sex is the sole indicator of spiritual and physical vitality in the novel. Those who are in touch with sexuality are in touch with their most primal desires, and the new literature is charged with bringing these desires to light through "the recording of all that which is omitted in books" (11). "We have evolved a new cosmogony of literature, Boris and I," Miller writes. "It is to be a new Bible—*The Last Book*. . . . Now we shall have a vessel in which to pour the vital fluid, a bomb which, when we throw it, will set off the world" (26).[9] The new literature is at once a religious "vessel"—a "Bible"—and a revolutionary "bomb" that will forever change the literary landscape. Great literature—like great sex—should be "capable of resuscitating the body and soul" (257). Only the "live wire of sex" can revive literature and humankind alike (249). In the transvaluation of values enacted here, sex is no longer a source of embarrassment; it is celebrated in explicit, carnal detail.

Of course, such an approach to song and sex in American literature finds an important precursor in Walt Whitman, whose *Leaves of Grass* is the only book Miller the author carries with him when he embarks for Paris (Turner 2012, 7). In *Tropic of Cancer*, Miller heralds Whitman as "the Poet of the Body and the Soul" and "the first and last poet," a literary shaman for whom Europe has no equivalent: whereas "Goethe is an end of something, Whitman is a beginning" (240). Whitman is an anachronism in his own time just as Miller is an anachronism in his, though it is difficult for the novel's characters to pinpoint just where these "poets of the body" belong. Miller writes of his friends, "Now and then they would compliment me on being alive, but in such a way that I felt embarrassed. They made me feel that I was alive in the nineteenth century, a sort of atavistic remnant, a romantic shred, a soulful Pithecanthropus erectus" (168–69). Miller's temporal dislocation from the literature and culture of his own milieu does not seem to grant him any special advantage. He is the sole survivor among the walking dead: "Boris especially seemed to get a great kick out of touching me," Miller continues; "he wanted me to be alive so that he could die to his heart's content" (169).

Even so, it is the role of the writer to rescue humanity from its own tyranny through artistic creation. "The race of artists," Miller writes, must "take the lifeless mass of humanity and by the fever and ferment with which they imbue it turn this soggy dough into bread and bread into wine and the wine into song" (254). The artist is depicted alternately as Promethean and Christ-like in his ability to give shape to lifeless matter and to perform miracles by turning the ordinary into the extraordinary. Like Prometheus and Christ, the artist sacrifices himself for the good of humanity, only to be repaid in violence: "A man who belongs to this race must stand up on the high place with gibberish in his mouth and rip out his entrails. It is right and just, because he must! And anything that falls short of this frightening spectacle, anything less shuddering, less terrifying, less mad, less intoxicated, less contaminating, is not art. The rest is counterfeit. The rest is humanity" (255). The martyrdom is public, graphic, and fatal to the artist. The image that Miller supplies is a man who literally bares his insides to his readership, only to destroy himself in the process.

In baring his own insides, Miller spares no detail of his sexual exploits, which are consistently depicted through the language of art in a way that fuses sexuality with creative production. The novel opens, for example, with a vivid description of Tania's genitals, staged as a lyrical apostrophe filled with mixed metaphors:

> O Tania, where now is that warm cunt of yours, those fat, heavy garters, those soft, bulging thighs? There is a bone in my prick six inches long. I will ream out every wrinkle in your cunt, Tania, big with seed. I will send you home to your Sylvester with an ache in your belly and your womb turned inside out. Your Sylvester! Yes, he knows how to build a fire, but I know how to inflame a cunt. I shoot hot bolts into

> you, Tania, I make your ovaries incandescent. Your Sylvester is a little jealous now? He feels something, doesn't he? He feels the remnants of my big prick. I have set the shores a little wider, I have ironed out the wrinkles. After me you can take on stallions, bulls, rams, drakes, St. Bernards. You can stuff toads, bats, lizards up your rectum. You can shit arpeggios if you like, or string a zither across your navel. . . . I will bite into your clitoris and spit out two franc pieces. (5–6)

The penis is figured as an iron, a lightning bolt, and a force of geologic erosion; the vagina becomes a vaquero, the rectum a jungle, and the clitoris a slot machine. The genitals are sites that bustle with activity, and proving that vital art begets still more art, they even yield music. Miller uses mixed metaphors of a very different type to depict Llona, whose cunt is too large to accommodate any lover: "Not a prick in the land big enough for her . . . *not one*. . . . A valise without straps. A hole without a key. She had a German mouth, French ears, Russian ass. Cunt international. When the flag waved it was red all the way back to the throat. You entered on the Boulevard Jules-Ferry and came out at the Porte de la Villette" (7). Llona's body is an international way station complete with its own street map. Feminists may cringe at these figurations, which position women as sexual receptacles, but the female body in all of its carnal detail becomes a source of staggering poetic inspiration for Miller. Staring between the open legs of a prostitute, he catches a glimpse of the "Absolute" in an epiphanic moment that approaches the Romantic sublime:

> A glance at that dark, unstitched wound and a deep fissure in my brain opens up: all the images and memories that had been laboriously or absent-mindedly assorted, labeled, documented, filed, sealed and stamped break forth pell-mell like ants pouring out of a crack in the sidewalk; the world ceases to revolve, time stops, the very nexus of my dreams is broken and dissolved and my guts spill out in a grand schizophrenic rush, an evacuation that leaves me face to face with the Absolute. . . . Great whore and mother of man with gin in her veins. Mother of all harlots, spider rolling us in your logarithmic grave, insatiable one, field whose laughter rives me! . . . When I look down into that crack I see an equation sign, the world at balance, a world reduced to zero and no trace of remainder. (246–47)

She is at once the Virgin Mary and Mary Magdalene, the "mother of man" and a "great whore." Her cunt is infinite—"the Absolute"—and yet finite, a mathematical equation that is perfectly reducible. The body of a woman is presented here through a series of paradoxical metaphors that align her with two extremes at once, the virginal and the infinite on the one hand, the sordid and the circumscribed on the other.

The sexualized body is understood in terms of art, and in turn, art is understood in terms of the sexualized body. This is most explicit when Miller channels Joyce, transforming Molly Bloom's motto—"I love everything that flows"—into a paratactic prose poem that celebrates the body, warts and all: "I too love everything that flows: rivers, sewers, lava, semen, blood, bile, words, sentences," he writes, placing linguistic artifice on the same plane as bodily fluids. "I love the amniotic fluid when it spills out of the bag. I love the kidney with its painful gallstones, its gravel and what-not; I love the urine that pours out scalding and the clap that runs endlessly. . . . I love everything that flows, even the menstrual flow that carries away the seed unfecund" (257–58). In another homage to an artistic contemporary, Miller depicts Matisse's impressionistic painting style through the language of sexual climax: "Even as the world falls apart the Paris that belongs to Matisse shudders with bright, gasping orgasms, the air itself is steady with a stagnant sperm, the trees tangled like hair" (166). Sex and art, for Miller, are inextricably linked; and, his extended metaphor argues, good art—like good sex—is revitalizing, an antidote to the "cancer" of complacency that characterizes modernity.

Tropic of Cancer, when not studied for its obscenity, is often studied as an exemplary novel of expatriation in the late modernist period. The novel's first half depicts Paris as the "incubator" that promotes the kind of artistic freedom and uninhibited sexuality Miller is unable to find in the United States (29). New York is a "hollow pit of nothingness," a "double-harness" that yokes Miller to the "treadmill" of daily living, but Paris palpitates like "a heart just removed from a warm body" (68–69; 63); it is "the very navel of the world to which, like a blind and faltering idiot, one crawls back on hands and knees" (182). Gradually, however, even Paris begins to lose its charm, especially from the vantage point of a starving artist living in squalor, plagued daily by lice and hunger. "Paris is a whore," Miller writes during one bout of depression. "From a distance she seems ravishing, you can't wait to have her in your arms. And five minutes later you feel empty, disgusted with yourself" (209). The city is particularly inhospitable—even "execrable" (219)—in the winter months: "The cold of a Paris winter is a cold unknown to America," he writes. "It is psychological, an inner as well as an outer cold" (240). The substance that Miller thought he had found in Paris turns out to be illusory; in fact, Miller even contemplates a return to the United States in the novel's closing pages. The disease that Miller initially detects in American culture loses its local specificity and becomes a global problem in the latter half of the novel. Gradually, Miller forgoes the language of the nation for the language of universal humanism, and his references to Americans and Parisians are replaced with references to "human beings" and "the world" at large. The rhetoric of expatriation is ultimately subsumed under Miller's sexual-aesthetic agenda, his quest to prove that "there has been a constant and steady decline of man in art, in thought, in action. The world is pooped out: there isn't a dry fart left" (249).

In 1940, a destitute Miller was commissioned to write smut stories for a dollar per page but "simply found that he couldn't write acceptable pornography," and quickly gave it up (Martin 1977, 341–42). Miller is not a pornographic writer, though this has been his legacy, even in the wake of the obscenity trials that cleared him of such charges. Unfortunately, Miller's reputation continues to confirm the thesis laid out in *Tropic of Cancer*: that human beings are deeply repressed, and that literature is "capable of resuscitating the body and soul," if only through controversy (257). *Tropic of Cancer* is a novel of ideas, even as it condemns the life of contemplation as a withdrawal from the world of the senses. In essence, it advocates a balance between theory and praxis, art and sex, precisely because of the reciprocal logic of metaphor. The metaphysical conceit that drives the novel—literature as sex, sex as literature—not only demonstrates its own thesis, but deliberately sets out to erase the very boundary between sex and literature that would, unfortunately, become the central focus of its own critical and legal reception.

In a sense, Russell Banks's *Continental Drift* (1985) is a continuation of Miller's experiments with scale, which range freely from the individual to the city to the nation to humankind and back again. In the first chapter of Banks's novel, we are introduced to Bob Dubois and his unhappy existence in a marriage and career that leave something to be desired; but the second chapter opens, quite unexpectedly, with an elaborate five-page conceit that guides the novel and inspires its title. The figuration likens human traffic to the movement of continents in a globalized world that increasingly resembles the planet as it has been modeled by geologists and meteorologists:

> It's as if the creatures residing on this planet in these years, the human creatures, millions of them traveling singly and in families, in clans and tribes, traveling sometimes as entire nations, were a subsystem inside the larger system of currents and tides, of winds and weather, of drifting continents and shifting, uplifting, grinding, cracking land masses. . . . We map and measure jet streams, weather patterns, prevailing winds, tides and deep ocean currents; we track precisely scarps, fractures, trenches and ridges where the plates atop the earth's mass drive against one another; we name and chart the Southeast and Northeast Trades and the Atlantic Westerlies, the tropical monsoons and the doldrums, the mistrals, the Santa Ana and the Canada High; we know the Humboldt, California and Kuroshio currents—so that, having traced and enumerated them, we can look on our planet and can see that all the way to its very core the sphere inhales and exhales, rises and falls, swirls and whirls in a lovely, disciplined dance in time. It ages and dies and is born again, constantly, through motion, creating and recreating its very self, like a uroborous, the snake that devours its tail. (34–35)

The conceit depicts human migration as something that is worthy of being "mapped," "tracked," "named and charted," and "known" in the same way as science records and analyzes the movement of land masses and weather currents. It also presents a bird's-eye view of humankind through which the lives of human beings are as patterned and cyclical as the natural currents of the planet. When viewed from a distance, individual lives appear to be swept up by larger forces that are beyond their control. Banks's narrator combines the rhetoric of geological science with the aesthetic purview of ancient Greek tragedy to create a metaphoric frame in which the transnational migrations of people, especially those from the third world, warrant a deterministic and, consequently, tragic reading:

> Seen from above, then, the flight of a million and a half Somali men, women and children with their sick and dying beasts out of the drought- and war-shattered region of Ogaden in the Horn of Africa would resemble the movement of the Southwest Monsoon Current. . . . The movement of the Somalis would seem inevitable, unalterable and mindless; and because we would have watched it the way we watch the weather, it would seem tragic. (35)

What is more, just as continental drift explains how geographically disparate parts of the world were once connected as Pangaea, so Banks's metaphor accounts for the interconnectedness of seemingly disparate human communities:

> Systems and sets, subsystems and subsets, patterns and aggregates of water, earth, fire and air—naming and mapping them, learning of the intricate interdependence of the forces that move and convert them into one another, this process gradually provides us with a vision of the planet as an organic cell, a mindless, spherical creature whose only purpose is to be born as rapidly as it dies and whose general principle informing that purpose, as if it were a moral imperative, is to keep moving . . . it's the only argument we have against entropy. And it's not truly an argument; it's a vision. (39)

The world is "an organic cell" whose parts serve some unseen vital and interconnected function. The human world, as modeled by continental drift, is sharply distinguished from the world as it appears on the surface, the realm of history and political science: fast-paced, war-torn, a constant influx of "news" that is filtered to the first world, only to be replaced by tomorrow's news in the form of another crisis: whereas "the metabolic rate of history is too fast for us to observe it," that of geology is "too slow" for human perception (36). One of the novel's goals, then, is to render human lives and their unexpected relationships in a global economy perceptible through the conceit of continental drift.

Continental Drift is a dual narrative in which two stories, unfolding in alternating chapters, "drift" toward one another before finally converging at the novel's climax. One depicts the unhappy life of the white, working-class Bob Dubois, who fixes oil burners for a living and who, disaffected with his wife and children, spends his nights getting drunk at the local bar and conducting a relatively meaningless affair with Doris Cleeve; the other chronicles Vanise Dorsinville, a Haitian refugee who flees her country with her nephew and infant child in fear for her life. Both Bob and Vanise cling to a vision of the American dream that will better their stations and give them the opportunity to start a new life under better circumstances. For Bob, this entails a series of career switches that gradually draws him into a world of criminal activity with the promise of money and leisure, both of which he imagines will bring his family closer. Vanise absconds from Haiti when her nephew steals a ham for their starving family and hence threatens their already tenuous safety from the local crime lord who controls the area. She hopes that a new life in America will finally secure their safety and freedom and help them escape abject poverty.

In the plot's most obvious parallel to continental drift, Bob and Vanise move toward each other geographically until finally meeting in the Florida Keys. Beginning with a job as a repairman for an oil company in Catamount, New Hampshire, Bob moves his family to Oleander Park, Florida to begin a new life manning a liquor store for his brother, who continually promises—and fails—to make Bob a co-owner. Disillusioned again, Bob moves to Moray Key to take up with an old friend, Avery, who runs illegal shipments of cocaine and, ultimately, immigrants along the coast for large amounts of money. Vanise begins in Haiti and spends all of her money on a boat ride that is supposed to take her to Florida but lands instead on North Caicos Island; she manages to embark on a second voyage to the Bahamas, where she is effectively forced into prostitution before finally securing a boat ride to Florida—from none other than Bob Dubois.

Ironically, their meeting suggests the fallaciousness, rather than the realization, of the American dream they have both been chasing, which has caused them to drift together. Vanise's nephew and fellow refugee, Claude, is hell-bent on America and the opportunities it represents, especially after having endured great hardship—starvation, rape, humiliation, exploitation—on the illicit voyages that brought them from Haiti to Florida. But when Claude and Bob stand face-to-face on the boat that will finally take Claude and Vanise to the United States, the narrator focalizes the scene's descriptors through Bob, who sees himself as the disillusioned product of the American dream that Claude will inevitably become:

> Claude stands next to Bob, and pointing out across the bow, says, "America?"
>
> Bob nods. . . . *America! Land, ho!* Only, like Columbus and all those guys looking for the Fountain of Youth, when you finally get

> to America, you get something else. You get Disney World and land deals and fast-moving high-interest bank loans, and if you don't get the hell out of the way, they'll knock you down, cut you up with a harrow and plow you under, so they can throw some condos up on top of you or maybe a parking lot or maybe an orange grove.
>
> Bob looks down at the boy's black profile, and he thinks, You'll get to America, all right kid, and maybe, just like me, you'll get what you want. Whatever that is. But you'll have to give something away for it, if you haven't already. And when you get what you want, it'll turn out to be not what you wanted after all, because it'll always be worth less than what you gave away for it. In the land of the free, nothing's free. (311–12)

Bob knows all too well the pitfalls of the Horatio Alger myth in which he, too, has become ensnared. No happier than he was at the beginning of the novel—actually, he is substantially less happy, and less stable, both materially and emotionally—Bob has come to realize that he has been chasing an unattainable ideal in abandoning the safety of New Hampshire for life on the edge as a trafficker of drugs and human contraband. He has also become acutely aware of the moral trade-offs he has made along the way. While the Haitian refugees would appear to have much more to gain from migration than Bob did, their sacrifices have been equally great. Both Claude and Vanise have traded not only all of their savings but also their bodies, their autonomy, and their dignity.

Claude's optimism in this passage is thrown into relief by Bob's cynicism, then undermined by the fate of the Haitians. When the boat is spotted by the coast guard as it nears the shore, Bob's partner pushes the refugees overboard in a desperate attempt to rid the boat of its human contraband, and all of the Haitians drown, save Vanise. Bob is so wracked with guilt by his unwitting role in the drownings that he tracks down Vanise and attempts to give her his share of the profit. When she refuses, Bob is immediately killed and robbed by the men who led him to her. Disparate lives indeed collide in *Continental Drift*, with tragic consequences. At the beginning of the novel, Bob and Vanise inhabit very different lives in very different parts of the hemisphere, but through the mechanism of "continental drift," their fates are inextricably tied together.

The conceit of continental drift calls into question the degree of control that Bob and Vanise have over their fates. If the activities of human beings, like geologic and weather patterns, are "inevitable, unalterable and mindless" (35), how could Bob, Claude, and the other Haitian refugees have possibly avoided their untimely deaths? This determinism in this framing metaphor would appear to detract from the novel's social critique of the illicit traffickers who profit from illegal immigration by treating human lives as commodities. This determinism, however, is illusory rather than substantive, a matter of perspective that results from the bird's-eye view of the novel's metaphoric passages. Human movement only "seems" inevitable from the remote vantage point of the narrator-geologist (35). From another, closer perspective, individual will remains intact: deliberations occur, choices are made, and consequences result from those choices.

Continental Drift attempts to balance these two perspectives: the distant view of the geologist and the proximate view of the novelist. The novel's conceit, which tracks human beings en masse, is countermeasured by the focus on individual lives that typically occurs in a novel. This balance is also at the forefront of Bob's mind as he contemplates the subject positions of the Haitians on his boat:

> Why do they do that? he wonders. Why do they throw away everything they know and trust, no matter how bad it is, for something they know nothing about and can never trust? He's in awe of the will it takes, the stubborn, conscious determination to get to America that each of them, from the eldest to the youngest, must own. But he can't put that willfulness together with what he sees before him—a quiescent, silent, shy people who seem fatalistic almost, who seem ready and even willing to accept whatever is given them. (305)

From a distance—that is, from Bob's external perspective as a cultural outsider—the refugees seem fatalistically shy, but even Bob marvels at the strength and sheer will that has caused them to risk their lives for a new start in the United States. The refugees, like all of the characters and events in the novel, are filtered through two perspectives: distance and proximity, the former examining people in aggregate, the latter examining people as individuals.

Novels typically focus on individual lives from close proximity—hence, we have characters—but the anchoring conceit of continental drift reframes these lives from a remote purview. Unlike the other novels treated here, *Continental Drift* works to widen, rather than close, the distance between its narrator and its characters. Such a gap, however, need not detract from our readerly sympathy. If we studied human lives from a geologic perspective, the conceit continues, "we could not argue over who was at fault or what should have been done; ideology would seem a form of vanity, a despicable self-indulgence" (35). Reserving judgment, readers should provide sympathy and aid to the novel's characters as if we they were real people: "We would rise from our shaded seat in front of our hut alongside the dusty road that leads from the treeless Damisa hills in Ethiopia to our village near the trading town of Samaso in Somalia, and we would step forward onto the road with a cup of water and a small bowl of millet and whey for the family we have been watching approach for the last hour." This example, of course, is deliberately metaleptic: as readers, we cannot offer water to these hypothetical

Somali characters any more than we can prevent Bob's fatal stabbing, but we can feel the requisite sympathy that would inspire these interventions, were they possible.

A conceit that relies so heavily on geology may seem to dwarf individual lives, but this distance also effectively erases particularities of place, race, and culture and, consequently, foregrounds areas of commonality and overlap. Continental drift points to common origins that render these differences accidental rather than essential. The metaphysical conceit framing Banks's novel encourages a very different reading practice from that to which we have become accustomed. Many critics have pointed to the relationship between readerly judgment and the novel as a form.[10] In contrast, Russell Banks explicitly discourages judgment, using a metaphoric frame to create enough distance between readers and his characters to elicit pity and compassion in its stead. The conceit of continental drift yields more than a vision or perspective—it yields a theory of reading. The novel concludes on this note, an extension of the earlier imperative to practice "distant" reading from the vantage point of the geologist:

> Knowledge of the facts of Bob's life and death changes nothing in the world. Our celebrating his life and grieving over his death, however, will. Good cheer and mournfulness over lives other than our own, even wholly invented lives—to, especially wholly invented lives—deprive the world as it is of some of the greed it needs to continue to be itself. Sabotage and subversion, then, are this book's objectives. Go, my book, and help destroy the world as it is. (366)

Sympathy, initially directed toward fictional lives, is imbued here with the power to change the world. In these closing lines, the novel's conceit broadens farther still, developing from a point of view to a reading practice to an ethical theory with the power to "destroy the world as it is" so that we might refashion it with greater compassion.

The novels treated here apply metaphoric frames to their plots in ways that foreground figuration and analogy over concrete action. These conceits cause the novels of Morrison and Hurston to hover between the realm of the literal and the realm of metaphor, but they become ever more distended in the works of Miller and Banks, stalling, rivaling, and even supplanting the narrative events that occur around them. *Tropic of Cancer* can hardly boast of a plot; without its overriding metaphor, the novel is largely a picaresque of Henry Miller's sexual conquests. Twin plots develop in Banks's *Continental Drift*, but they are dramatizations of the axioms laid forth in the novel's introductory conceit. In their own elaborations of metaphor, the metaphysical poets are important literary-historical precursors to these novelists; the conceits of these poets are so extensive, so intricate, that one questions whether the metaphor frames the poem or vice versa. Likewise, the novels in this chapter rely extensively on framing metaphors that compete with, rather than serve, the plot.

Reading for the plot is often taken to be a "passive" form of reading by which readers simply follow a series of events to their conclusion without necessarily pausing to consider complexities like abstract themes or tropes.[11] By contrast, figuration engages both the imagination and the intellect of its readers, who must apprehend the rich, multidirectional connections that inhere between the terms of the analogy. The metaphysical conceits developed in novels by Morrison, Hurston, Miller, and Banks facilitate dynamic interactions between pairings of objects and concepts that do not bear obvious relations to one another. To understand grief in terms of a gray ball hovering just outside one's peripheral vision, marriage in terms of an intricately blossoming pear tree, literature in terms of sexual vitality, and human lives in terms of continental drift is to perform a type of abstract, philosophical labor that ventures far beyond plot when we approach these novels through the type of lyrical engagement they demand.

Finally, these novels invite us to reconsider the fraught nature of mimesis in both lyric and narrative forms. As Seo-Young Chu reminds us in her study of science fiction, some concepts simply "elude representation" and require more creative forms of exemplification (2011, 2). The lyric tradition, because of its rich involvement with metaphor and analogy, encompasses a reserve of poetic tropes that can supply just that. Yet Chu insists that narrative and lyric must work in tandem to realize this ambition: "Only a narrative form thoroughly powered by lyricism possesses enough torque—enough twisting force, enough *verse* (from 'vertere,' Latin for 'to turn')—to convert an elusive referent into an object available for representation. Only a form in which poetic *tropes* (from 'tropos,' Greek for 'turn') are systemically turned into narrative literalities can accommodate referents ordinarily averse to representation" (15). The novels of Morrison, Hurston, Miller, and Banks are dramatic departures from the science-fictional texts Chu includes in her study, but they too are fueled by the reader's—indeed, the text's—suspension between literal and figurative realms via plots that are never squarely or even comfortably situated in the concrete realm of narrative action.

Chapter 5

✦

Dramatic Personae

Thanks to its ubiquity in critical discourse surrounding modernist and postmodernist novels, the concept of the unreliable narrator has become quite familiar to readers and scholars of narrative prose. The term's prevalence in classrooms and in scholarship has also, however, diluted its application and efficacy since its initial deployment in Wayne Booth's *The Rhetoric of Fiction* ([1961] 1983)—and contrary to Booth's account, it has become virtually synonymous with first-person narration. This chapter seeks to restore our understanding of unreliable narration as a special manipulation of the reader that warns against naively literal readings of plot. It does so by resituating the device within the Victorian dramatic monologue's upending of the relationship between subjectivity and authority that largely characterized the Romantic meditative lyric. Unreliability generates considerable ontological tension between the real and the imagined, which prompts readers to reevaluate and even reconstruct the type of action that can be taken for granted in most narrative fiction, particularly as unreliable character-narrators tend to reveal more about themselves and their psychology than about the (fictional) world around them. Plot deteriorates in these novels until it becomes scarcely distinguishable from characterization. The realm of action becomes the realm of subjectivity.

The dramatic monologues of Robert Browning play a key role in the development of prose fiction's unreliable narrator. Whereas Romantic lyrics typically feature speakers who are extensions of their authors, Browning altered the poetic relationship between subjectivity and authority by creating lyric-drama hybrids in which fictional speakers work hard to mask their untrustworthiness. His dramatic personae anticipate the unreliable character-narrators of the twentieth century in compelling readers to recast events in light of their calculating manipulation or psychological instability. Four exemplary novels display their indelible imprint: Henry James's *Turn of the Screw* (1898), Vladimir Nabokov's *Lolita* (1955), Bret Easton Ellis's *American Psycho* (1991), and Chuck Palahniuk's *Fight Club* (1996). These works, arranged in order of their increasingly unstable ontologies, urge readers toward figurative understandings of external events as their plots buckle under the strain of their unhinged character-narrators.

Because they reflect and intensify subjectivity, lyric forms in general—and the Victorian dramatic monologue in particular—have influenced narrative fiction by subordinating action to the realm of characterization. Like the works examined in the previous chapter, the novels of James, Nabokov, Ellis, and Palahniuk demand that we venture beyond the literal plane of story events to read figuratively. They also demonstrate, with increasingly radical results, the diffusion of unreliability through multiple narrative levels. Narrators are placed under careful scrutiny, but so is the event structure that undergirds plot, and finally, the notion of character itself. Just who is Tyler Durden's alter ego, the nameless, self-deluded narrator of *Fight Club*? Unreliability defies us to parse real events from a character-narrator's delusions, but it can also violate ontological boundaries by blending and erasing the identities of character-narrators. Taken to the extreme, unreliability not only compromises the integrity of the narrator but also compromises plot and characterization, the building blocks of narrative fiction.

The aim of Booth's seminal 1961 study, *The Rhetoric of Fiction*, was to unearth the partiality that underpins not only unreliable narration but all narration, however objective or transparent it may seem. "The author's judgment is always present," Booth writes, "always evident to anyone who knows how to look for it" (20). Its legacy, however, has been its attention to dramatized narrators generally and to the "unreliable" narrator in particular, a section that spans only ten pages of text and leaves room for much elaboration. When Booth coined the term, he reserved it for narratives that exhibited stark contradictions in fact or moral value between narrator and implied author: "I have called a narrator *reliable* when he speaks for or acts in accordance with the norms of the work (which is to say, the implied author's norms), *unreliable* when he does not" (158–59). The distance between the narrator's perspective and that of the implied author is what Booth identifies as irony, which—within this richly complex rhetorical triangle of reader, author, and narrative perspective—effectively places the reader in alignment with the implied author at the narrator's expense: "The author and reader are secretly in collusion, behind the speaker's back, agreeing upon the standard by which he is found wanting" (304). Unreliable narration, as Booth conceived it, places a great hermeneutical burden on readers, who must identify the signposts of narrative irony and adjust their readings accordingly. As Greta Olson argues, "One reads literally until textual markers and indications force one to revise one's interpretation" (2003, 95).

Booth's articulation of unreliable narration and the demands it makes on readers initiated a flurry of studies that elaborated on this concept and applied it widely to nineteenth- and twentieth-century fiction. The term's increasingly expansive application, however, has undermined its usefulness as a special category that separates truly untrustworthy narration from other types of character-narration. Critics such as William Riggan (1981), for example, extend it to include narrators whose perspectives are limited by such factors as age, though Greta Olson (2003) has convincingly argued that narrators might be fallible for any number of reasons that do not necessarily make them untrustworthy, including inexperience, bias, or limited access to information (101, 103). In part, the overuse and subsequent diminished utility of the notion of narrative unreliability results from Booth's own definitional vagueness. "Our terminology for this kind of distance in narrators is almost hopelessly inadequate," he concedes (158). Critics have used this slackness, however, as an occasion for lightening the interpretive burden that Booth's concept was meant to place on the reader. Both Riggan and Monika Fludernik have argued, for example, that all homodiegetic narrators are unreliable by virtue of the "human limitations of perception and memory and assessment" and the "lack of objectivity" inherent in every first-person account (Riggan 1981, 920; Fludernik 1999, 76). Such critical assessments not only flatten reader response but rely on the fallacious premise that to tell a story from a subjective perspective is to sacrifice one's rhetorical credibility.

Within the lyric tradition, subjectivity and authority are not as discordant as scholars of modern fiction tend to assume. In wake of the Romantic revolution enacted by Shelley, Coleridge, and Wordsworth, lyric poetry has been increasingly identified with the realm of private consciousness as articulated through a first-person speaker. Wordsworth famously championed the lyric as a wellspring of emotional subjectivity in the preface to his lyrical ballads, where he characterized the genre as "the spontaneous overflow of powerful feelings" ([1801] 2007, 82). The philosophy of the period also placed a heavy emphasis on interiority as a foundation for ontology. The idealism espoused first by Kant and then by Fichte, Schelling, and Hegel established subjective perception as the primary frame of reference with regard to an external world that is otherwise inaccessible to us—what Kant referred to as the *noumena*, or "things-in-themselves." According to the epistemology that undergirds idealism, subjectivity—the realm of the *phenomenal*—is our only gateway to the world of the *noumenal*, which is ultimately unknowable except through personal experience. Subjectivity, then, actually yields epistemic authority, since we gain reliable knowledge of the world only through the direct access our senses and ideas afford. Likewise, as readers, we have no cause to doubt the integrity of the subjective experiences articulated by the Romantic poets, including Wordsworth's impressions of the landscape near Tintern Abbey or the opium-induced dream that inspired Coleridge's "Kubla Khan." To be sure, such perspectives might prove fallible, as Marjorie Levinson demonstrates in her famously political reading of "Tintern Abbey," which challenges Wordsworth's ellision of key landscape features, including vagrants and industrial pollution. Yet these intensely personal meditations are not intended to deceive; rather, as David Bromwich puts it, "the poet has told one story and the critic knows of another he might have told" (1998, 75).

The Victorian lyric saw a significant shift in the relationship between subjectivity and authority in the mask lyrics and dramatic monologues that gained momentum during this period. As Ralph Rader has noted, the lyric "I" that reigns over these poems differs markedly from that of the "expressive" lyric that dominated the Romantic period (1976, 150). Whereas the "expressive" speaker is, by and large, an extension of the poet, the speaker in a dramatic monologue is a fully developed character with a personality, identity, and temperament of his or her own. According to Robert Browning's formulation in an advertisement for the first edition of his *Dramatic Lyrics* in 1842, these persona poems were a hybrid of lyric and drama, "for the most part Lyric in expression, always Dramatic in principle, and so many utterances of so many imaginary persons, not mine" (quoted in Howe 1996, 5). Scholars continue to dispute the definition of the dramatic monologue, some arguing for a more capacious understanding that includes persona poems such as Tennyson's "Ulysses," while others try to restrict the term to those poems that include "oral discourse, presence of an auditor, and psychological self-revelation" (Howe 1996, 3). For Browning, however—the primary practitioner of the form and a model for Pound, Eliot, and other mask poets of the modernist period—the key to the dramatic monologue was its disassociation from the poet. Whatever one might say of the speaker's voice, his early advertisement insists, it is "not mine."

One should certainly hope not—Browning's speakers are duplicitous, psychotic, narcissistic, even murderous. They are also distinguished from Browning the poet through their individuated fictional or historical identities, which are flagged by their titles: "Porphyria's Lover" (1836), "Fra Lippo Lippi" (1855), and the Duke of Ferrara in "My Last Duchess" (1842). These are not the vaguely universal "I" speakers of the Romantic lyrics; they are personalities with unique occupations, reputations, and psychologies, and they are agents who actively participate in the dramas that unfold. They are, in effect, the lyrical equivalent of character-narrators. As such, they are equidistant from poet and reader, as Elisabeth Howe has argued: "Dramatic monologues assume a certain separation or *distance* between poet and speaker on the one hand and between reader and speaker on the other" (1996, original emphasis, 6); or as William Rogers puts it, "We feel the 'otherness' of the speaker's voice as a difference not only from the author, but from ourselves" (1983, 82).

This distance is exacerbated by differences in value and perception between dramatic and "implied" speakers, to borrow Booth's terminology. Readers of the dramatic monologue, like readers of unreliable narration, find themselves in collusion with the poet at the expense of the speaker, who gradually reveals himself to be rhetorically untrustworthy. Contradictions emerge between the poem's state of affairs and the speaker's evaluations of them, between the speaker's perception of himself and the way he presents himself to the reader, and between the speaker's sense of authority and the reader's mounting skepticism. In some cases, the speaker is duplicitous, deliberately seeking and cultivating the reader's trust, though he is unworthy of it. One of the more famous instances of this type is Browning's Duke of Ferrara. In the opening lines of "My Last Duchess" (1842), the Duke beguiles his addressee, an envoy for the Count, through a combination of civility, flattery, and feigned intimacy:

> That's my last duchess painted on the wall,
> Looking as if she were alive. I call
> That piece a wonder, now: Frà Pandolf's hands
> Worked busily a day, and there she stands.
> Will't please you sit and look at her? I said
> 'Frà Pandolf' by design, for never read
> Strangers like you that pictured countenance,
> The depth and passion of its earnest glance,
> But to myself they turned (since none puts by
> The curtain I have drawn for you, but I)
> And seemed as they would ask me, if they durst,
> How such a glance came there; so, not the first
> Are you to turn and ask thus. (1981, 349)

Beginning with a polite invitation—"Will't please you sit and look at her?"—the Duke disarms the envoy by claiming to disclose his motives ("I said / 'Frà Pandolf' by design") and placing the addressee in the company of others who have likewise wondered about the Duchess's "countenance." By the time he brings himself to critique the Duchess's moral character, he does so with authority and artfully feigned delicacy: "She had / A heart—how shall I say?—too soon made glad, / Too easily impressed" (349–50). The litotes in these lines, however, are offset by the gross exaggeration that follows: "She liked whate'er / She looked on, and her looks went everywhere" (350). The Duke transforms his duchess's graces into flaws, commending her etiquette only to recast it as a personal affront: "She thanked men—good! but thanked / Somehow—I know not how—as if she ranked / My gift of a nine-hundred-years-old name / With anybody's gift." Though he cannot detect her disloyalty with any precision ("Somehow—I know not how"), her greatest crime seems to be her lack of reverence for the Duke's noble ancestry. Browning also invites us to consider the Duke's duplicity on a formal level: as Howe points out, the Duke's speech works to disguise the poem's form, since its syntactic punctuation does not align with the poem's line breaks, giving the monologue a conversational cadence that masks its otherwise regular form (11). And just as it becomes clear that the Duke has murdered his last duchess for her ostensibly wandering eye—"I gave commands; / Then all smiles stopped together. There she stands / As if alive"—he diffuses this tension by insinuating that he has merely been discussing art all along: "Notice Neptune though, / Taming a sea-horse, thought a rarity, / Which Claus of Innsbruck cast in bronze for me!"

Earlier critics of the poem such as Robert Langbaum tend to read the Duke as a delusional character who is more worthy of sympathy than of judgment (quoted in Rader 1976, 135–36). Ralph Rader persuasively argued against this reading in his now-classic essay, "The Dramatic Monologue and Related Lyric Forms." The Duke, Rader contends, knows exactly what he's doing: he "reveals himself with deliberate calculation, for a specific purpose," to warn a future wife of the previous duchess's fate through the oblique hints he drops to the envoy (136). According to Rader, understanding this monologue as a manipulative admonition creates a more powerful experience for the reader. "The revelation is more massive; probability and surprise are both increased as the Duke's motives become completely cogent and more deeply hidden" (138). As Rader describes it, the experience of reading a dramatic monologue is akin to reading a detective novel. The reader identifies traces of a crime, pieces together a larger picture of the truth, and eventually uncovers the criminal's motives.

Other, equally powerful monologues, however, feature speakers who are less manipulative than they are unstable. Consider, for example, Browning's "Porphyria's Lover," which appeared alongside "My Last Duchess" under the subheading *Dramatic Lyrics* in the same collection (1842). The speaker in this lyric does not make the pretenses of authority and trustworthiness that are made by the Duke, though he is no more reliable in his evaluation of his lover. After describing Porphyria's selfless efforts to start a fire in his hearth after entering from a storm—indeed, she only "withdrew the dripping cloak and shawl" from her shoulders once the fire is lit for him—the speaker accuses her of "pride" and vanity (1981, 380). Though she assures him of "how she loved [him]," he decides that the only way to secure her is in death: "All her hair / In one long yellow string I wound / Three times her little throat around, / And strangled her" (381). The speaker faults Porphyria for her unwillingness to "give herself to [him] for ever" (380)—perhaps, as Monique R. Morgan speculates, a hint that "she is unwilling to give up her family and their wealth to marry her less prosperous lover" (2009, 161). Yet the speaker's characterization of Porphyria seems inconsistent with her selfless behavior, and his own actions betray his desire for control. Prior to her strangulation, she had "made her smooth white shoulder bare, / And all her yellow hair displaced, / And, stopping, made my cheek lie there"; afterward, their roles are reversed, and the speaker becomes the caretaker: "I propped her head up as before, / Only this time my shoulder bore / Her head, which droops upon it still" (381). Rader insists that we react to the delusional speaker, in contradistinction to the deceitful speaker, with "comic condescension" (1976, 139), but there is nothing "comic" about our apprehension of the speaker's unreliability in "Porphyria's Lover." In fact, the progression here looks quite similar to that of "My Last Duchess": a speaker depicts a loving relationship before taking a sharp, criminal turn that displays his unreliability.

Both monologues discourage prima facie readings that uncritically accept the perspective of the speaker. Instead, they introduce contradictions that can be resolved only by readings that venture beyond the literal. It would be a mistake to assume that the women in these lyrics are fickle lovers who deserve their lot, as the Duke and Porphyria's lover would have it. In fact, these lyrics are not really about the Duchess or Porphyria at all, since—like most unreliable narration—they reveal far more about the psychology of their speakers than about the events they purport to describe.

The link between the unreliable speaker of the dramatic monologue and the unreliable narrator of the modern novel may seem obvious, but it has only been so much as hinted at in literary scholarship.[1] In fact, the connection is primarily drawn by scholars of lyric poetry in protest of our critical tendency to read all lyrics in light of the dramatic monologue and, hence, the novel. Jonathan Culler asks that we stop treating every lyric speaker "as a character in a novel whose motivations must be elucidated" and that we adopt a long view of the lyric that recovers its roots in the rhetoric of ancient Greece, situating the speaker instead "as a performer picking up traditional elements and presenting them to an audience" (2008, 204). Virginia Jackson too asks that we diversify our notion of the lyric to be more responsible to historical practice: "The notion of the lyric I as a speaker in a dramatic monologue came to dominate modern interpretation—and, in my experience, still does" (2008, 183). Both critics rightly point out that the popularity of the novel with both academic and commercial audiences has led to the novelization of lyric poetry, in which we force lyric poems to "assimilate . . . to the form of narrative fiction" (Culler 2008, 201). What is more, they underscore the literary-historical significance of the dramatic monologue, which does not stand in for lyricality but represents a shift in the tradition that sharpens and dramatizes the distance between lyric speaker and poet. Certainly, poets wrote from the perspective of fictional personae prior to the nineteenth century: examples include "epistolary forms of monologue" in which lyrics positioned themselves as letters from, say, Dido to Aeneas or Penelope to Odysseus (Howe 1996, 18). The dramatic monologue, however, extends the distance between poet and speaker by exploring the psychological—and ontological—dimensions of unreliability, calling into question not only the mental stability of the speaker but the very fabric of the world he narrates.

Unreliability deliberately severs subjectivity from authority to facilitate a particular reading practice. It asks that we read beneath the surface of the text to make sense of its incongruities, though in so doing, we begin to lose our ontological footing. The Duke's accusations of infidelity with regard to his last duchess are dramatically undermined by his vacillations between litote and exaggeration as he tries to account for her behavior. Likewise, the charge of vanity issued against Porphyria by her lover is indirectly contradicted by her behavior in the poem, which instead demonstrates devotion and self-abnegation. Perhaps the duchess was indeed flirtatious, and perhaps

Porphyria did refuse a prior marriage proposal; but our access to these possible events remains blurred and stymied by unreliable narration. Such is the challenge of reading through the prism of unreliability, which introduces doubt but fails to replace it with anything in the affirmative. As Henry James said of Browning's art, we are faced with "a deposit of stated matter, a block of sense already in position and requiring not to be shaped and squared and caused any further to solidify, but rather to suffer disintegration, be pulled apart, melted down, hammered, by the most characteristic of the poet's processes, to powder" (1914, 388).

Truly unreliable narration produces conflicting readings that effectively erase, or at the very least obscure, the event structure that is foundational to narrative fiction. As the previous chapter has established, narrative fiction would typically have us track characters through a plot that is to be read more or less literally. The radically unstable narrators of the twentieth century, however—James's governess, Nabokov's Humbert Humbert, Ellis's Patrick Bateman, and the unnamed narrator of Palahniuk's *Fight Club*—demand that we, as readers, continually revise what we think we know about these character-narrators and the fictional worlds they simultaneously inhabit and narrate. While James and Nabokov have created highly manipulative narrators who take pains to establish their authority and credibility before introducing markers of unreliability, the narrators in Ellis and Palahniuk—more in line with Porphyria's lover than with the Duke—are deeply mentally ill, though neither seems to understand the depth and extent of his illness. All four novelists urge readers toward increasingly figurative understandings of their ontologically dubious story worlds, in which our only access to plot is filtered through highly unreliable perspectives.

The ability of unreliable narration to produce twin contradictory readings was a major feature of Tzvetan Todorov's classic study *The Fantastic: A Structural Approach to a Literary Genre* (1975). Here, Todorov analyzes a large body of fantastic fiction that facilitates two readings: either the supernatural events are real or they are products of a protagonist's imagination. For Todorov, this dichotomy lies at the very heart of the fantastic, which often plays with or oscillates between these two extremes. The hesitation of the protagonist, who struggles to choose between these two interpretations, is meant to mirror that of the reader (31). Ultimately, however, the reader is pressed to make a choice:

> The fantastic, we have seen, lasts only as long as a certain hesitation: a hesitation common to reader and character, who must decide whether or not what they perceive derives from 'reality' as it exists in the common opinion. At the story's end, the reader makes a decision even if the character does not; he opts for one solution or the other, and thereby emerges from the fantastic. If he decides that the laws of reality remain intact and permit an explanation of the

> phenomena described, we say that the work belongs to another genre: the uncanny. If, on the contrary, he decides that new laws of nature must be entertained to account for the phenomena, we enter the genre of the marvelous. The fantastic therefore leads a life full of dangers, and may evaporate at any moment. It seems to be located on the frontier of two genres, the marvelous and the uncanny. (41)

Todorov does not prescribe one reading over the other, though he does require readers to select and subscribe to a single interpretation, as evidenced by his insistence on the verb *to decide*. Since different readings entail different generic consequences, the act of deciding is paramount to Todorov's point about the broad spectrum on which genres overlap and diverge: one selection lands readers in the realm of the fantastic, while another lands them in the realm of the uncanny, while still another turn of the screw may lead them toward the marvelous. Each reading and subsequent genre contains its own tone, tenor, and ontology. In fact, Todorov explicitly rejects any symbolic reading that attempts to reconcile dual readings through metaphor or allegory. This, he argues, would be the realm of the "poetic," which is insufficient for handling questions of ontological significance that occupy the fantastic and simply "do not come up" in lyric poetry, where there is no pressure to parse and resolve such ambiguities. "The fantastic implies, then, not only the existence of an uncanny event, which provokes a hesitation in the reader and the hero, but also a kind of reading, which we may for the moment define negatively: it must be neither 'poetic' nor 'allegorical,'" he insists (32).

Narrative theorists since Todorov have adopted a similar model for dual readings in which readers are pressed to select an interpretation, however arbitrary that choice might be. Peter Rabinowitz's article "Truth in Fiction: A Reexamination of Audiences" (1977) parses the issue by dividing audiences into four types: the *actual* audience, or the flesh-and-blood readers who understand stories to be fictional; *authorial* audience, or the author's ideally constructed, hypothetical readers who still understand stories to be fictional; *narrative* audience, or an audience that possesses a deep knowledge of literary history and generic forms but understands stories and their characters to be "real"; and the *ideal narrative* audience, which is ideal from the narrator's point of view, "roughly analogous to the way that the authorial audience relates to the actual audience" (134). Just as genres yield different readings for Todorov, each audience yields a different reading for Rabinowitz, who productively teases out the tensions that exist among, between, and even within these various levels. Depending on which "narrative audience" we posit for James's *Turn of the Screw*—that is, whether James writes for a narrative audience accustomed to the realism that permeates his other works or posits "the narrative audience traditionally implied by gothic novels, one able to believe in ghosts"—we arrive at either realist or fantastical readings of the novella, respectively (137). Too hastily, however, does Rabinowitz argue that "it ultimately makes little difference which one chooses," since, even if the narrative audience accepts the presence of ghosts, "the authorial audience is apt to treat them as in some sense symbolic when called upon to interpret the novel." Here, Rabinowitz appear to shortchange his own carefully delineated categories, failing to account for tensions between two very different narrative audiences or how an authorial audience would necessarily "correct" the shortcomings of the former audience. Instead, he devotes the rest of his article to a nuanced reading of Nabokov's *Pale Fire* that showcases "more difficult" ambiguities of this experimental novel and why his audience-based model "explains the novel's persistent ability to interpret the novel."

Yet *The Turn of the Screw* and the other novels examined in this chapter exhibit serious exegetical difficulties that are not resolved by the arbitrary selection of one reading over another nor by any automatic "correction" made among a layering of implicit audiences. This is largely because, unlike *Pale Fire*, a metafictional text that revolves around exegesis as a theme and practice, the novels examined here hinge on a traditional plot structure that is simultaneously developed and erased by their unreliable narrators. These plots, in other words, are established only to unfold in ways that, by design, prevent readers from selecting any one reading over the other. Todorov tells us that either reading is possible, but we *must* choose, and choice determines genre; Rabinowitz tells us that either reading is possible, and that we *can* and *do* choose, even if the choice is arbitrary. The novelists treated in this chapter tell us instead that *neither* reading is possible and hence we *cannot* choose. The twin readings they generate are not only contradictory and mutually exclusive when paired together, but they are contradictory and sparse even when pulled apart and examined separately. Plots are established only to deteriorate so rapidly that they seem to disappear altogether, folded as they are into the complex psychology of a disturbed character-narrator.

The context of the dramatic monologue helps us grapple with the alternating manipulations and delusions of character-narrators who establish, undermine, and ultimately dismantle the event structure upon which readers of narrative fiction have come to rely. Because dramatic monologues foreground the vexed and even inverse relationship between character psychology and event ontology, they provide a model, if not a solution, for navigating works in which action gives way to interiority and stymies the reader's access to plot. This cross-generic understanding of unreliability poses a challenge to the often-cited multidimensional update of Booth's model put forth by James Phelan and Mary Martin, who, like Rabinowitz, try to sort through the problem of dual readings by creating categories that establish various levels and degrees of unreliability. According to Phelan and Martin (1999), the conflict between the narrator and the implied author or audience that transpires under unreliable narration may occur on any or all of three general levels or axes: misreading, or contradictions between the narrator's perception of events and the implied author's perception of them (the axis of perception);

misreporting, or contradictions between the narrator's reportage of events and the facts of the events in the fictional world (the axis of facts); and misregarding, or contradictions between the narrator's moral evaluation of events and the implied author's evaluation of them (the axis of values). In his book *Living to Tell about It* (2004), Phelan adds another layer of unreliability to this taxonomy: under-reporting, under-reading, and under-regarding, in which readers do not necessarily reject the narrator's point of view but must seek out supplemental information for a more complete account (51). Phelan and Martin freely admit that their taxonomy is heuristic and that narrators may exhibit more than one brand of unreliability, but the neat separation of misreporting and misreading in their analysis of Ishiguro's *Remains of the Day* glosses over the complex ways in which these two concepts interact with and even constitute one another. Because a narrator's (mis)perception of reality necessarily contributes to a distorted picture of the fictional world he is narrating, misreading quickly yields to misreporting in ways that are often too difficult and too complex for readers to disentangle, as this chapter's textual analyses will demonstrate. In other words, the novels here pivot around an axis of facts that are never made fully available to readers. Indeed, the greater the distortion in a homodiegetic narrator's perception, the more distorted the fictional world will be, and some narrators—unlike Stevens—never fully realize the extent of their derangement.

To some extent, Browning's monologues corroborate Phelan's delineations of the ways in which radically distorted fictional worlds require extensive reconfigurations on the part of the reader, who must not only identify the markers of narrative unreliability but also subsequently determine which facets of the plot are concrete events occurring in the storyworld and which are extensions, or projections, of the narrator's fraught mental state. Yet the novels treated in this chapter amplify the dramatic monologue's conflation of ontology with character psychology by making that determination onerous or even impossible, showcasing unreliability's potential to wreak ontological havoc in ways that present a serious stumbling block for readers of fiction who are searching for plot. To borrow Phelan and Martin's terminology: these writers deliberately obscure the boundary between misreading and misreporting that typically separates plot from its representation by a character-bound narrator, such that their stories virtually crumble between our fingers with each turn of the screw.

Henry James's *The Turn of the Screw* ([1898] 1999) systematically tantalizes, manipulates, and ultimately stymies our understanding of narrative action by tethering it to an untrustworthy character-narrator who reports events that may or may not be happening. Criticism of the novella—especially early criticism—attempts to locate a stable plot by determining whether the ghosts that populate this gothic novella are "real" or the delusional imaginings of the unnamed governess who presides over the story. One strain of scholarship, beginning with prominent early critics such as F. O. Matthiessen, Allen Tate, and even Wayne Booth, argues for more or less "straight" readings of the governess's first-person account. "When she says that she saw Peter Quint and Miss Jessel, or that she felt a gust of icy air in a sealed room, there is no reason to suppose her hysterical," concurs Alexander E. Jones (1959, 121). "At most, the governess can be charged only with ambiguity," he maintains; otherwise, "the governess' testimony is generally reliable." The other strain, beginning with Edmund Wilson and Harold Goddard, argues for Freudian readings in which the ghosts are hallucinations resulting from "a neurotic case of sex repression" (Wilson [1938] 2007, 90). The question driving these analyses—"Are they or aren't they?"—is a cogent attempt to resolve the novella's ambiguities, but it creates a false dichotomy that the text itself does not bear out. Readings that take into account only one of these extreme positions necessarily suppress those textual details that support the alternative. Rather than urging readers to declare for one of two possible readings, *The Turn of the Screw* paradoxically asks us to inhabit both and neither, setting up deliberate ambiguities that prompt these questions of ontology versus psychology but do not admit an answer.[2]

James achieves this manipulation through his contradictory characterization of a governess who is authoritative at times and unreliable at others, a tension that he builds into the novella's very framing. Much like the stories that make up *The Canterbury Tales*, the main plot of *The Turn of the Screw* is an embedded narrative positioned as one of several stories exchanged by guests who have gathered together at an old country house on Christmas Eve. Most critics refer only to the governess's narration, but the novella contains a complex tiered structure involving three discernible narrators: the governess, who commits her first-person account to the written page; Douglas, who relates her account to the group; and the unnamed first-person narrator who relates the account, in turn, to us. Though the other character-narrators take pains to establish the governess's credibility in light of her tale's phantasm, these added narrative layers simultaneously widen the rhetorical and epistemological distance between the governess and the reader. Each transmission of the story introduces room for error, but more than that, each transmission draws attention to the artifice of storytelling.

Just as the Duke of Ferrara tries to secure the trust of the envoy, so the elaborate frame surrounding the governess's story works to establish its veracity despite its tertiary distance from the events relayed. Having known the governess personally, Douglas attests to her character, informing the group that she was prepared for the hardships at Bly and that she did not take her charges lightly, taking several days before finally accepting the position. The elaborate frame James provides for the governess's account includes an episode in which Douglas refuses to paraphrase her words and sends instead for her manuscript, which remains under lock and key at his home and which—much to the irritated suspense of his fellow travelers—takes three days to arrive. Yet James reintroduces doubt when Douglas confesses in this prefatory material that the manuscript is a transcription of the governess's faded original. The transcription and narrative embedding place readers at a fourth remove from the story events of *The Turn of the Screw*. Thus, the promise of a reliable and authoritative narrative becomes increasingly strained not only as these additional layers are introduced but as inconsistencies and contradictions emerge in the governess's first-person account, which takes up the rest of the novella.

The governess's initial encounter with the apparitions at Bly seems reliable enough, since she does not yet understand them to be ghosts. Startled by the appearance of a strange man on the grounds, she takes him to be an intruder and "a horror" until she learns of Peter Quint, a former servant at Bly whose description matches that of the stranger (22). Mrs. Grose divulges that Quint had been conducting an affair with the former governess, Miss Jessel, who left under mysterious circumstances. "Quint was much too free," she suggests, evoking a "sudden sickness of disgust" in the governess (25). As Bruce Robbins has argued, Mrs. Grose may refer here to Quint's "class transgression" (1986, 200): a servant carrying on a relationship with the governess is not being properly servile. Mrs. Grose's euphemism also, however, implicates Quint as a pedophile, as Ellis Hanson has argued (2003). Whatever the offense—a crucial detail that James deliberately obscures—the governess believes that the ghosts, as she understands them, continue to threaten the children's well-being. She becomes fiercely protective of Miles and Flora: "I was a screen," she explains. "I was to stand before them. The more I saw, the less they would" (27).

The following encounter with Miss Jessel's apparition, however, calls her discernment into question. For one, her perception is now guided by premonition: "There was no ambiguity in anything; none whatever at least in the conviction I from one moment to another found myself forming as to what I should see straight before me and across the lake as a consequence of raising my eyes" (28). The language of certainty is undermined here by the governess's use of the subjunctive mood—not what she *did* see, but what she anticipates she *should* see. Nor is she the only witness to the scene: this visitation occurs as a distracted Flora plays on the edge of a lake. Though the girl is only "ten yards away" from the apparition, she never looks up from her play. Flora's reaction, or lack thereof, yields a number of plausible interpretations, including the possibility that she has not noticed the ghost, or—more likely, given her proximity—that the ghost was never there at all. The governess, however, jumps to a third conclusion: "Flora *saw* . . . [and] she kept it to herself" (29).

This scene marks a shift not only in the governess's perception of the ghosts but also of her two young charges. When first introduced to Miles and Flora, she is overwhelmed by their innocence: Flora seems to her one of "Raphael's holy infants" (8), and Miles too is described as an "angel"

(19). She has unshakable faith in their good intentions, though Miles has been expelled from his school under mysterious circumstances. She recalls her first meeting with him: "What I then and there took him to my heart for was something divine that I have never found to the same degree in any child—his indescribable little air of knowing nothing in the world but love. It would have been impossible to carry a bad name with a greater sweetness of innocence" (13). Following the pivotal scene at the lake, however, the governess becomes equally convinced of their malevolence. She insists to Mrs. Grose that Miles and Flora are not only aware of the ghosts but in collusion with them: "They *know*—it's too monstrous: they know, they know!" she cries. Approaching the children with renewed skepticism, she now sees their innocence as a form of concealment, a "play . . . at perfect propriety" (45). Reversing her earlier estimation of Miles and Flora as virtuous angels and victims of predatory behavior, she now senses in them a "secret precocity—or whatever I might call the poison of an influence that I dared by half-phrase" (61). In fact, the governess becomes wildly speculative in her assessments of the children, reporting events to which she cannot possibly have access. She intuits, for instance, that "whatever I had seen, Miles and Flora saw *more*—things terrible and unguessable and that sprang from dreadful passages of intercourse in the past" (51). Convinced that the children are communicating with the ghosts in secret, she hazards to Mrs. Grose—resorting again to the subjunctive mood—that the children "say things that, if we heard them, would simply appall us" (66).

Neither Miles nor Flora seems to display the changes that the governess ascribes to them, but the governess's erratic and contradictory behavior places their relationship under gradual strain. She becomes at once fiercely protective and almost violently punitive as her lingering dedication to guarding the children from malice is now matched by her urge to castigate them as if they were willing participants. Her emotional outbursts vacillate between tenderness and wrath. "There were moments when I knew myself to catch them up by an irresistible impulse and press them to my heart," she confesses (37)—and yet, convinced that Flora is lying when she denies having seen Miss Jessel by the lake, her fury is palpable: "Why not break out at her on the spot and have it all over?—give it to her straight in her lovely little lighted face?" (41). Always on her guard, she is unable to sleep or relax, sitting up at night "till I did n't know when" and hovering over the two children "like a gaoler with an eye to possible surprises and escapes" (41, 43). The children become fatigued by her attentions: "You know, my dear, that for a fellow to be with a lady *always*—!" declares an exasperated Miles, contradicting the governess's insistence that "they never resent my inexorable, my perpetual society" (52).

As contradictions accrue between the children's behavior and the governess's increasingly hysterical perspective, we are pressed to question our narrator's grip on reality. Does she continue to protect the children with heroic dedication, or has she unwittingly slipped into the role of villain? The children become apprehensive around her, effectively shifting the focus of this gothic tale from the ghosts to the governess herself. "We must do nothing but what she likes," Miles tells Mrs. Grose—an avowal that the governess takes for affectionate loyalty. Flora's anxiety even causes her to become psychosomatically feverish from "fears that had for their subject not in the least her former but wholly her present governess" (71). Mrs. Grose whisks Flora away from Bly at the end of the novella, but not before she insinuates that the governess has been inappropriate with Flora in a way that is reminiscent of Peter Quint. Speaking in oblique fragments, she declares that Flora has been telling her "really shocking" things about the governess: "It's beyond everything for a young lady; and I can't think wherever she must have picked it up— . . . Well, perhaps I ought to . . . since I've heard some of it before!" (74). It remains unclear from these fragments whether Mrs. Grose refers to Flora's language, the governess's behavior, or some combination of both. Either way, Mrs. Grose's reaction positions the governess as a double for Peter Quint, perhaps even positioning her as the new antagonist.

Whatever these "shocking" linguistic utterances or behaviors might be is deliberately obfuscated by the novella's circuitous dialogue, as are so many other critical plot points: Miles's expulsion from school; the bizarre no-contact rule imposed by the children's guardian; and the many ambiguities surrounding Peter Quint and Miss Jessel, including why they left Bly, under what circumstances they died prematurely, and the nature of their relationship with the children and with each other. While Mrs. Grose seems to imply that Miss Jessel left after becoming pregnant with Quint's child—"She could n't have stayed. Fancy it here—for a governess! And afterwards I imagined—and I still imagine. And what I imagine is dreadful" (32)—she also insinuates that their relationship may not have been consensual: "I've never seen one like him. He did what he wished," Mrs. Grose says of Peter Quint. "With *her*?" the governess asks, referring to Miss Jessel, to which Mrs. Grose obliquely replies, "With them all." Our uncertainty about the story's event structure stems not only from the governess's frazzled mental state, then, but also from the stilted dialogue of the novella's other characters, such as Mrs. Grose.

Nor can we easily discount the governess's narration as a consequence of her unreliability, since a number of passages corroborate her observations. It is Mrs. Grose, after all, who identifies the first apparition as Peter Quint based on the governess's description. At times, the governess's instincts about the children are quite accurate. When she intuits that Flora has taken the boat across the lake to visit with Miss Jessel, she finds Flora exactly there. When she suspects that Miles has stolen the letter she has written to his guardian, Miles confesses that he has done exactly that. The governess's intuitions, unfounded as they may seem, do have undeniable predictive power. James marshals just enough evidence to substantiate her perceptions. Just as we are warned against taking the governess's word for granted, we are also warned against discounting it.

Thus, James has created a novella that frustrates, from a variety of angles, the reader's drive to locate plot. Ambiguities are introduced and dramatized, mutually exclusive perspectives are presented without resolution, and we are hard pressed to determine which events are a part of the fabric of this fictional world and which a product of the governess's psyche. The novella's dramatic final scene brings this confusion to a climax. Convinced that she sees Peter Quint in Miles's bedroom window, the governess clutches the child to her as she points to the window:

> But he had already jerked straight round, stared, glared again, and seen but the quiet day. With the stroke of the loss I was so proud of he uttered the cry of a creature hurled over an abyss, and the gasp with which I recovered him might have been that of catching him in his fall. I caught him, yes, I held him—it may be imagined with what a passion; but at the end of a minute I began to feel what it truly was that I held. We were alone with the quiet day, and his little heart, dispossessed, had stopped. (85)

Has Miles died of shock because he too sees the apparition? Has the governess frightened him to death by suggesting the return of his molester? Has she suffocated him to death as she presses him to her "with what a passion"? Those who angle for a "straight" reading will argue that Miles's response corroborates her vision while those who are convinced that the governess is insane will read the ending as a homicide. To adopt either reading at the expense of the other, however, would be to flatten a deliberately byzantine text that lends support to both possibilities. James forces us to live with these ambiguities and contradictions, an aesthetic strategy that will frustrate readers who gain traction in fiction by relying on concrete story events. "'The story *won't* tell,' said Douglas; 'not in any literal vulgar way'" (3)—and indeed, it won't. *The Turn of the Screw* is devoted instead to the elaboration of a lyric persona who, like the speaker of "Porphyria's Lover," demonstrates the type of unwitting unreliability that obstructs our access to plot. Rather than reading for events, we are drawn instead to the complex psychology of our enigmatic character-narrator, whose motives—and sanity—are continually called into question.

Vladimir Nabokov's *Lolita* ([1955] 1997) is frequently cited as an exemplar of unreliable narration, though critical discussions tend to center, for obvious reasons, on Humbert's distorted sense of morality and the ethical position of the reader who is beguiled by Humbert's artful narration but repulsed by his behavior.[3] Much like James's novella, however, *Lolita* experiments with ontological unreliability by toying with the permeable boundary between plot and character psychology, and Humbert's penchant for wordplay further distorts the event structure that lies somewhere beyond his narration. Readers and critics have constructed radically different accounts of this controversial novel's plot based on their divergent readings of its characters and events. Lionel Trilling famously argued that *Lolita* is "not about sex, but about love" and suggested that the romance between Humbert and Lolita is as mutual and heartfelt as it is illicit (1958, 15). Stanley Kubrick's 1962 film adaptation also takes Humbert's perspective seriously, depicting—with hilarious black humor—the story of a sexually advanced coquette who seduces a vulnerable older man. (Adrian Lyne's 1997 version adopts a similar plotline without the humor.) *Lolita*'s detractors regard the novel as a sordid story of kidnapping, captivity, and routine sexual child abuse; for this reason, *Lolita* was turned down by a number of American publishers before finally being published—and quickly banned—in France. Still another strain of criticism, pioneered by Wayne Booth, argues for a more nuanced understanding in which the novel begins as a story of seduction but concludes as a story of rape based on Humbert's gradual realization and "recantation" of his crimes ([1961] 1983, 391). How can such fundamentally different plot summaries emerge from the same novel? A deeper exploration of Humbert's unreliability can better parse those ambiguities that prevent readers from readily accessing the events that give shape to *Lolita*'s plot.

Humbert Humbert—even his pseudonym is a playful ruse—is one of Western literature's most manipulative narrators. Eloquent, refined, well educated, witty, and charming, he is also a master wordsmith whose facility with language produces some strikingly gorgeous prose. "You can always count on a murderer for a fancy prose style," he quips, admitting that his behavior is at odds with his aesthetic sensibility (9). Such contradictions abound in his character, and critics have only begun to plumb the depths of his multidimensional unreliability. Peter Rabinowitz (2004) provides a compelling rhetorical account of Humbert's efforts to silence Lolita despite her "unrelenting expressions of outrage," concentrating on the ways in which critics have mostly followed Humbert's lead (326). Lisa Zunshine (2006) offers a fascinating analysis of Humbert's cognitive designs on the reader: among other strategies, Humbert manages to impute pedophiliac states of mind to the reader to deflect our attention from his own sexual perversion (103, 106). I would like to build on these accounts by focusing on the stylistic dimension of Humbert's untrustworthiness. Humbert's logophilia, which he shares with Nabokov, blurs his delineation from the author and calls into question the ontological status of places and characters integral to the novel's plot. Before we can readily assess what is ethical, we must determine what is real—a task that launches readers into a seemingly infinite regress of ontological uncertainty.

As in *The Turn of the Screw*, these uncertainties are built into the novel's framing material. Many forget that *Lolita* too is positioned as a "found manuscript" penned by an incarcerated Humbert as he awaits trial. The text features a foreword written by a fictitious academic named John Ray, Jr., who has been asked by Humbert's lawyer to compile and edit the text of *Lolita* per Humbert's request. While the frame in James's novella works to validate and authenticate the governess's account, however, Ray's foreword aims to discredit Humbert's perspective by positioning *Lolita* as a "case history" that "will become, no doubt, a classic in psychiatric circles" (5). The ensuing narrative, he cautions, is "shocking," and the "desperate honesty that throbs through [Humbert's] confession does not absolve him from sins of diabolical cunning" (5). Nabokov—via Ray—alerts us to Humbert's unreliability at the outset, yet Nabokov has also commented on Ray's unreliability in his famous rejoinder to the novel's detractors: "I am neither a reader nor a writer of didactic fiction, and despite John Ray's assertion, *Lolita* has no moral in tow," he wrote in a now-classic essay, "On a Book Entitled *Lolita*," which is appended to most editions of the novel (314). Thus, *Lolita*'s nested structure reflects nested forms of unreliability in which Humbert's moral failure is encased in, and even distorted by, by John Ray's exegetical deficiencies, for—like many of James's critics—Ray flattens the ethical and aesthetic complexities of a novel that dwells in the realm of ambiguity.

Ambiguity also surrounds the novel's other characters, and Ray's foreword sets into motion the type of linguistic play that will infuse Humbert's narration and cause us to question the very existence of the text's major players. Though Ray—with sarcastic though dubious use of quotation marks—gently mocks readers who cling to verisimilitude before updating us on the "destinies of 'real' people beyond the 'true' story," he reports on characters to whom we have yet to be introduced (4). Vivian Darkbloom's biography, "My Cue," is unrecognizable until we learn about Clare Quilty and his cognomen, "Q." The homonym suggests that Nabokov has planted these and other signals or "cues" for readers to untangle. Vivian Darkbloom herself is another such "cue": her name is an anagram for the author, Vladimir Nabokov. Even Lolita's name is disguised in Ray's preface, since she does not become "Mrs. Richard Schiller" until the end of the novel. Thus, as Lisa Sternlieb has argued, the novel itself—like the anagram Vivian Darkbloom—must be read both forward and backward, and Ray's preface is not entirely coherent until we have finished the novel (2008, 159–60). Yet even then, questions remain about the status of these characters in Nabokov's fictional world. Does Vivian Darkbloom have an existence beyond that of her writing partner, Clare Quilty? Is she a clever stand-in for Nabokov? Or is she merely a "cue" to readers that Nabokov routinely violates fictional conventions so that a number of his characters—including Humbert—are not so easily distinguished from their author?[4] The preface's play with wording and grammar does not, as it claims, provide closure for its characters so much as it subjects them to further inquiry. In fact, the very function of the preface via Nabokov's "impersonation of suave John Ray" (Nabokov [1955] 1997, 311) may be to groom readers for the depth and variety of ontological instability they will experience as they navigate Humbert's story.

Like Browning's Duke of Ferrara, Humbert attempts to disarm readers by establishing his authority as a reliable judge and providing rationalizations that mitigate his crimes. His purported narrative audience, after all, is the grand jury to whom Humbert presumed he would present his account "in toto" at his impending trial (308). Many of his rationalizations are not only, as Phelan has put it, "obviously literally false" (2007a, 235)—among them his bizarre theory of "nymphets," those demonic young girls who cast sexual spells over unwitting adult aesthetes—but they contradict one another in ways that render then internally inconsistent. Humbert moves seamlessly between characterizing pedophilia as an artist's affliction to describing it as a common practice in non-Western cultures: "Marriage and cohabitation before the age of puberty are still not uncommon in certain East Indian provinces. Lepcha old men of eighty copulate with girls of eight, and nobody minds" (19). Even in the West, he continues, the age at which a girl enters puberty is too wildly variant for the state to define the age of consensual sex with such rigidity: "The median age of pubescence for girls has been found to be thirteen years and nine months in New York and Chicago. The age varies for individuals from ten, or earlier, to seventeen. Virginia was not quite fourteen when Harry Edgar [Edgar Allan Poe] possessed her" (43). Relying on dubious science, he even argues that this age may be contingent on climate: "'In such stimulating temperature climates [says an old magazine in this prison library] as St. Louis, Chicago and Cincinnati, girls mature about the end of their twelfth year.' Dolores Haze was born less than three hundred miles from stimulating Cincinnati. I have but followed nature. I am nature's faithful hound" (135). Thus, Humbert relies on three separate and incongruous arguments for the origins of pedophilia: if it is supernatural, it cannot be rooted in nature or culture; if it is natural, it cannot be culturally contingent; and if it is determined by the relativity of cultural norms, it cannot be said to "follow nature."

Perhaps his most convincing defense is one that is explicitly embedded in the lyric tradition, providing our first indication that Humbert may be manufacturing characters for his own benefit. Humbert presents "exhibit number one" to his juridical audience (9): his lost love, Annabel Leigh, whose name—and story—are suspiciously close to that of the titular figure in Edgar Allan Poe's lyric, "Annabel Lee" (1849). Humbert's Annabel, like Poe's, dies before the two child-lovers can consummate their romance. In fact, Humbert essentially pirates Poe, lifting entire lines and phrases from the poem without attribution and using them to articulate his own narrative of thwarted love. His assertion that the seraphs envy the purity of the love between himself and Annabel echoes a very similar line from Poe's verse: "With a love that the winged seraphs in heaven / coveted her and me" (Poe 1984, 738). He also uses the poem's opening line as a springboard for developing his theory of nymphets: "When I was a child and she was a child, my little Annabel was no nymphet to me," he plagiarizes, insisting that his lust for girls began quite innocently as a love between two peers of the same age (17). In fact, Humbert establishes himself as his own best psychoanalyst. "I am convinced . . . that in a certain magic and fateful way Lolita began with Annabel," he writes (13–14). "Twenty-four years later, I broke her spell by incarnating her in another" (15). Here, Humbert attributes his pedophilia to a tragically foiled childhood romance that has emotionally encased him in an irretrievable past. Though he continues to age and advance physically, sexually, and intellectually, the Annabels he continues to seek out are, like their prototype, prepubescent children. Here, he mobilizes the lyric tradition in an appeal to stasis that justifies, and even romanticizes, his illicit desire. Given the deliberate, extensive, and undocumented intertextuality of his account, one wonders whether Humbert's Annabel Leigh ever existed at all. "All I want to stress is that my discovery of [Dolores] was a fatal consequence of that 'princedom by the sea' in my tortured past," he insists again, (mis)quoting from Poe's lyric once more (40), but the pedophile doth protest too much. Referring in another wordplay to "Annabel Haze, alias Dolores Lee, alias Lolita," Humbert not only scrambles their names and hence their identities, but fails to provide the alternate spelling of Annabel's surname (Leigh) that separates her, albeit superficially, from Poe's creation (167).

Yet to whom do we attribute Annabel Leigh's intertextuality—Humbert or Nabokov? One of the characteristics that makes Humbert such an unusual narrator is Nabokov's decision to allow Humbert to "share" in his "stylistic virtuosity," as Phelan puts it (2007a, 234). Typically, artfulness is one of those authorial functions that separate the creator from his creation; we do not credit Nick Carraway for the beauty of F. Scott Fizgerald's prose. The potential for unreliability along the axis of aesthetics, however, is once again foreshadowed by Browning's Duke of Ferrara. "Even had you skill / In speech—which I have not," he declares to the envoy, suddenly drawing attention to the poem's rhymed couplets and iambic pentameter (1981, 350). Ralph Rader argues that there are two ways to read this statement. If the Duke is sincere—and after all, as Rader points out, the regularity of the poem's meter is "concealed" by its enjambment (1976, 138)—then the Duke reveals himself to audiences "by accident" and without ulterior motive. If he is ironic, however—that is, if Browning's submerged stylistic virtuosity signifies the Duke's submerged rhetorical virtuosity—then the Duke's revelation is calculated, and the camouflaged couplets are evidence of the Duke's cunning and symbols of his "hidden purpose" (139).

There is certainly evidence that Humbert, like the Duke, has been given stylistic control over his narrative in ways that allow him to manipulate language and, in turn, manipulate his readers. As Sternlieb points out, Humbert deliberately spells Hourglass Lake incorrectly ("Our Glass") until he visits there with Charlotte, "although he obviously knows how to spell the lake by the time he writes *Lolita*" (2008, 158). Here, she argues, Humbert relies on homophone to "play games with retrospection" as does Nabokov—or rather

John Ray?—when he tinkers with character names in the novel's preface. This deliberate incoherence on Humbert's part is matched by other games that suggest uncanny coherence: for example, the room number assigned to Humbert and Lolita at the Enchanted Hunters is the same as the Hazes' house number and—as Alfred Appel points out—appears in quotation marks, suggesting that it may be a fiction (1991, 118n3). The name of the hotel is also echoed in the title of Clare Quilty's play—another inexplicable coincidence. Humbert's wordplays are too frequent, and their contexts too intricate, to enumerate here; I will not attempt to compete with the wonderfully exhaustive annotations Alfred Appel, Jr., provided in his edition of *Lolita.* The ontological implications of these linguistic "cues," however, are manifold. Are they Humbert's attempt to protect the identities of the "'real' people beyond the 'true' story"? Or is Humbert, like Ray, gently mocking our hunger for verisimilitude by toying with concrete details such as room and house numbers? Or is Humbert leaving "cues" that these people and places never existed, even within the bounds of his fictional world? "Oh, my Lolita, I have only words to play with!" he apostrophizes in the novel's opening pages (34). If so, then the fabric of *Lolita*'s plot quickly unravels.

At the center of this mysterious ontology is the ubiquitous Clare Quilty, who leaves throughout the novel traces of his presence that can only be understood retrospectively because Humbert delays in disclosing his identity.[5] Many of these early appearances are incidental: he is featured, for example, in a cigarette ad that adorns Lolita's bedroom wall (69). Yet as Humbert becomes increasingly involved with Lolita and, subsequently, more paranoid about his dual role as father and lover, Quilty begins to appear with greater frequency and magnitude. He materializes at the Enchanted Hunters hotel, where Humbert consummates his relationship with Lolita; he appears again at Beardsley while attending rehearsals for a performance of his play, *The Hunted Enchanters*, though Lolita refers to him as "some old woman" to disguise his identity—and gender—to an ever more jealous Humbert (209); and when Humbert and Lolita flee Beardsley, he appears to follow them on their circuitous cross-country travels, though he is mistakenly identified again by Humbert as his father's cousin, Gustave Trapp (216).

The sheer number of Quilty's appearances—and the variety of forms he takes—suggests that he is ever-present, but there is also some question as to Humbert's psychological reliability here. His recognitions of Quilty become increasingly strained: after finally losing Quilty's red convertible, he is convinced that Quilty—"a veritable Proteus of the highway"—has traded it in for a series of rentals (227). When even the driver appears to change, he concludes that Quilty has hired accomplices to pursue them. Humbert's frazzled condition in part 2, exacerbated by heavy drinking, causes him to lose control of the polished narrative voice that dominates part 1. When Lolita makes her escape in chapter 22, his paragraph breaks disappear, his sentences become run-ons, and his punctuation becomes harried and stilted, filled with dashes and ellipses. In these passages, Humbert resembles the Duke of Ferrara less than Porphyria's lover, manic and unhinged as he anticipates a treacherous lover's departure.

Unlike Porphyria's lover, however, Humbert's paranoia is not unfounded. When Lolita finally disappears from Humbert's life, it is Clare Quilty who takes her away, signing her out of the hospital under the guise of her uncle Gustave. But when Humbert obsessively retraces his steps across the country and checks the ledgers of the inns he had stayed at with Lolita, he imagines not only that he finds Quilty's signature—or that of an accomplice—in every ledger, but that Quilty has, as Humbert puts it, "planted insulting pseudonyms for my special benefit" (248). The pseudonyms are tailored precisely to his "mind and manner": "[Quilty's] genre, his type of humor—at its best at least—the tone of his brain, had affinities with my own. He mimed and mocked me. His allusions were definitely highbrow. He was well-read. He knew French. He was versed in logodaedaly and logomancy. He was an amateur of sex lore" (249–50). So remarkable are their similarities, so strong their psychic connection, that one wonders whether they inhabit the same mind—and body. When Humbert arrives to murder Quilty, the latter is wearing a purple robe identical to Humbert's; when the two wrestle each other to the ground for control of Humbert's gun, their identities are confused, then conflated as Nabokov deliberately plays with pronouns: "He was naked and goatish under his robe, and I felt suffocated as he rolled over me. I rolled over him. We rolled over me. They rolled over him. We rolled over us" (299).

Based on these and other passages, many critics understand Quilty to be Humbert's even more unscrupulous doppelgänger. A pedophile without any of Humbert's belated misgivings, he outdoes Humbert by trying to involve Lolita in child pornography. Nor does he take care of her in the way Humbert does when, for better or for worse, he assumes the role of her guardian: "It was all drink and drugs [with Quilty]. And, of course, he was a complete freak in sex matters," Lolita explains (276). This information simply floors Humbert, who relishes the feeling of holding Quilty at gunpoint. "To have him trapped, after those years of repentance and rage . . . to know that this semi-animated, subhuman trickster who had sodomized my darling—oh, my darling, this was intolerable bliss!" he cries in a most hypocritical judgment. Humbert seems to have channeled all of his self-loathing onto Quilty, who—as a selfish, sex-crazed child molester—embodies Humbert's own worst qualities.

This reading would explain the uncanny coincidence of Humbert and Quilty's thoughts and behavior, but it yields problematic consequences for other aspects of the novel's plot. If Quilty doesn't exist per se—if he is an extension of Humbert's warped psyche, perhaps a mechanism through whom Humbert copes with his crimes against Lolita—then how are we to understand the frame narrative in which Humbert has landed himself in jail for Quilty's murder? Is the entire frame, too, an elaborate figment of Humbert's imagination? One critic speculates that Humbert never committed murder and is serving time instead for statutory rape and transporting a minor across state lines (Tekiner 1979, 468). Yet even the prison library's *Who's Who in the Limelight* features an entry on none other than Clare Quilty (Nabokov [1955] 1997, 31). Is this too a delusion or fabrication, or is Clare Quilty a bona fide playwright upon whom Humbert has projected his own pedophilia and duplicity? The question of how far we may reasonably extend Humbert's unreliability is a slippery slope that quickly threatens to unravel the entire novel. If Quilty doesn't exist, and if the record of Quilty in the prison library is also a projection of Humbert's mind, then the same might be said for the prison itself, and for Humbert's crimes, his identity, John Ray's preface, and so on.[6]

Quilty is only one of many nodes that will cause Humbert's entire edifice to collapse if we lean on it too heavily. As Sternlieb has argued, Nabokov "overturns the most basic of novelistic conventions" when he defies us to distinguish between one character and another or between character and author: "By turns he makes it virtually impossible to distinguish between Vivian and Quilty, Quilty and Humbert, Humbert and John Ray, Jr., Annabel and Lolita, Lolita and Charlotte, and himself and Vivian Darkbloom" (2008, 161). This blurring of characters and narrative levels renders the plot of *Lolita* more fluid and amorphous than critics have typically suggested. Humbert is so enamored with his own wordplay, the "palliative of articulate art," that one is hard pressed to imagine what the events of this novel would look like apart from his stylish narration—and his endless attempts at self-exculpation (283). In a final, desperate validation of his behavior, Humbert claims that he still loves Lolita, now seventeen, pregnant, and far beyond her prime as a "nymphet." "I insist the world know," he declares on record, "how much I loved my Lolita, *this* Lolita, pale and polluted, and big with another's child, but still gray-eyed, sooty-lashed, still auburn and almond, still Carmencita, still mine" (278). In the end, even Humbert cannot reliably divorce his own perception from his rationalizations—and neither can we.

We may never wrangle a plot from *Lolita*, which instead delivers a multivalent portrait of a character-narrator who suffers from a debilitating case of solipsism. Azar Nafisi argues in her memoir *Reading Lolita in Tehran* (2003) that "Humbert was a villain because he lacked curiosity about other people and their lives, even about the person he loved most, Lolita. Humbert, like most dictators, was interested only in his own vision of other people" (48–49). Indeed, Humbert's worldview—like those of Browning's dramatis personae—is a reflection of his innermost desires (Lolita as willing "nymphet") and fears (Quilty as her unsavory predator). *Lolita*'s ambiguous ontology makes it difficult to discern whether Humbert is guilty of murder, or rape, or neither; but his egocentric narrative indicates that he is certainly guilty, as Nafisi suggests, of blotting out others.

Bret Easton Ellis's *American Psycho* (1991) joins *Lolita* as a novel whose unreliable character-narrator generated a firestorm of controversy that caused some hiccups in its initial publication. Simon and Schuster dropped the novel after several of its most violent and misogynistic passages were leaked to the press, appearing alongside editorials "decrying the decision to publish the book" (Freccero 1997, 48). Within days, the novel was picked up by Random House, and the controversy surrounding Ellis's depiction of Patrick Bateman—a remorseless serial rapist and murderer—raged on. Tammy Bruce, the head of the Los Angeles chapter of the National Organization of Women, famously called for a nationwide boycott of Random House, summarizing the novel as "a how-to manual on the torture and dismemberment of women" (quoted in Freccero 1997, 50). To emphasize her point, she chose an illustrative excerpt from the novel that played on loop over the NOW chapter's phone line.

In too readily conflating the values of Bateman with those of the author (and then with those of the publisher), Bruce fails to recognize the markers of unreliability that generate the novel's satire of the disaffected, materialistic, heteromasculine culture of Manhattan's Wall Street financiers in the late 1980s. In fact, she provides precisely the kind of naively literal reading against which the novel is pushing. As C. Namwali Serpell (2010) has argued, however, critics have tended to overcompensate for this reading by amplifying the text's postmodernist elements, including its fixation on consumer name brands and other simulacra as well as Bateman's own gestures toward self-erasure.[7] Elizabeth Young, one of the novel's pioneering scholars, characterized the narrator as a "void. He is the abyss. He is a textual impossibility, written out, elided until there is no 'Patrick' " (1992, 119). "His psyche is nonexistent," concurs Mark Storey. "Instead, Ellis gives us a central identity created by external forces, a fictional world encased in the language of the society that created it and told through the voice of a man who in real terms is not actually there" (2005, 58). The cornerstone for these postmodernist readings is Bateman's assertion in a particularly hazy passage that "there is no real me, only an entity, something illusory. . . . *I simply am not there*" (Ellis 1991, 376–77). Yet Bateman's declaration, as Serpell points out, "is an ontological impossibility: a speaking 'I' is necessarily somewhere" (2010, 50). In what follows, I attempt to bridge the two poles of this critical debate—the murders occurred and Bateman is a threat, the murders never occurred and Bateman is "not there"—by reading Bateman's unreliability in the context of Browning's dramatic personae.[8] *American Psycho* presents a richly layered portrayal of a character-narrator who, beneath his suave veneer of power and control, is incredibly self-conscious: a cross between the Duke of Ferrara and Porphyria's lover, Bateman is both "there" and "not there" as he attempts to conceal his frailties beneath the persona of a brazen criminal madman. Unlike these monologues, however, Ellis's novel includes a wide cast of minor characters whose opinions of Bateman differ markedly from Bateman's self-presentation. Much as the Duke's and the lover's accounts of fickle women include litotes, exaggerations, and unconfirmed suspicions that cast doubt on their reliability, so the reactions of Bateman's lovers, colleagues, and acquaintances cast doubt on his. A closer examination of these minor characters will help us to better parse the nature of Bateman's unreliability and its consequences for *American Psycho*'s plot.

Though Bateman's identity is ultimately far less stable than Humbert's, he too presents himself as a raconteur who is in complete control of his narrative—and, by extension, of the life he narrates. Materialistic, vain, obsessive, and pedantic, he overwhelms readers with the tedious particulars of his beauty regimen, gym routine, and strategies for coordinating his suits with his shirts, ties, vests, and socks. Other characters are introduced according to their clothing and accessories, which Bateman assesses carefully as a reflection of their worth. He itemizes the meals they order at expensive restaurants and peppers his narrative with authoritative music reviews of dated rock bands.[9] He never fails to tell us who was featured on the *Patty Winters Show* each morning, a tic that becomes an index for his mounting unreliability. ("On *The Patty Winters Show* this morning," he claims at the end of the novel, "a Cheerio sat in a very small chair and was interviewed for close to an hour" [386].) Even before the murders, Bateman's self-presentation should arouse suspicion, since he catalogs things that seem superficial or irrelevant to most readers while neglecting to report on things that seem important. His descriptions of clothing become surrogates or placeholders for his relationships with other characters. In a very brief and potentially tender scene in which Bateman visits his mother in a sanitarium, for example, Bateman reveals virtually nothing about their relationship: "I don't say anything. I've spent the last hour studying my hair in the mirror I've insisted the hospital keep in my mother's room. . . . She sits on her bed in a nightgown from Bergdorf's and slippers by Norma Kamali that I bought her for Christmas last year" (366). Even his job gets surprisingly short shrift in this novel of careerist social climbing. We never witness Bateman actually working in his office—here he is, assigning trivial tasks to Jean; there he is, lifting weights; and there he is again, completing crossword puzzles, listening to his Walkman, and reading *Sports Illustrated*.

Gradually, Bateman reveals his murderous tendencies to readers who may have been lulled into complacency by his giant compendiums of name-brand clothing and his mind-numbingly superficial conversations with colleagues.[10] Initially, his sado-sexual fantasies are buried casually in subordinate clauses, such as his disclosure that he "rerent[ed] *Body Double* because I want to watch it again tonight even though I know I won't have enough time to masturbate over the scene where the woman is getting drilled to death by a power drill since I have a date with Courtney at seven-thirty at Café Luxembourg" (69). Violent anticipations soon give way to confusing flashbacks, also casually obscured by their subordinate position in his statements: "Anne Smiley and I share a mutual acquaintance, a waitress from Abetone's in Aspen who I raped with a can of hairspray last Christmas" (94) Ultimately, these violent flashbacks extend all the way back to Bateman's days at Harvard: "A young girl, a freshman, I met in a bar in Cambridge my junior year at Harvard told me early one fall that 'Life is full of endless possibilities.' I tried valiantly not to choke on the beer nuts I was chewing. . . . Needless to say, she did not live to see her sophomore year. That winter, her body was found floating in the Charles River, decapitated, her head hung from a tree on the bank" (241). His sexual perversities reach back farther still. Retreating to his "own private maze" of thoughts while dining with Evelyn, he recalls "the Christmas Eve when I was fourteen and had raped one of our maids" (342).

These flashbacks reinforce the violence Bateman commits in the novel's present-tense narration by establishing a history of psychosis for this character-narrator. The present-tense murders betray the ethical and emotional unreliability that lurks beneath his tightly controlled narration, but they also reveal more about Bateman's character by betraying his deepest anxieties. The first fatality—Bateman's senseless maiming and torture of a black homeless man with whom he becomes frustrated because they "don't have anything in common" (131)—is predictable enough, since he is a symbolic victim of the same capitalist market of which Bateman and his cronies are beneficiaries. The latter have spent much of the novel taunting the homeless, offering bills only to withdraw them as they leave exclusive, five-star restaurants. Bateman shames his murder victim into believing his destitution is his own fault: "'Get a goddamn job, Al,' I say earnestly. 'You've got a negative attitude. That's what's stopping you. You've got to get your act together'" (130). To complete the execution, Bateman must convince both himself and his victim that the life he is about to take is worthless. The homeless, as Bateman understands them, are naturally unfit "member[s] of the genetic underclass" (266). The same principle governs his execution of prostitutes Christie, Torri, and Tiffany: uneducated and unrefined, they are dispensable largely because they are totally uninterested in the materialistic accoutrements that Bateman typically uses to impress women.

Other executions, however, indicate the fragility of Bateman's sense of superiority, which appears to falter whenever he senses a competitor. He kills what he thinks to be a Japanese delivery boy following Charles Murphy's invective against the growing threat of Japanese economic supremacy. When Murphy asserts that the Japanese have purchased both the Empire State Building and a popular nightclub in Manhattan called Nell's—"*Nell's*, can you believe it, Bateman?"—Bateman reveals that the tirade "moves something in me, it sets something off" (180). The delivery boy is in fact Chinese, but Bateman's violent overreaction to a perceived threat begins a thread that ties together a number of subsequent killings. He beats a "blond hardbody" nearly to the point of decapitation because the only music she listens to is gangster rap, the antithesis of the yuppie lifestyle Bateman has cultivated for himself. ("Haunted" by her taste in music, he buys "ninety dollars' worth of rap CDs but, as expected, I'm at a loss: niggerish voices uttering ugly words like *digit*, *pudding*, *chunk*" [256].) He also murders a rival mergers and acquisitions financier named Paul Owen who has landed the coveted "Fisher account." Paul Owen's success indirectly points to Bateman's failings as a Wall Street yuppie. Though they are the same age, Owen has the personal driver, the nicer apartment, and the disposable income to buy his girlfriend a diamond necklace from Tiffany's (mistakenly taken by Evelyn to be Bateman's gift to her). Consumed by envy, Bateman becomes obsessed with Owen, even asking Jean to start a file on Owen's Fisher account; Owen, for his part, cannot even remember Bateman's name. Thus, each victim seems to illuminate something about Bateman's most deep-seated insecurities.[11]

The murder victim who reveals the most about Bateman's character—the other dimension of Bateman that lurks beneath the suave exterior—is Bethany, the college sweetheart who knew him before he was a Wall Street big shot. His behavior around Bethany is markedly different from the persona he has created for himself and for readers. "Extremely nervous" to see her again, Bateman becomes suddenly uncertain about his looks, obsessively worried over the new mousse he has decided to use in his hair: "Since I last saw my hair, seconds ago, it feels different, as if its shape was somehow altered on the walk from bar to table" (231). Seated across from Bethany, he finds himself trembling and twitching uncontrollably. "Calm down," she pleads, covering one of his hands with her own. "You look like a wild man" (232). He babbles uncontrollably, uttering disjointed thoughts in nervous fragments as Bethany listens in worried silence. His leg jerks uncontrollably, shaking the table. This is not the smooth-talking, smugly self-assured Bateman with whom readers have become familiar. Bethany's ability to see through Bateman—a skill that amounts to a death sentence—makes him feel vulnerable. In a rare moment of honesty, Bateman confesses to Bethany that he hates his job, though he cannot bring himself to quit because of his true objective: "I . . . want . . . to . . . fit . . . in," he admits.

Bateman's admission prompts us to recast his egotism as a series of pathetic attempts to assimilate to the Wall Street crowd. After all, he and his colleagues dress exactly alike, donning similar double-breasted suits, silk ties, slicked-back hair, suspenders, and horn-rimmed glasses; they are all recreational coke users; they all seem to have the new Talking Heads album. Superficially, they are totally interchangeable, which is why Paul Owen mistakes Bateman for one of his colleagues, Marcus Halberstam. "It seems like a logical faux pas," Bateman concedes, "since Marcus works at P & P also, in fact does the same exact thing I do, and he also has a penchant for Valentino suits and clear prescription glasses and we share the same barber at the same place, the Pierre Hotel" (89).[12] Nor is this the only instance in which Bateman is mistaken for one of his many yuppie doubles. Harold Carnes misidentifies him as "Davis" and inadvertently reveals what he really thinks about Bateman. "Your joke *was* amusing," he tells Bateman, referring to his confession, on Carnes's voicemail, of the murders he has committed. "But come on, man, you had one fatal flaw: Bateman's such a bloody ass-kisser, such a brown-nosing goody-goody, that I couldn't fully appreciate it. . . . Why else would Evelyn Richards dump him? You know, really. He would barely *pick up* an escort girl, let alone . . . what was it you said he did to her? . . . Oh yes, 'chop her up'" (387–88).

Carnes—like Bethany—depicts a version of Bateman that runs counter to the self-image Bateman has been cultivating with tedious care. A far cry from the polished Casanova who moonlights as a serial killer, Carnes's Bateman is groveling, obsequious, and laughably clumsy around women. Carnes also contradicts Bateman's insistence that he ended the relationship with Evelyn by sending "a small box of flies along with a note, typed by Jean, saying that I never, ever wanted to see her face again and, though she doesn't really need one, to go on a fucking diet" (382–83). This startling discrepancy between Carnes's perception of Bateman and Bateman's perception of himself overturns everything we thought we knew about this character-narrator. In a final turn of the screw, Carnes offers one more piece of evidence that undermines Bateman's credibility: Bateman couldn't have killed Paul Owen because Carnes "had . . . dinner . . . with Paul Owen . . . twice . . . in London . . . *just ten days ago*" (388, ellipses and italics original).

Carnes's revelation, if it is to be believed,[13] casts doubt on whether Bateman committed *any* of the murders he narrates. This thesis that Bateman merely hallucinates or fantasizes about these killings has its fair share of textual support, though behind every piece of evidence lurks another piece that seems to corroborate the murders. In the chapter "Dry Cleaners," for instance, Bateman harangues the Chinese owners of a dry cleaning business he patronizes because they have failed to remove the blood splatters from his laundered sheets. While one owner yells back in her native tongue, the other takes the sheets and "stares at them dumbly" as if he sees nothing there at all (82). The episode is interrupted by an appearance from Bateman's acquaintance, who looks closely at the stains that Bateman has been describing. "'Oh my, I see,' she murmurs. . . . 'What *are* those?'" (84). Are there or aren't there bloodstains on the sheets—or are the sheets, as Bateman tells his acquaintance, discolored by red wine? Similarly, when Bateman visits Paul Owen's apartment "one hundred and sixty-one days" after killing and mutilating two prostitutes there, he discovers that the apartment is now on the market, the previously blood-soaked furniture "spotless" and "intact" without any trace of foul play (366, 368). Has Bateman lost his mind—or is the real estate agent willing to conceal a crime scene to sell a lucrative piece of property? ("*How much is Owen's apartment worth?*" Bateman muses [367–68].) The novel is peppered with these ambiguities and double entendres, including Bateman's murderous dialogue, which often goes unheard by the novel's other characters. Bateman confesses to a new acquaintance that he works in "murders and executions"; hearing "mergers and acquisitions," she asks, "Do you like it?" (206). Is Bateman's dialogue misunderstood—or does it remain unspoken, except in Bateman's own tormented mind?

Carnes's testimony about Paul Owen opens up broader questions about the novel's ontology, since it was Bateman—and not Ellis—who decided to "send the bastard to England" while inventing a story to conceal the murder (218). Is it sheer coincidence that Owen (or an Owen lookalike) was actually seen in London? Or does Ellis—like Nabokov—allow Bateman to share in his author-function here? Perhaps Owen is *American Psycho*'s version of Clare Quilty, a ubiquitous presence who may be a personified projection of the narrator's anxieties. If so, then the ontological groundwork for this novel unravels in an equally chaotic fashion: which characters and events are "real," and which are manufactured by Bateman?

Bateman himself seems unsure, since—unlike Humbert—he repeatedly questions his grip on reality. Frequently complaining of tension, he even narrates "a major league anxiety attack" in a chapter titled "A Glimpse of a Thursday Afternoon," the indefinite article of which implies an iterative event that may be a regular occurrence for Bateman (148). Bateman is frantic in this section, which is almost devoid of punctuation; in fact, the chapter ends abruptly when Bateman trails off without completing his sentence. To avoid these panics, he increasingly relies on dangerous cocktails of liquor, pain relievers, and antianxiety pills, and his experience begins to verge on the surreal: as he asserts variously that "I find myself dreaming while still awake" (86), "I think I'm losing it" (214), "I'm really dreaming all this" (231), and "I was simply imitating reality, a rough resemblance of a human being, with only a dim corner of my mind functioning" (282). Eventually, his erratic behavior is no longer confined to the murders he purports to commit. "There's no use in denying it: this has been a bad week," he reports near the end of the novel. "I've started drinking my own urine. I laugh spontaneously at nothing. Sometimes I sleep under my futon. I'm flossing my teeth constantly until my gums are aching and my mouth tastes like blood" (382). In the closing pages, he attributes malicious intent to inanimate objects: "My automated teller has started *speaking* to me, sometimes actually leaving weird messages on the screen, in green lettering, like 'Cause a terrible scene at Sotheby's' or 'Kill the President' or 'Feed Me a Stray Cat,' and I was freaked out by the park bench that followed me for six blocks last Monday evening and it too spoke to me. Disintegration—I'm taking it in stride" (395–96).

What really happens in *American Psycho*? And who is Patrick Bateman? These are not easy questions to answer because of the way Ellis has interlaced plot with character psychology. Reading the narrator in terms of plot—understanding Bateman in light of the murders—yields a novel chronicling the exploits of a misogynistic serial killer. When we read plot in terms of the narrator, however—understanding the murders in light of Bateman—these crimes become projections of a warped mind, a fantasy of power and control hallucinated by a character who feels he has none. Ellis, like James, undermines plot by suspending us between these two possibilities, but he also undermines character by presenting us with two Patrick Batemans. Which is the "real" Bateman—the homicidal Casanova or the nervous wreck? Ellis makes it impossible for us to decide, which is another reason why the naively feminist reading of *American Psycho* falls flat. The misogyny of Bateman the "homicidal Casanova" may be animated, after all, by the repressed homosexuality of Bateman the "nervous wreck," a reading I will develop here to demonstrate the complexities of Bateman's bifurcated personality.

Heavily stigmatized in the 1980s through the emergence and rapid spread of the AIDS virus, homosexuality haunts Bateman's interactions with women and with his colleagues. Erroneous rumors about the transmission of AIDS circulate in the early pages of *American Psycho*. Tim Price relays a popular "theory out there now" whereby "if you can catch the AIDS virus through having *sex* with someone who *is* infected then you can also catch *any*thing, whether it's a virus per se or not—Alzheimer's, muscular dystrophy, hemophilia, leukemia, anorexia, diabetes," and even "dyslexia, for Christ sakes" (5). David Van Patten relays an erroneous article stating that men are essentially not at risk: "Our chances of catching [AIDS] are like zero zero zero zero point half a decimal percentage or something, and this no matter what kind of scumbag, slutbucket, horndog chick we end up boffing," he reassures the other men (34). Though Bateman's male circle of friends feigns a smug sense of security, the women in the novel are openly paranoid. McDermott complains that a "Vassar girl" refused to have intercourse at all for fear of AIDS: "She would only give me a hand-job, and get this . . . she kept her *glove* on" (34). In wondering why Tim Price has suddenly disappeared—"rehab," Bateman speculates—Evelyn begins to panic: "'You don't think it's'—and she looks around the restaurant before leaning in, whispering—'AIDS?'" (120). Their fears are aggravated by the fact that none of these men use prophylactics. Courtney forces Bateman to wear protection during intercourse, but he demonstrates his unfamiliarity with condoms when Courtney scolds him for failing to leave a "receptacle tip," or space for his ejaculation (103).

Bateman appears to distance himself from the stigma of homosexuality by consistently referring to other gay men as "faggots" and singing the praises of reproductive sex: "'Well, my theory's always been,' I start, 'men are only here to procreate, to carry on the species, you know?'" (91). Not surprisingly, Bateman's "theory" runs totally counter to his practice. As he drops a reluctant Jeanette off at an abortion clinic, he boasts, "This is, I think, the fifth child I've had aborted, the third I haven't aborted myself" (381). Despite his many protestations of heterosexuality—and here again, the narrator doth protest too much—he seems to attract the attention of nearly every gay man he encounters. At the gym, he rather revels in the idea that he is being studied: "Already some faggot is behind me, probably checking out my back, ass, leg muscles" (68). While checking his messages in a phone booth, "a couple of skinny faggots walk by . . . one of them whistles at me, the other laughs: a high, fey, horrible sound" (128). Standing alongside a gay pride parade, he "began to receive fey catcalls from aging, overmuscled beachboys with walruslike mustaches" (139). A waiter at a restaurant playfully "bats his eyelashes" while taking down his order (215). A department store worker "flirts and asks if I'm a model" (179). He describes Evelyn's masseur as "some scary faggot who lived down the road with a famous book publisher and who flirted openly with me" (281). For someone who avers to be staunchly heterosexual, Bateman, inadvertently or not, seems to regularly invite homosexual advances.

At times, he even flirts back. He stops and chats with a man who gives him "the once-over with a quizzical smile" as he walks his shar-pei (164). Bateman "grin[s] boyishly" at the man, who playfully corrects his pronunciation of the dog's breed. Predictably, Bateman ends this flirtatious episode by killing both the dog and its owner, but other encounters yield very different endings. Seated front and center at a U2 concert, Bateman becomes convinced that he and Bono have made some sort of singular connection, that "we share a bond"; the rest of the band and crowd seem to fade away as Bono conveys a message tailored exclusively for Bateman, whose response is intensely erotic: "I'm nodding back, everything getting clearer, my body alive and burning, on fire. . . . I'm left tingling, my face flushed, an aching erection pulsing against my thigh" (147). Bateman's most intense homosexual encounter occurs with his colleague Luis Carruthers in the men's bathroom of a restaurant. As Bateman turns to strangle Carruthers to death, Carruthers misreads his body language as a sexual advance, and responds with tender eagerness. "'God, Patrick,' he whispers. 'Why *here*?'" (159). Bateman is "paralyzed"—with shock, fear, or pleasure?—and finds that he can't strangle Luis after all: "I *can't* do it, my hands *won't* tighten, and my arms, still stretched out, look ludicrous and useless in their fixed position" (159). Luis insists that his feeling is mutual. "I've seen you looking at me," he tells Bateman in the bathroom; during a later encounter in a department store, he insists, "Just because you won't admit . . . certain feelings you have doesn't mean you don't have them. . . . I know you feel the same way I do" (293). If Luis is wrong, then why is Bateman, a self-professed serial killer, suddenly incapable of murder?

Even Bateman's heterosexual practices point to queer desire. He is incapable of sustaining an erection during intercourse, as Courtney appears to suggest: "'I want to fuck you again,' I tell her, 'but I don't want to wear a condom because I don't feel anything,' and she says calmly, taking her mouth off my limp shrunken dick, glaring at me, 'If you don't use one you're not going to feel anything anyway'" (105). Instead, Bateman's desires revolve around anal play and fellatio. One of his favorite porno flicks, *Inside Lydia's Ass*, features a woman who is anally penetrated by a vibrator while a man with a "huge cock" ejaculates on her face (97–98). He becomes erect when Sabrina sniffs Christie's asshole, upon his request (173); his orgasm with Christie is prolonged when Sabrina sticks her tongue in his rectum (176). There is even a strong homoerotic element in Bateman's misogynistic torture scenes. Twice—once with Bethany, and again with Torri—he brings himself to climax by manipulating their bloody mouths around his penis (Bethany is tongueless, Torri decapitated) in a grisly parody of fellatio. In a similar parody of anal penetration, he nails a dildo that he's "tied to a board" into Tiffany's rectum using a nail gun (305). Read this way, Bateman's violence toward women, horrific as it may be, becomes a dark caricature of his own closeted desires.

We may only speculate on Bateman's sexual hang-ups, as with any other aspect of his personality; this unreliable narrator remains so deluded about his own identity that it is impossible to locate the "true" Bateman apart from the persona he has created. Bateman's instability, like that of Porphyria's lover, challenges readers to reevaluate his narrative in light of these and other insecurities. As James R. Giles has argued, "The essential ambiguity of Bateman's murders leaves open at least three possible readings: all of the murders . . . actually occur, Bateman killed some limited number of people and has fantasized the rest . . . or all of the murders are sheer fantasy" (2006, 171). Because he provides textual support for all three possibilities, Ellis suggests that plot is ancillary to the development—and unraveling—of Bateman's dramatic persona. The events of *American Psycho*, real or imagined, become figurative markers of this character-narrator's aspirations to become the powerful persona he inhabits when he suppresses Bateman the nervous wreck to channel Bateman the homicidal Casanova.

If Ellis presents an unreliable narrator who is figuratively bifurcated, Chuck Palahniuk ventures even farther by physically splitting his into two separate characters. *Fight Club* (1996) chronicles the development of an anarchic organization called Project Mayhem, which is formed and implemented by the narrator and his fearless new "friend," Tyler Durden. Tired of feeling demeaned and exploited in low-level, low-paying jobs, Tyler begins to rebel through small acts of sabotage: splicing children's movies with frames of giant erections, urinating in the soup he delivers to a guest's hotel room. Eventually, he and the narrator form Fight Club, where men meet in secret to exchange blows in a cathartic exercise of violence that offsets their otherwise unfulfilling lives. As Tyler attracts followers (dubbed "space monkeys"), the enterprise escalates into an anarcho-terrorist group that bombs buildings, castrates city officials, and eventually commits murder. As the organization's violence reaches its peak, the narrator discovers that he has a split personality and that Tyler is merely a persona he has created to cultivate a more aggressive and authoritative version of himself. One character has been parading as two; what appears to be a dialogic narrative has been monologic all along.

Palahniuk introduces more of a twist here than what we have seen in the novels of James, Nabokov, and Ellis, offering no discernible clues that Tyler and the narrator are the same character until the narrator is suddenly confronted with the news toward the end of the novel, first by a bartender, then by his girlfriend Marla, and finally by Tyler himself. The narrator's self-diagnosed insomnia may cause readers to question his reliability—"Three weeks without sleep, and everything becomes an out-of-body experience," he confesses (19)—but only a retrospective reading will unearth those details that suggest his split personality. "I know this because Tyler knows this," he is fond of saying after he rehearses a fact, though this phrase appears to suggest codependence more than coidentity (12). A number of similarly cryptic statements take on new meanings. "Tyler had been around a long time before we met," he writes at one point. "I had to know what Tyler was doing while I was asleep. If I could wake up in a different place, at a different time, could I wake up as a different person?" (32–33). "I did this to myself," he insists with ironic truth when he appears at work with a swollen face, bruised and battered after a fistfight with Tyler (48). Like Nabokov's wordplay, these utterances demand a retrospective reading, since we cannot appreciate their double entendres until we learn the narrator's true relationship to Tyler Durden.

The narrator's surprise revelation manipulates ontology in a way that distinguishes it from the novels of James, Nabokov, and Ellis. In short, it violates our most basic notions of character and characterization by disguising one person as two. The concept of character in the twentieth-century novel has been largely shaped by E. M. Forster's distinction between "round" and "flat" characters. Both types, he argued, are necessary for all serious fiction, and each has its virtue, but characters that are thoroughly fleshed out are more dynamic and human-like because of their complexity ([1927] 2005). Like any human being, rounded characters carry with them some measure of unpredictability that keeps readers guessing: "The test of a round character," he maintained, "is whether it is capable of surprising in a convincing way" (41). Contemporary narrative theorists have built on Forster's understanding of fictional characters by emphasizing the rounded or mimetic qualities that cause them to resemble actual people; indeed, readers of the novel have come to expect some measure of growth or change from its characters as a narrative progresses.[14] On the other hand, characters must also display personalities that, as Mieke Bal puts it, "make psychological and ideological descriptions possible" (1997, 115). That is, they must remain static enough to render themselves legible to readers. Terry Eagleton reminds us that the concept of character "derives from an ancient Greek term meaning a stamping tool which makes a distinctive mark" (2013, 48). Hence, people—real or fictional—who deviate from this mark are said to behave "out of character."

Fight Club's narrator surprises us in a way that undermines rather than develops or "rounds" his character. By collapsing himself into Tyler Durden—or rather, by showing that the differences between these characters were only illusory—he forces us to reconcile two contrary sets of character traits that even he cannot properly parse. By day, he is a drone who is a little too attached to his effeminately adorned apartment and who works unhappily as a "recall campaign coordinator," conducting cost-benefit analyses that consider whether the lawsuits that accompany a product malfunction would exceed the cost of a recall. By night, he is Tyler, hypermasculine, assertive, aggressive, and fearless; Tyler gets what he wants, tells people what he really thinks, and even succeeds in bedding Marla. The narrator longs for the sweet release of death, wishing for a crash every time his airplane lands; Tyler yearns for life. The narrator is the ego and Tyler is the id. The narrator is weak and Tyler is strong. The narrator abides by the law and is generally "good"; Tyler is a wild-card anarchist who is unconcerned with moral consequences. On its face, *Fight Club* is an updated version of Robert Louis Stevenson's *Dr. Jekyll and Mr. Hyde*, in which a scientist bifurcates his personality to indulge his darkest desires while preserving his reputation in Victorian high society.

This artificial bifurcation, however, is not as neat as the narrator would have us believe: there are elements of Tyler in the narrator and vice versa. The narrator, for example, exhibits dark tendencies that help pave the way for Tyler's anarchic violence. He spends the early part of the novel haunting various support groups, exploiting the ailments and tragedies of others so that he can have a safe space in which to exercise his otherwise repressed emotions. "We work so hard all the time. This is the only place I ever really relax and give up," he narrates as he cries on the shoulder of a testicular cancer patient (18). He justifies these incursions into the lives of the terminally ill by callously equating their physical pain with his own existential suffering: "On a long enough time line, the survival rate for everyone will drop to zero" (17). Conversely, the platform for Project Mayhem reveals Tyler's surprising soft spot for humanity. Both Fight Club and Project Mayhem are designed to empower the everyday "Joe on the street" (119): "'What we have to do, people,' Tyler told the committee, 'is remind these guys what kind of power they still have'" (120). Tyler's projects have democratizing aims that grant importance to those individuals—service industry drones, blue collar workers—who are lost and ignored in the current system. Project Mayhem's goal may be "the complete and right-away destruction of civilization," but toward an end that is actually utopian: "It's Project Mayhem that's going to save the world. . . . Like fight club does with clerks and box boys, Project Mayhem will break up civilization so we can make something better out of the world" (125).

Subsequently, the division between the good narrator and bad Tyler is a bit messy, though it serves a number of purposes for this unreliable narrator. Tyler provides the narrator with an opportunity to reinvent himself. "From the first night I met her, Tyler or some part of me had needed a way to be with Marla," he confesses. Inspired, he creates a better version of himself through his alternate persona: "I love everything about Tyler Durden, his courage and his smarts. His nerve. Tyler is funny and charming and forceful and independent, and men look up to him and expect him to change their world. Tyler is capable and free, and I am not" (174). Tyler also, however, serves another important function: he allows the narrator to avoid culpability for his actions. "Tyler does this," the narrator insists after splicing the erection into the children's film (30). "It wasn't me. It was Tyler," he maintains again when Marla discovers that he's stolen her "collagen trust fund"—fat rendered and saved from her mother's liposuction surgeries—and turned it into soap, the proceeds of which will fund Project Mayhem (93, 91). As the narrator finds himself blackmailing the manager of the Pressman Hotel, he is shocked by his own brazenness, which he once again attributes to Tyler: "Tyler's words coming out of my mouth. And I used to be such a nice person" (114).

In fact, the narrator continues to play the blame game even *after* he is confronted with the truth about his split personality. He uses Tyler as a device for parsing his mixed feelings, for example, upon discovering that he has planted an explosive in his office computer, killing his boss. "The problem is, I sort of liked my boss. If you're white and Christian and living in America, your father is your model for God. And sometimes you find your father in your career. Except Tyler didn't like my boss" (186). When Marla informs the narrator that he has embarked on another violent rampage while sleepwalking as Tyler—"You shot the mayor's special envoy on recycling!" she yells—the narrator continues to evade responsibility, silently correcting her with some measure of flippancy: "Tyler shot the mayor's special envoy on whatever" (196).

The narrator simply refuses to deal with the moral consequences of his discovery that he is Tyler Durden, but more importantly for our purposes, he also fails to deal with its ontological consequences when he continues not only to inhabit Tyler but also to hallucinate him. The novel begins and ends with a climactic scene in which Tyler presses a gun to the narrator's throat. Tyler disappears as Marla enters, and the narrator stands holding a gun in his own mouth. "I'm not killing myself," he tries to reassure her. "I'm killing Tyler" (205). Because the narrator never really seems to accept the reality of his split personality—that he and Tyler are one person; that he (and not Tyler) loves Marla; that Marla loves him; and that he is responsible for the destruction, violence, and murder that has been wreaked in Tyler's name—he remains unreliable even after his revelation.

Unlike *Dr. Jekyll and Mr. Hyde*, which unfolds chiefly through a third-person narrative focalized through a lawyer named Gabriel Utterson, *Fight Club* unfolds through a first-person narrator whose unreliability poses another potentially infinite regress of ontological uncertainties. Some critics consider Tyler's "space monkeys" to be part of his delusion. Paul Kennett maintains that "the space monkeys also represent a split of the Narrator's subjectivity—they encapsulate the part of the Narrator that is debased and abused by his boss, who is represented by Tyler. . . . [The] characters involved in Project Mayhem may be considered as projections of the Narrator's fragmented self" (2005, 57). Kathryn Hume extends the narrator's unreliability farther still. "Because of his mental problems," she argues, "we cannot be sure about anything he says. Tyler's many monk-like acolytes, for instance, may just be his hallucinations. Or they may be real, in which case the fictional world is in trouble, because these followers happily throw off previous obligations and rules and luxuriate in physically assaulting others who still live by those rules" (2011, 147). As Hume suggests, the magnitude of the narrator's delusion may compromise the integrity of Palahniuk's entire fictional world. "Everybody in Project Mayhem is part of Tyler Durden, and vice versa," the narrator asserts (155). Is Project Mayhem itself then also just part of Tyler Durden's psyche? What about Marla—does she exist? The ontological contours of the plot become cloudy once we attempt to delineate reality from the narrator's delusions. "Every once in a while," the narrator insists from a psychiatric ward on the novel's final page, "somebody brings me my lunch tray and my meds and he has a black eye or his forehead is swollen with stitches, and he says: 'We miss you Mr. Durden' " (208). Has Fight Club taken hold even in the wake of the narrator's institutionalization, or does the narrator continue to hallucinate his other persona? Because the narrator never quite comes to terms with his psychosis, Palahniuk has made it impossible for us to decide.

Deprived of stability at the level of plot, we return to the question of character. The unreliable narrators of *The Turn of the Screw, Lolita,* and *American Psycho* complicate or even block our access to plot, but they provide fascinating psychological studies of character: a frazzled governess who buckles under the twin pressures of isolation and maternal responsibility, a defensive pedophile who must justify his behavior to others, and an obsequious Wall Street banker who fantasizes about power, violence, and control. What does *Fight Club* divulge about its narrator? We are never provided with a clear picture. Tyler Durden is described in far more detail, which is why, as Palahiunk writes in his afterword, he has become such a cultural phenomenon: "Young men around the world took legal action to change their names to 'Tyler Durden' " (211). Because the narrator is characterized only in contradistinction to his alter ego, it is difficult to understand him except as a person who is conflicted about his feelings. The narrator loathes Marla, but Tyler desires her; the narrator likes his boss, but Tyler hates him; the narrator works in middle management, and Tyler works in the service industry. Both have fathers who are largely absent, and both seem discontented with their white-collar jobs, which causes them to feel powerless and emasculated. Beyond this, we learn very little, especially since the narrator refuses to reconcile his dual (and dueling) personalities. He even remains unnamed, a feature that adds to his cryptic anonymity and that separates him from other dramatic personae who are individuated with great care. The result is a peculiar character portrait of a man who, despite his first-person narration, remains as much a mystery to readers as to himself.

Fight Club—and, to a lesser degree, *American Psycho*—demands what David Richter calls "late reconfiguration" on the part of its readers (2001). Timing matters, he argues: "The closer to the denouement one places the event which causes the alternative configuration to come into focus the greater the danger of driving the gentle reader beyond the bounds of patience." The film adaptation of *Fight Club* attempts to resolve this problem by replaying scenes in which the narrator has previously inflicted violence on others but, post-revelation, is now seen inflicting it on himself. (Mary Harron uses a different approach in her adaptation of *American Psycho*; in effect, she authenticates the murders with a detective plot in which Bateman is tracked by an investigator.)[15] Audiences are most forgiving of this trick, Richter maintains, when "plot isn't the most important factor in the progression." To be sure, the kinship these novels share with the dramatic monologue reveals that they instead hinge on the elaboration of their character-narrators rather than events, which ultimately collapse under the weight of characterization. The residual frustration we may experience upon finishing *Fight Club*, then, stems not from an absence of plot but from its dissatisfying portrait of our unnamed narrator, with whom we only become intimate through his alter ego, Tyler Durden.

The novels treated in this section are frequently described as having a "surreal" quality because they suspend readers somewhere between the real and the imagined.[16] This quality is largely a function of the ontological instability introduced when a novel departs from the literal components of plot to develop the psychological complexity of an unreliable narrator. Readers must continually ask themselves whether the "reality" depicted by these narrators is merely the projection of an unstable mind. Critics have been tempted to resolve these ambiguities by creating binary readings and staking out one or the other position: Do ghosts exist, or don't they? Is Lolita a seductress, or is she a rape victim? Does Bateman commit the murders, or doesn't he? Do Fight Club and Project Mayhem exist apart from Tyler Durden, or don't they? Eager to resolve the ontological confusion these novels generate, critics and readers arrive at partial readings to lend stability to these fictional worlds. Yet these worlds are inherently unstable because of their character-narrators, whose fears and desires cause them to engage in mental acrobatics ranging from rationalizations to wish fulfillment to hallucinations and split personalities. The memorable elements of these novels, after all, are not their disappearing plots but their dramatic personae. The frazzled governess, Humbert Humbert, Patrick Bateman, and Tyler Durden have become synecdoches for the novels from which they are derived, as Ellis reminds us: "The band Limp Bizkit bannered their website with 'Dr. Tyler Durden recommends a healthy dose of Limp Bizkit' " (Palahniuk 1996, 211).

The reading strategies we deploy for dramatic personae also recall the reading strategies outlined in chapter 4. Because these quasi-surrealistic novels subordinate plot to character, we are urged—contra Todorov—toward figural rather than literal understandings of their plots. The ghosts of James's *The Turn of the Screw* become figures for the governess's fragile mental state and, perhaps, for her own abuse of Miles and Flora. Humbert's theory of nymphets and rivalry with Clare Quilty point to his struggles to rationalize his pedophilia. Patrick Bateman's killing rampage may or may not be real, but it indicates his disaffection with the yuppie, heteromasculine culture of Wall Street in the wake of his failure to "fit in." Likewise, Tyler Durden does not "exist" except as a projection of the narrator's fantasies of power and masculinity in *Fight Club*. These extremely unreliable narrators push us to filter characters, events, and other concrete staples of narrative through tropes of figuration that preserve the ambiguities that cannot be disentangled from these fictional worlds. Such figurative and character-driven understandings of plot dovetail with Monique R. Morgan's argument about the dramatic monologue in *Narrative Means, Lyric Ends* (2009). The dramatic monologue, she maintains, urges us to focus on the "revelation of character" above all else, though she also charts this revelation through the dimension of time (159). Whereas the unreliable speaker of the dramatic monologue may (or may not) remain "static," his or her witting or unwitting revelation of character to the reader is dynamic. That is, the dramatic monologue subordinates plot to characterization because it "emphasizes the act of storytelling at least as much as the story events" (163). In this sense, Morgan argues, the dramatic monologue has narrative dimensions, since—unlike "pure lyric"—this type of telling "unfolds over time" (163).

Yet lyric time is not necessarily static, as chapter 2 establishes, especially as repetitions urge us to read both forward and backward. In fact, dramatic personae demand to be read in much the same way: because we are unable to fully appreciate the degree and nature of a narrator's unreliability until we finish a novel, we are compelled, like detectives, to return to the text for clues that push us toward more figurative readings. Thus, as Morgan argues, we experience temporal progressions, though in the case of dramatic personae, the progression may paradoxically lead us backward. Like the dramatic monologues that supply their structure, these novels invite any number of readings based on their internal contradictions and ambiguities. With whom do our sympathies lie? Whom do we trust, why, and to what extent? How do we parse the ontological paradoxes presented in the text? This chapter offers its own speculative readings, but the answers to these questions will naturally vary from one reader to another, which is why these novels remain so powerful—and so controversial.

Chapter 6

Exclusive Address

"So. Now vee may perhaps to begin. Yes?" (Roth [1969] 1994, 274). Thus, the line that famously concludes *Portnoy's Complaint*, uttered by the silent analyst Doctor Spielvogel, punctuates the tortuous and otherwise unbroken monologue in which Portnoy recounts his innermost secrets, grievances, and hang-ups in embarrassing detail. Flagged by Roth as the novel's "PUNCH LINE"—the ending marking the beginning of Portnoy's counseling—the rhetorical frame of the therapy session is often cited but rarely analyzed by critics, who tend to fold it into the novel's comedy.[1] Spielvogel's dialogue, however, carries serious ethical as well as narratological implications for our understanding of the text, since it serves as a powerful reminder that Portnoy has not been directing this intimate confession at a general audience. In effect, it transforms readers into eavesdroppers, even involving us in a breach of doctor-patient confidentiality.

Readers of narrative fiction are typically invited to the text as welcome participants, a truism addressed at length by critical works including Garrett Stewart's *Dear Reader: The Conscripted Audience in Nineteenth-Century British Fiction* and James Phelan's *Narrative as Rhetoric: Technique, Audiences, Ethics, Ideology*. These studies place narrative fiction within rhetorical communication models in which authors actively engage readers through techniques that range from direct address—"gentle reader" (Stewart 1996, 8)—to subtler versions of engagement in which authors extend "a multidimensional (aesthetic, emotive, ideational, ethical, political) invitation to a reader who, in turn, seeks to do justice to the complexity of the invitation" (Phelan 1996, xi).[2] Novels such as *Portnoy's Complaint*, however, pose a special problem for these models, since they ask readers to participate in a different and more limited capacity. We are both there and not there, detected by authors but not by their narrators, who disclose sensitive or shocking material to an intimate listener under the guise of privacy. What reading strategies are recommended by texts that relegate readers to the liminal and morally awkward position of the overhearer?

This chapter examines works by novelists who have forgone the narrative model of communication for a lyrical model based on exclusive address.

In the past five decades, works as diverse as Philip Roth's *Portnoy's Complaint* (1969), Gloria Naylor's *Mama Day* (1988), Louise Erdrich's *Tracks* (1988), and Marilynne Robinson's *Gilead* (2004) have cultivated the illusion of privacy in which a character-narrator delivers delicate subject matter to a trusted, character-bound addressee. This particular constellation of contemporary American novels spans an important political timeline with regard to privacy and the law. With the exception of *Portnoy's Complaint*, published at the end of a decade known for "free love," these novels followed on the heels of the famous Supreme Court decision in *Bowers v. Hardwick* (1986) that upheld antisodomy laws criminalizing private sexual activities between consenting adults—a decision finally overturned in *Lawrence v. Texas* (2003), which established privacy as a fundamental right protected under the law with regard to consensual conduct. The relationship between privacy and consent necessarily informs these novels, in which readers are invited to "invade" the privacy of unsuspecting character-narrators—a dilemma that carries significant ethical as well as political weight in this context. To what degree are we, as readers, invited to the text in these confessional contexts; and to what degree might character-narrators be said to "consent" to our eavesdropping?

The reliance on exclusive addressees also has significant implications for our understanding of narrative fiction. Not only does it diminish the importance of plot, which is submerged under the relational dynamic between narrator and addressee, but it dramatically alters the role of the reader, who is displaced and sidelined by the presence of an intimate, albeit fictional, target audience. By examining the form and function of the exclusive direct address, this chapter traces the complex ways in which we reader-overhearers are pressed to negotiate positions for ourselves at the margins of these confessional texts. Exclusive address not only reconfigures the degree and nature of our participation in these texts, but also shapes the way we approach character-narrators who do not intend their narratives, at the intradiegetic level, for us.

The concept of the narratee—narratology's term for the person to whom the narrator directs the story—remains somewhat underdeveloped in narrative theory, which has until lately largely focused on texts and narrators.[3] Many texts, after all, do not feature discernible narratees, in the same way that texts with extradiegetic narrators do not necessarily feature discernible speakers. If the presence of a narrator is generally announced by the first-person pronoun I, the narratee is marked by the second-person pronoun you—a voice that is often used in self-help manuals and guidebooks but rarely in narrative fiction. As a result, the sudden postulation of a narratee within a work of fiction may well startle its readers ("Who, me?"). In some cases, the narratee is indeed aligned with the actual reader: Robyn Warhol has argued that Victorian women writers used the device of the narratee to address an audience directly during a time when public speaking was prohibited or unavailable to women (1989). When the narratee is sharply distinguished from the reader, however, the effect can be quite disorienting. To whom is the narrator speaking? When is the narrator relaying this story? To what extent does the narrator assume the narratee's familiarity with the fictional world she is narrating? In this sense, the introduction of an unknown narratee can work in opposition to narrative form, which typically roots itself in particularities of time, place, and character during its exposition.

To some extent, fictional narratees perform pragmatic functions: as Gerald Prince has argued, they act as mediators who "relay [information] between the narrator and the reader(s), or rather between the author and the reader(s)" ([1973] 1980, 21). That is, the narratee can provide an alternate means by which the author transmits story material to the reader. "Should certain values have to be defended or certain ambiguities clarified, this can easily be done by means of asides addressed to the narratee," he explains. Narrators who overshare under the assumption of privacy, however, complicate this disclosure function. Oblivious to authors and readers alike, these narrators extend exclusive invitations only to trusted, character-bound narratees. Subsequently, as Phelan argues, communication—especially in character narration—occurs along "two tracks": the narrator-narratee track and the narrator-reader track, in which "the narrator unwittingly reports information of all kinds to the [reader]," since "the narrator does not know that [the reader] exists" (2004, 12).

The division between these two tracks—exaggerated by the authors examined here—yields important rhetorical as well as ethical distinctions that impact our reading experience. To clarify, we might rephrase the division between narrator and narratee in terms of what sociolinguist Erving Goffman calls the "ratified participant" and the "overhearer" (1981, 131–32). Naturally, these two positions entail radically different responses, the latter of which is fairly complicated. When we inadvertently observe a private conversation, Goffman argues, we tend to "disavail ourselves" of the opportunity to eavesdrop, "practicing the situational ethic which obliges us to warn those who are, that they are, unknowingly accessible, obliging us also to enact a show of disinterest, and by disattending and withdrawing ecologically to minimize our actual access to talk" (132). This situational etiquette, he continues, arises from our instinctual urge to preserve the privacy of a conversation's ratified participants. Yet eavesdropping—or the "desire to sample, even to experience, the private lives of others" (Locke 2010, 13)—also carries an illicit appeal that may even have origins in our evolutionary history. Biolinguist John L. Locke ventures an argument that would explain and even justify our penchant for spying on our neighbors. "Eavesdropping," he maintains, "is a deeply biological trait, with ancient roots. . . . When our own species was evolving, and the modern human brain was under construction, those who knew what their associates were doing, or might do with the future, were more likely to survive to reproductive age and to pass on their genes" (16). As we began to erect social barriers, however, to better protect ourselves—literal as well as metaphorical walls—this biological impulse was gradually occluded by our conflicting desire for privacy. Consequently, it also became more difficult to satisfy: "Where casual observation had been sufficient, new and more invasive intake strategies became necessary" (17).

Hence, the natural urge to listen in and the social urge to disengage are at war in the eavesdropper, who must negotiate both the pleasures and prohibitions of overhearing messages intended for someone else. Our deeply rooted desire to pry not only compromises the privacy of the speaker but causes us to "steal" information that is not freely given. The conflict between these opposing reflexes is nicely dramatized in John Cheever's short story "The Enormous Radio" ([1953] 1979), in which a married couple find that they are able to hear the conversations of those in neighboring apartments through a glitch in their new radio. Though Irene knows that she should not listen in, she finds herself unable to turn the radio off as she overhears acquaintances and strangers unwittingly air their dirty laundry: "Everybody's been quarreling," she tells her husband. "They're all worried about money. Mrs. Hutchinson's mother is dying of cancer in Florida and they don't have enough money to send her to the Mayo Clinic. . . . And some woman in this building is having an affair with the handyman—with that hideous handyman" (39). "It's indecent," her husband chides her. "You know you don't have to listen to this sort of thing. You can turn it off." Yet Irene continues to eavesdrop, satisfying a craving that begins to color her worldview and adversely affect her relationships with others: sitting across from a friend over lunch, she "looked searchingly at her friend and wondered what her secrets were" (38).

While Cheever demonstrates the conflicted position of the overhearer at the level of plot, other authors model this conflict on more dramatic and formal levels, even involving readers in these breaches of privacy, propelling us forward at the expense of the character-narrator's privacy. In effect, they coerce us into leaving the radio on. The scenario of Portnoy's therapy session may be fictional, but our affective response is the same: we cringe when Portnoy reveals too much, yet we read on to see what more he might reveal. "We laughed and mocked and blushed," recalls Bernard Avishai about his first encounter with Roth's novel in 1969 (2012, 13). Texts that make use of the diegetic situation of the "overheard" narrator, then, demand a complicated hermeneutic response that involves some mixture of pleasure and shame: they may truly generate "guilty pleasures," since we are forced to square our compulsion to read against socially conditioned rules of privacy and propriety that would ordinarily cause us to turn away.

Fortunately, lyric poetry provides just such a model for navigating this difficult balance. The lyric has been labeled the realm of the "overheard" by critics dating back to John Stuart Mill, who likened the lyric poem to "the lament of a prisoner in a solitary cell, ourselves listening, unseen in the next" (Mill [1833] 1996, 350). Following Mill, Northrop Frye famously maintained that the lyric individuated itself from other genres through "the concealment of the poet's audience" from the speaker, who is usually "speaking to someone else: a spirit of nature, a Muse . . . a personal friend, a lover, a god, a personified abstraction, or a natural object" (1957, 249). Subsequently, he argues, the poet deliberately isolates the reader-eavesdropper from the poem's message: "The poet, so to speak, turns his back on his listeners" (250). As Jonathan Culler points out, these formulations essentially conflate the genre of the lyric with the device of the apostrophe—though not without good reason. The apostrophe, he argues—however "embarrassing" due to its "poetic pretension" (1981, 143)—is the genre's chief staple, creating an "I-Thou" drama that serves as the engine of the poem. Apostrophes may evoke a variety of subjects, some of them nonhuman, but when a lyric speaker calls upon an intimate auditor, they "imply our exclusion from the private situation between speaker and listener" (Ferry 1996: 120). Consequently, we readers must weigh our exclusion by the speaker against our inclusion by the design of the author since, as Culler points out, the apostrophe effectively conceals "the fact that a poem is a verbal composition which will be read by an audience" (135, 141).

Contrary to Mill's formulation, however, exclusive address does not attempt to obliterate the reader so much as it raises critical questions about reader response. As William Waters has argued, "The topic of the pronoun *you* and the topic of reading (what it is like to be a person reading a poem) become two sides of a single coin" (2003, 2). Thus, poems featuring a conspicuous addressee prompt readers to focus on their own positions within the complicated rhetorical context of a poem. To be sure, a poem's various subject positions—author, reader, speaker, and addressee—are fluid and amorphous, and as Waters argues, the reader may well inhabit multiple positions simultaneously: "We may, in reading, 'blur' ourselves into the addressee position even where the logic of discourse deters such identification" (47). Some poems, however, are engineered to place pressure on precisely this "blurring" of diegetic distinctions. Consider, for example, a poem such as Robert Graves's "The Reader over My Shoulder," which reinforces Mill's conception of the solitary poet by openly expressing contempt for its reader: "You, reading over my shoulder, peering beneath / My writing arm—I suddenly feel your breath / Hot on my hand or on my nape" (1977, 43). The reader is positioned here as a voyeur who interferes with the creative process. The speaker goes on to lament the "blurring" of the line between poet and reader that occurs through the process of literary analysis in which the two parties battle for control over the text: "What now, old enemy, shall you do / But quote and underline, thrusting yourself / Against me, as ambassador of myself, / In damned confusion of myself and you?" Poet and speaker are collapsed together here, as are reader and addressee, so that the poet can address the reader directly—in this case, to issue a rebuking reminder to the reader seen as a burden, even an "enemy." The poet-speaker is putting the reader in her place, so to speak—and that place is a decidedly marginal one.

"The Reader over My Shoulder"—albeit an extreme example—is one of many twentieth-century poems that reinforce rather than contest the division between poet and reader through the device of exclusive address. As Deborah Nelson (2002) has argued, confessional poetry simultaneously guarded and flaunted its private content in the oppressive atmosphere of surveillance that permeated the Cold War era; consequently, its disclosures were often framed by strategic use of intimacy. The term *confessional*, after all—coined by M. L. Rosenthal in a review of Robert Lowell's *Life Studies*—recalls the Catholic sacrament in which parishioners privately confess their sins to a priest in exchange for absolution. So exclusive is the information exchanged here that its confidentiality is protected under U.S. law by a rule of evidence called "confessional privilege," an outgrowth of the First Amendment. The same dynamic underpins physician-patient privilege, which serves as the context for *Portnoy's Complaint* ([1969] 1994) and which many confessional poets knew all too well. Both W. D. Snodgrass and his student Anne Sexton were urged by their therapists to use poetry as a means of working through their personal struggles. Exclusive direct address enhances the already deeply personal content of confessional poems by reminding us of these religious and therapeutic contexts, since they coerce readers into eavesdropping on a private revelation that is delivered to a trusted confidant.

Sharon Olds's painfully intimate "Miscarriage" from her collection *The Dead and the Living* ([1984] 2009) is a poem in the confessional tradition that makes pointed use of the exclusive address. A moving meditation on pregnancy and loss, the poem depicts the physical event of the speaker's miscarriage in graphic detail, including the shape and texture of the "clots of blood" that appear beneath her in "the pale / green swaying water of the toilet." Midway through the poem, Olds's speaker shifts from first-person singular to plural, revealing the poem's addressee to be her husband. Labeled "private" under one of the collection's subcategories, "Poems for the Dead," the lyric is the speaker's elegy for the spontaneously aborted child and her attempt to make symbolic sense of this loss. The final lines recast the miscarriage as an ominous bodily "messenger" that is delivered to the speaker and her husband. Their unfortunate ability to "botch something" together foreshadows their eventual divorce, chronicled in Olds's equally intimate collection *Stag's Leap* (2013).

Exclusive address in this poem prompts readers to consider their own positions based on a number of rhetorical cues. First and foremost, our rhetorical omission from the address formally transforms us from hearers into overhearers. There is also, however, the subject matter: alongside the speaker, we bear witness to an exclusive event, "the only appearance made by that / child." Exclusivity of both address and event underscores our special access to a uniquely painful and private experience. Olds's speaker also creates intimacy through her language and tone, which are remarkably, even brutally, unguarded. Her description of the miscarriage is frank, pitiless, and nearly clinical; she even seems to assume culpability for the "botched" pregnancy. (The same self-lacerating technique is used with greater drama and complexity in the apostrophic poem that follows, titled "The End." The poem depicts an abortion, the deliberate nature of which reverberates against "Miscarriage.") By combining the intimacy of the poem's subject matter and addressee with the vulnerability of its speaker, Olds—like many confessional poets—reconfigures readers into eavesdroppers.

What sort of reading practice does a confessional work suggest when it relocates us to the margins of the text? As reader-overhearers, we inhabit a difficult position somewhere between presence and absence, engrossed as we are in this intimate moment even as we recoil from it. Our experience here is akin to what Locke calls "liminal intimacy" because our relationship to overheard material is so difficult to define: "Is it the experience of operating *near* a boundary, or crossing it, or *being on the other side of it*?" (2010, 215, original emphasis). Or, to rephrase in literary terms: are these writers involving us in acts of "perceptual trespassing" in which we cross a boundary between public and private (210) of which the poem's speaker, who is operating only in the realm of the private, is unaware? It is hard to say, since this boundary is purposely obscured by the complex relationship between the intra- and extradiegetic layers of confessional literary texts: no matter how "private" the speaker understands the situation to be, the author has created both situation and speaker with readers in mind. Rather than asking us to decide one way or the other, these writers explore the ethics and hermeneutics of eavesdropping by deliberately drawing our attention to the boundary itself.

Texts that feature exclusive direct address also toy with the "tension between sympathy and moral judgment" that characterizes the dramatic monologue (Langbaum 1957, 85). Positioned as outsiders looking in, we reader-overhearers must determine what proportion of compassion and censure is warranted for confessional speakers who are unaware of our presence. I contend that, like the therapist or priest in other confessional contexts, we are compelled to listen to these speakers with suspended judgment and heightened compassion. Such a response runs counter to prevailing accounts of readerly engagement articulated by narrative theorists such as Phelan, who insists that judgment is "crucial to our experience—and understanding—of narrative form" (2007b, 3). Phelan links judgment to genre, arguing that narrative positions us as "outsiders" and adjudicators to the fictional world of the text:

> The authorial audience perceives the characters as external to themselves and as distinct from their implied authors, and the authorial audience passes interpretive and ethical judgments on them, their

> situations, and their choices. The audience's observer role is what makes the judgment role possible, and the particular judgments are integral to our emotional responses as well as to our desires about future events. (7)

Phelan countermeasures this response against that elicited by the lyric, which urges us "toward fusion with the speaker—or, to put it in more measured terms, toward adopting the speaker's perspective without any irritable reaching after difference and evaluation" (22). Yet the exclusive direct address in narrative fiction collapses this distinction by presenting novels in which we are both observers and sympathizers, discouraged from identifying with either narrator or addressee but encouraged nonetheless to listen with patience and understanding. Thus, these texts simultaneously place pressure on our reading practices and on the model of genre from which they emerge.

The character-narrators examined here employ exclusive address to reveal intimate secrets in various rhetorical contexts that are all justified through the frame of confidentiality. Alexander Portnoy may seek sympathy from his analyst, but he also seeks help and direction; Nanapush of Erdrich's *Tracks* delivers an intimate family history to Lulu so that she does not repeat the mistakes of her predecessors; Cocoa and George, separated by death, reveal their true feelings for each other through dual addresses in Naylor's *Mama Day*; and John Ames couches his confession as a didactic letter to his young son in Robinson's *Gilead*. As we navigate these texts, we must not only relax our notions of plot, since narrative action is subsumed here by the relational dynamics between mutually constitutive narrators and addressees; we must also reckon with our position as overhearers, which necessarily shapes the way we approach and understand character-narrators who place a premium on privacy.

Tracks (1988) is the story of the Turtle Mountain Chippewa (Anishinabe)[4] after the turn of the century as they struggle to hold onto their land in the face of government policies designed to take it away. The Burke Act of 1906 and its follow-up legislation, the Declaration of Policy of 1917, extended fee patents to "competent" Indians, requiring them to pay property taxes on their land. As a result, many American Indians lost their land through tax foreclosure sales.[5] Erdrich's novel contains dual—and dueling—narrators who depict and interpret these events from very different vantage points in alternating chapters. Nanapush, an aging patriarch who is deeply concerned with the future of the Anishinabe, is melancholic about the loss of land and tradition these government policies have caused; Pauline is a shy, young, orphaned, mixed-blood Anishinabe who seeks relief for her marginalized status in her culture by renouncing her heritage and fleeing to the Catholic Church, and she sees the loss of land as not only inevitable and deserved but divinely ordained: "Surely that was the work of Christ's hand," she remarks as surveyors for the lumber company prepare to raze Fleur's timber-filled plot to the ground at the end of the novel (204). Critics such as Nancy J. Peterson have noted the use of oral techniques in Nanapush's narrative that appear to protest those written documents—treaties, maps, legislative acts, and commercial contracts with the logging industry—used to encroach on Anishinabe territory (1994, 985).[6] Nanapush's narrative is, however, also a pointedly private address to Lulu, the daughter of his adopted child, Fleur. "Granddaughter, you are the child of the invisible, the ones who disappeared," he writes, paradoxically rendering her visible through the direct address (1). Reading his chapters in contradistinction to Pauline's through the framework of the exclusive address reveals the personal stakes of his narrative, which seeks both to heal the rift between Lulu and her mother and to prevent her from abandoning her family and culture as Pauline has done.

One of Nanapush's primary motivations for telling this story is to cultivate Lulu's sympathy for her estranged mother, Fleur. By divulging the family history of the Pillager ancestral line, he is able to depict Fleur's hardships, including her orphaning and near death during a tuberculosis outbreak, her sexual abuse by the men of Argus, and her fight to defend her family's plot of land against the interests of government as well as the Turcot lumber company. These turbulent scenes—interspersed with domestic scenes that reveal Fleur's tenderness toward her young daughter—enable Nanapush to establish a rationale for Fleur's decision to send Lulu away to a government boarding school, a decision that Lulu has erstwhile understood as an act of abandonment and betrayal. Yet Nanapush places these scenes in a broader cultural context to demonstrate his concern with a new generation of Anishinabe who are severing their ties to their tribal heritage and their birthright, the timber-filled land that surrounds Matchimanito Lake.

Nanapush signals the communal nature of his narrative by beginning in the first-personal plural: "We started dying before the snow, and like the snow, we continued to fall" (1). His narration begins with the story of the Turtle Mountain Chippewa and their triple-pronged plight: plagued first by smallpox and then by government exile, they are beleaguered in 1912 by an outbreak of tuberculosis that wipes out much of the tribe, including Fleur's family. When Nanapush finally invokes Lulu to build an "I/thou" drama that constricts his narration to the first- and second-person singular, he does so by proxy as the sole survivor of a community ravaged not only by disease but by government encroachment:

> My girl, I saw the passing of times you will never know.
>
> I guided the last buffalo hunt. I saw the last bear shot. I trapped the last beaver with a pelt of more than two years' growth. I spoke aloud the words of the government treaty, and refused to sign the settlement papers that would take away our woods and lake. I axed the last birch that was older than I, and I saved the last Pillager.
>
> Fleur, the one you will not call mother. (2)

This shift in address, nested in Nanapush's pronoun shift from *we* to *I* and back again, places both Nanapush and Lulu in conversation with larger communities—first with the Anishinabe, and finally with the Pillager family, of which Lulu and her mother are the sole living descendents. In stark contrast, Pauline's narration seems to exist only for her own benefit. She never names an addressee but uses her chapters to vindicate herself for disavowing her Anishinabe heritage. Her sections become increasingly *I*-centered as she alienates herself from her tribe and joins the Catholic order of nuns. Even there, she continues to distinguish herself through self-inflicted suffering, which ironically leads to self-aggrandizement rather than the self-effacement that her order promotes: "I knew there never was a martyr like me," she smugly declares after immersing her hands in a cauldron of boiling water (192). Pauline's narration enacts an important grammatical turn, however, as she begins to refer to her people in the third person, a rhetorical choice that contrasts with Nanapush's rhetorical connection to his community. "'The Indians,' I said now, 'them.' Nevermind *neenawind* or us" (138). Pauline must renounce her heritage and pass as Caucasian to become a nun, but she also internalizes this pronoun shift, imagining that God visits her to explain that she "was not one speck of Indian but wholly white" (137). Eventually, Fleur and Nanapush respond to her behavior accordingly: "[They] treated me as they would a white. I was ignored most of the time. When they did address me they usually spoke English" (145–46). Outwardly, Pauline has successfully shed her Indian heritage, though her masochistic behavior suggests that she is not at peace with her decision.

Nanapush's exclusive address to Lulu contains urgency as he expresses his concern that she is following the wrong path, which will inevitably lead to the kind of assimilation and self-loathing that Pauline represents. In particular, he feels deeply apprehensive about Lulu's impending marriage to an unnamed member of the Morrissey family. Many of his direct appeals to her are admonishing. "Take a lesson from what an old man knows and think about this Morrissey twice!" he cautions (180). The Morrisseys have distinguished themselves from the Pillagers through their controversial decision to sell their land to the Turcot lumber company. To Nanapush, this decision demonstrates their greed and indolence, evidenced also by the state of their home, which has fallen into terrible disrepair: "Their windows were broken out with planks and dirty oiled paper hung in their place. Garbage, the snapped bones of muskrats, crushed cans and splinters of crates were littered in the crusted snow. . . . Granddaughter, if you join this clan, I predict the union will not last. Listen to experience and marry wisely. I always did" (181–82). The Morrissey home, Nanapush suggests, functions metonymically for their attitude toward Anishinabe land and culture: they take it for granted and do not properly care for it; as a result, they are instrumental in its destruction.

By marrying into the Morrissey clan, Lulu will align herself with a family that, as Nanapush depicts it, has turned its back on Anishinabe culture.

Nanapush is also concerned, however, that a Morrissey will turn his back on his own family. "You . . . will need a mother once the Morrissey fills you with child and whines in your ear and vanishes," he warns her, alluding again to her rift with Fleur (211). Morrisseys are not just terrible Anishinabe, he stresses; they are also terrible fathers and husbands. In *Tracks*, ties of kinship run laterally as well as vertically; allegiance to culture is as important as allegiance to one's immediate family, and vice versa. To sever ties with one is to sever ties with the other.

Like the Morrisseys, Lulu risks severing ties with both. "You, heartless one, won't even call Fleur mother or take off your pointy shoes, walk through the tough bush, and visit her," Nanapush chastises her in the present tense (210). Lulu's shoes become a powerful synecdoche for a rift that easily slips from cultural to familial. Nanapush impresses this upon her with another anecdote from her childhood. When Fleur nearly dies at the hands of an incompetent Pauline while delivering a stillborn child, Lulu must run through the snow to Nanapush's cabin for help, but she is wearing impractical, Western-style shoes made of vinyl. Her feet are so frozen when she arrives that her life too appears to be in danger. Nanapush recalls the incident with another admonishment couched in the exclusive direct address:

> Vain girl, you wore your fancy shoes once you did not have to answer to your mother.
>
> "Damn Eli for buying them!" Margaret yelled when she plucked off the pretty shoes. She was so mad she threw open the stove door and stuffed them into the fire. But soon they began to melt and stink, so she snatched them from the flames with a meatfork and threw them smoking into the snow. (166)

Lulu's vinyl shoes are an act of cultural as well as filial rebellion, but they quickly backfire on her. Because they trade utility for vanity, they fail to protect her feet during her crucial trek to save her mother's life. Their cheap, synthetic quality is also highlighted by their chemical reaction to the fire, which causes them to "melt and stink." In betraying her people, Lulu has only hurt herself; yet her choice of shoes in the present moment indicates that she still has not learned her lesson. Nanapush scolds her for wearing "such shoes as you have on at this moment—those heels, like tiny knives, and your toes sticking through!" (166). He does not have the language to describe Lulu's peep-toed high heels, and he is clear about what he would prefer to see on her feet instead: "Footwrappings made of rabbit fur for protection, and no fine stockings either" (166).

At times, Nanpush's urgency gives way to desperation. Painfully aware of his dwindling authority within the community, he has lost confidence in his ability to persuade the new generation of Anishinabe to heed his warnings: "It is embarrassing for a man to admit his arms have thinned, his capacities diminished, and maybe worse than that, his influence over the young of the tribe is gone for good" (109). Even his granddaughter Fleur has ceased to listen, despite his best efforts: "I made her sit down and listen just the way you are sitting now. . . . I told her things she could not hear. . . . I saw the barrier of her obstinate pride had kept my words safely beyond belief" (178). Nanapush is concerned that Lulu, like her mother, will erect a "barrier" that will prevent her from really hearing his entreaties, despite his attempts to reach her through his exclusive address.

In contradistinction to the *I*-centered soliloquy showcased by Pauline, Nanapush's sections indicate outreach, even if they do not expect or even admit a response from their addressee. The plural first-person pronoun that opens the novel ("We started dying before the snow") joins his narrative to a cultural history, and the direct address ("Granddaughter, you are the child of the invisible") joins him to Lulu. His audience, however, remains exclusive: Nanapush divulges for Lulu an intimate ancestral saga that includes some very sensitive incidents, including Fleur's brutal beating and gang rape at the hands of the butchermen of Argus and Margaret's humiliation when Clarence Morrissey forcibly shaves her head (as a bound and helpless Nanapush watches, no less). While direct address only occasionally punctures his narrative—perhaps one of the reasons critics have overlooked the novel's lyricality—these moments are significant reminders of the sensitive personal and cultural nature of Nanpush's address.

Culturally particular or "minority" literature, Doris Sommer writes, often makes strategic use of difference and distance to redirect readerly desire for intimacy toward more cautious interactions that are based on "modesty and respect" (1999, xi). In these contexts, she suggests, our automatic inclination toward empathy may be misguided and even presumptuous; as mainstream readers, we cannot assume that we possess the background and knowledge that would enable such engagement. Likewise, by positioning Lulu as the narratee of *Tracks*, Erdrich highlights personal as well as cultural differences between reader and addressee that lead us closer to sympathy than to empathy. Discouraged from completely identifying with either Nanapush or Lulu, we are called instead to overhear their communication as compassionate observers of an intimate family saga in which tribal members must choose a path in the wake of federal and industrial encroachment on their land. Pauline chooses self-abnegation and assimilation; the Morrisseys choose money. Nanapush devotes his exclusive address to Lulu in hopes that she will mend her rift with Fleur and, like her mother, choose resistance.

Like *Tracks*, Gloria Naylor's *Mama Day* ([1988] 1993) features a culturally specific exclusive address that creates tension with its mainstream readership; and, like *Tracks*, it contains multiple narrators who tell strikingly different versions of the same events. Critics typically focus on the novel's setting in the small fictitious Gullah island of Willow Springs and "the island inhabitants' retention and transmission of African-derived traditions and values . . . in the face of cultural forces that would efface them" (Lamothe 2005, 156). The novel also boasts a complex narrative structure, however, in which alternating sections are narrated respectively by Cocoa and George, a couple experiencing strife following a whirlwind courtship and marriage that has left them feeling like strangers to each other. Their first-person narratives, which are addressed to each other, are tempered by a third, extradiegetic narrator who chiefly focalizes the story through Miranda, or "Mama Day," as Cocoa's grandaunt is affectionately called. The novel opens, however, with prefatory material featuring a fourth, intradiegetic narrator, an unnamed voice that identifies itself only as a resident of Willow Springs. This narrator's use of the plural first-person, much like Nanapush's, positions readers as outsiders to the culture of Willow Springs, but the prefatory material ends with a striking address to the reader. Remarking disdainfully on a Willow Springs native who returned from college to perform an ethnographic study on the residents, the narrator mocks the boy's overly clinical approach to the rich history that is brought to life through narrative: "He coulda listened to them the way you been listening to us right now. Think about it: ain't nobody really talking to you. We're sitting here in Willow Springs, and you're God-knows where. It's August 1999—ain't but a slim chance it's the same season where you are. Uh, huh, listen. Really listen this time" (10). Readers are called to "listen" in a way that diverges from the methods of the ethnography student—an admonition that calls to mind Erdrich's exclusive address in *Tracks*—but perhaps more importantly, we are simply called to listen. This prefatory material, which acknowledges our alienation from the fictional world of Willow Springs, ends nonetheless with a provocation that invites us to the text as sympathetic overhearers.

The dual address in *Mama Day* effects a chronological alteration, catapulting Cocoa and George backward in time to tell the story of their courtship and marriage and its gradual disintegration through alternating chapters that betray very different perspectives on the same events. To some extent, their divergent perspectives are a function of their personalities: George is an optimist and Cocoa a pessimist; George is generally forthright, whereas Cocoa is emotionally restrained. Their divergent narratives also, however, reveal the miscommunication inherent in their failed relationship. George and Cocoa's sections may be addressed to each other, but they are not in dialogue. Instead, they are one-sided utterances in which each confesses his or her true feelings only in the absence of the other and without any possibility of a response.

Their inability to communicate is not only a formal feature of the novel; it is a problem highlighted by Cocoa in one of her sections. Though Cocoa is initially quite guarded—her early sections are steeped in sarcasm and cynical humor, and she hardly allows herself to admit her feelings for George—her later sections are more open and confessional, and she expresses frustration that George does not make himself vulnerable in return. "You wouldn't talk to me," she laments. "I had told you about where I grew up. . . . I did open up fully to share my feelings about my father running off and my mother dying so young. I talked to you about loneliness—all kinds. About my day-to-day frustrations with the job, the plans I had for my future—going back to college and getting a history degree. . . . I talked and talked, but getting you to say anything about yourself was like pulling teeth. . . . I thought you didn't trust me enough to share those feelings" (126–27). In the following section, George offers a confession that addresses Cocoa's complaint. Raised in a group shelter with other orphans, he feels as though he has no biography to share with her: "I was always in awe of the stories you told so easily about Willow Springs. To be born in a grandmother's house, to be able to walk and see where a grandfather and even great-great-grandfather was born. You had more than a family, you had a history. And I didn't even have a real last name" (129). George's address to Cocoa in this section is gentle and honest, but when he tells Cocoa about his upbringing in real time, he is brutal, even violent. After slapping her for sleeping with an old boyfriend while the couple has taken a break from each other, he chooses this, of all moments, to finally bare his soul. "My mother was a whore. And that's why I don't like being called the son of a bitch," he tells her gruffly. He then takes her on a macabre tour of the city, pointing out the brothel where he was born, the café where his mother abandoned him, and the shoreline where her body was found. Cocoa recalls the forcefulness of his grip as he "drag[ged]" her up the street, "crushing" her hand all the while (130). George suddenly softens, however, when he recalls his mother's absence:

> You see, when I was growing up, there was no reason for me to neglect her on the days that would have been important: her birthday, anniversary, or the second Sunday in May. I didn't forget to call now and then to ask her how she was doing. I didn't find her demands annoying, or her worries unnecessary. I was the kind of son who didn't refuse to share my friends, my interests, or my hopes for the future with her. Yeah, that's pretty close to the kind of son I was. (131)

This episode in which George tenderly refers to his mother in the third person reveals that George is much more comfortable communicating through indirect address, a fact that heightens our sensitivity to George's vulnerability as we bear witness to his exclusive direct addresses to Cocoa.

As reader-eavesdroppers, we bear witness to other ugly, violent episodes between the couple as well, including a bitter quarrel that is depicted very differently in their sections. "Our worse fight ever. And it was all your fault," they both begin, though their agreement ends there (230, 232). The conflict begins, literally and metaphorically, over cosmetics. Upon telling Cocoa that her foundation is "too dark" for her skin, George insists that he is only being frank after Cocoa pressed him to be honest: "I had told you a thousand times—not once, not a dozen—a thousand: if you don't really want my honest opinion (about your hair, clothes, shade of eyeshadow, or the latest fashions for Pygmy women) *don't* ask me for it. And you kept pushing, didn't you?" (230). For her part, Cocoa complains that George deliberately failed to give her the simple affirmation she craved: "You refused to tell me when you knew I needed so desperately to hear. Of course that foundation wasn't the right shade, but couldn't you lie? I had to be perfect that evening and I was shattered" (233). In this way, the structure of the dual address in *Mama Day* enhances character focalization, since we are able to directly access the conflicting perspectives of George and Cocoa. The argument quickly escalates, however, into issues of race and sexual jealousy: George's white, red-headed ex-girlfriend; George's caramel-colored fantasy woman; Cocoa's insecurities regarding the hue of her skin, exacerbated by George's criticisms. "And you're the one painting yourself with tar? Don't you preach to me about values until you learn to accept what you are and wipe that crap off your face," he retorts (235).

Readers are invited to identify here with Abigail and Mama Day, sidelined observers who overhear the fight in a section narrated by an extradiegetic narrator. "The voices behind the closed bedroom door been rising and falling, rising and falling, for a good twenty minutes," it begins (232). Both women pretend not to listen as they go about their party preparations. Their divergent reactions, however, reflect the split position of the reader. "Miranda realizes there's a whole world in there that she ain't got nothing to do with. Abigail spreads the lace tablecloth and wrings her hands, sets out the punch bowl and wrings her hands, while Miranda keeps slicing up peach pie as calmly as if she was at a church supper." Like Miranda, we acknowledge our distance from George and Cocoa, though like Abigail, we are nonetheless drawn into their domestic strife, wringing our hands as tensions escalate. What, then, do we make of the intradiegetic narrator in the novel's preface who invites us to "listen, really listen this time"? Unlike Miranda and Abigail, who are only able to catch select words and phrases, we are granted privileged access to narrative events like the "worst fight ever" through George and Cocoa's retrospective reflections. Because of our unfettered access, however, we are also called to exercise balance in judgment. The novel alternates evenly between George's and Cocoa's sections in a way that defies readers to side with one character over the other. Their first-person narratives invite us to share in their perspectives even as their exclusive addresses simultaneously preserve their distance from us. Neither character is wholly at fault for the failing marriage that is put on display in *Mama Day*, though each would have us believe that the other is culpable. As outside arbiters who witness their direct dialogue as well as their private soliloquies, we are able to see how, when, and why they routinely miscommunicate.

Their private addresses to each other are much more tender and honest than their flesh-and-blood interactions. When their "worst fight ever" results in a cold war, Cocoa puts herself in the hands of a jealous local woman named Ruby, who braids her hair with nightshade. Though George refuses to comment out loud, his direct address to Cocoa in this section reveals his abiding love and admiration for her: "Your hair looked gorgeous. The braids were like the ones I'd seen on prints of African women with those colored beads draped over the necks and crossed under high, tilted breasts. You should really wear it like that all the time. I wanted to follow you in the house and tell you, but that's sort of hard to do when you're not talking to someone" (247).

Only when we finish *Mama Day* do we realize that George and Cocoa's sections *cannot* be in dialogue with one another because George has died at the end of his narrative. He has sacrificed his life for Cocoa's in an act of altruism after Ruby uses the nightshade in Cocoa's hair to place a hex on her that Mama Day, a conjure woman, is unable to lift by herself. His death also explains the disembodiment of George and Cocoa's voices and the ambiguity of their locations in time and space, since they are addressing one another from opposite sides of the grave. George even narrates his own death in his final section: "I want to tell you something about my real death that day. I didn't feel anything after my heart burst. As my bleeding hand slid gently down your arm, there was total peace" (302). Cocoa, for her part, is rooted more firmly in time and geography. She reveals in her final section that she is living near Charleston, South Carolina, and she is just shy of forty-seven. Nearly twenty years after first meeting George, she is still devastated by his loss. "It sits permanently in your middle," she writes of her grief, "but it gets less weighty as time goes on and becomes endurable" (308). She continues to struggle with the disparity that has always existed between her perspective and that of George. "When I see you again," she signs off, "our versions will be different still. . . . What really happened to us, George? You see, that's what I mean—there are just too many sides to the whole story" (311).

George's death amplifies the poignancy of George and Cocoa's alternating sections, but their addresses also reveal how alienated they had become from one another even during their marriage. Both narrators are dislocated in time and space from the events of the novel, though they depict their thoughts and feelings as if these events were still unfolding. "Each time I go back over what happened, there's some new development. . . . I guess one of the reasons I've been here [to George's grave site] so much is that I felt if we kept retracing our steps, we'd find out exactly what brought us to this slope near The Sound," Cocoa confesses (310). As George and Cocoa each attempt to retrace and rediscover the contours of their relationship through exclusive direct address, readers are along for the ride at the invitation of the novel's intradiegetic narrator, though we remain invisible to its character-narrators.

In contrast to both *Tracks* and *Mama Day*, which prime their readers with prefatory material about the time, place, and culture of the fictional world they are entering, Marilynne Robinson's exclusive address in *Gilead* (2004) begins in medias res: "I told you last night that I may be gone sometime, and you said, Where, and I said, To be with the Good Lord, and you said, Why, and I said, Because I'm old, and you said, I don't think you're old" (3). The narrator is John Ames, a seventy-six-year-old preacher who is suffering from chest pains and heart failure. He has married a much younger woman who has borne him a son, age seven at the time of narration, which is sometime in the 1950s.[7] Because Ames does not know how much longer he might live, he addresses his narrative to his son in the form of a long letter (or series of letters, depending on how one reads the section breaks), though the narrative does not contain any of the formal signals of epistolary writing—no greetings, no closings, and as in *Mama Day*, no possibility of a response.

Because Ames anticipates the passage of at least ten years' time between the composition and reception of his letter, his narrative does not have the rhetorical urgency of Nanapush's addresses to Lulu. "If you're a grown man when you read this—it is my intention for this letter that you will read it then—I'll have been gone a long time," he writes (3). Instead, much of *Gilead* is devoted to anticipations of loss—his anxiety over what his absence as husband, father, and provider will mean for his family, and his regret that he will never live to see his son grow up. As a corrective, his letter serves as a deeply intimate proxy for his presence:

> For me writing has always felt like praying, even when I wasn't writing prayers, as I was often enough. You feel that you are with someone. I feel I am with you now, whatever that can mean, considering that you're only a little fellow now and when you're a man you might find these letters of no interest. Or they might never reach you, for any number of reasons. Well, but how deeply I regret any sadness you have suffered and how grateful I am in anticipation of any good you have enjoyed. That is to say, I pray for you. And there's an intimacy in it. That's the truth. (19)

As Ames indicates here—"I feel I am with you now"—the letter itself is something of a surrogate parent to the young boy, a compressed account of the fatherly counsel Ames might have offered him in life. "I'm trying to make the best of our situation," Ames writes. "That is, I'm trying to tell you things I might never have thought to tell you if I had brought you up myself, father and son, in the usual companionable way" (102).

Critics have rightly focused on the novel's religiosity, but *Gilead*'s unusual form enhances another ethical dimension of the work by revealing the difficulty of finding compassion without judgment.[8] The novel is a fragmented assortment of family stories and anecdotes, personal meditations, and pieces of advice and admonition as Ames tries to parse his life's lessons for the benefit of his son. These fragments, like Ames's state of mind, are somewhat chaotic: stories are frequently interrupted by a moral or a piece of information that seems more pressing, only to be picked up again much later. In this sense, they reflect Ames's struggle to prioritize all of the messages he wishes to communicate. Yet the letter takes a very different turn midway through as Ames becomes increasingly fixated on Jack Boughton, the prodigal son of his neighbor and closest friend, who has returned home after a twenty-year absence. When Jack reappears in his hometown of Gilead, Iowa, Ames is distrustful, especially when Jack begins to bond with Ames's family. "My impulse is strong to warn you against Jack Boughton. Your mother and you," he writes. "He is not a man of the highest character. Be wary of him" (125).

Ames's verdict, which is unconfirmed by Jack's present behavior, clashes with the Christian principles that otherwise permeate Ames's narrative: forgiveness, humility, judge not lest ye be judged. In fact, Ames often tries to twist his rants about Jack into crude aphoristic lessons for his son. "Avoid transgression. How's that for advice," he writes with bitterness after one such diatribe (122). His discussions of Jack, however, seem to be less and less for his son's sake. In his more candid moments, Ames admits that his acrimony is partly fueled by envy. After all, Jack is a generation younger than Ames—and so is Ames's wife. On some level, Ames fears that Jack will take his place within the family unit. As he stands at his pulpit, looking down at his family seated next to Jack, he shifts his address to Boughton: "You looked to me like a handsome young family, and my evil old heart rose within me, the old covetise I have mentioned elsewhere came over me, and I felt the way I used to feel when the beauty of other lives was a misery and an offense to me" (141).

As he slips into this confessional mode, revealing jealousies, vanities, and other insecurities that, albeit human, are unbefitting of a man of the cloth, Ames becomes more honest with his son—and with himself—than he had intended to be. He is intensely self-conscious, for example, about his age: "You read the dreams of an anxious, fuddled old man," he writes at one point (53); "How I wish you could have known me in my strength," he writes at another (94). The novel is filled with comments like these. "The fact is," he admits candidly, "I don't want to be old. And I certainly don't want to be dead. I don't want to be the tremulous coot you barely remember. I bitterly wish you could know me as a young man" (141). He frequently compares himself to Abraham. He even fantasizes about becoming young again in the afterlife, an indulgence not without vanity. "I believe the soul in Paradise must enjoy something nearer to a perpetual vigorous adulthood than to any other state we know. . . . I certainly shouldn't mind the thought of your mother finding me a strong young man," he declares with more than a hint of sexuality (166).

As these and other insecurities emerge, Ames admits that he is losing sight of his original rhetorical aims: "I have been looking through these pages, and I realize that for some time I have mainly been worrying to myself, when my intention from the beginning was to speak to you. I meant to leave you a reasonably candid testament to my better self, and it seems to me now that what you see here is just an old man struggling with the difficulty of understanding what it is he's struggling with" (202). His rhetorical dilemma here is paradoxical: the narrator's addressee has become buried under his quest for self-discovery, but Ames would never have explored these feelings so deeply without the frame of the exclusive address. Confessional writing without an audience would likely strike Ames as self-indulgent. "Here I was a pastor of souls, hundreds and hundreds of them over all those years, and I hope I was speaking to them, not only to myself," he writes of his sermons (41). Nor would he feel comfortable, however, sharing details of his personal life with any of the members of his parish. "I want you to realize that I am not by any means a saint," he tells his son, perhaps unduly castigating himself, like the speaker of Olds's "Miscarriage." "I get much more respect than I deserve. This seems harmless enough in most cases. People want to respect the pastor and I'm not going to interfere with that. But . . . my reputation is largely the creature of the kindly imaginings of my flock, whom I chose not to disillusion" (39–40). Ames emphasizes here a distinction between public and private that reminds us of the line we straddle as reader-overhearers. The artistry of the exclusive address also, however, liberates Ames from the vocational constraints that might ordinarily prevent him from indulging in the act of memoir writing. As a result, he is free to explore thoughts and emotions that would otherwise be prohibited to him, though he is always careful to couch this self-exploration as being for the benefit of his young son.

Gilead becomes a nested confession in the final section, in which Ames reveals Jack Boughton's secret history, which Jack has divulged to Ames, his confessor, in strict confidence. Jack has acquired another family, a "wife" and son for whom he cares very deeply. Because she is black and their son is mixed race, however, antimiscegenation laws have made it impossible for them to cohabit peacefully, let alone marry, in Saint Louis. To make matters worse, her father deeply disapproves of their relationship, and Jack finds it difficult to keep a job once his employers discover that he is in a mixed-race relationship. He has returned to Gilead, he confesses to Ames, to see if he "might find some way to live with my family here, I mean my wife and son. I have even thought it might be a pleasure to introduce Robert [Jack's son] to my father. I would like him to know that I finally have something I can be proud of" (229). He has not, however, told his father or any of his family about his wife and child and, in view of his father's poor health and old age, worries that the shocking news would "kill him" (229).

Jack has revealed his secret to Ames to seek his counsel. Should he tell his father, or should he continue to allow his wife and child to remain a secret? Do they have a future here in Gilead? "What about this town? If we came here and got married, could we live here? Would people leave us alone?" he asks (231). Unfortunately, Ames does not have any easy answers, and the town's own dubious racial history—a mysterious fire erupted just outside a black church, causing many of Gilead's black residents to leave town—does not seem promising for Jack.

Why does Ames repeat Jack's intimate disclosure in his letter to his son—a secret that is subsequently disclosed to readers? "You might wonder about my pastoral discretion, writing this all out," he admits. "Well, on one hand it is the way I have of considering things. On the other hand, he is a man about whom you may never hear one good word, and I just don't know another way to let you see the beauty there is in him" (232). The imperative to represent Jack Boughton fairly, Ames suggests, outweighs the imperative of confidentiality, but Ames's defensive comments here also indicate some remorse regarding his own unforgiving depiction of the young Boughton. Whatever his motives—and Ames acknowledges that "I conceal my motives from myself pretty effectively sometimes" (147)—readers are made privy to an aspect of Jack Boughton that would be inaccessible to us save through Ames's breach of confidentiality, which is justified in terms of the exclusive direct address.

As a preacher, Ames is acutely aware of the ways a shift in audience can change the rhetorical framework of a text. "At times . . . I might not care particularly whether people are listening to what I have to say, because I know what their thoughts are," he says of his Sunday sermons. "Then if some stranger comes in, that very same peace can seem like somnolence and like dull habit, because that is how you're afraid it seems to her" (20). Strangers have a way of heightening our self-consciousness and magnifying our insecurities. In a confessional narrative that Ames describes as an "experiment with candor" (7), the text of *Gilead* would be changed indeed if Ames were aware of our presence. Ames is ill at ease in his new role as penitent: previously the confessor, he is now in the position of confessing his own flaws to his (future) adult son. He is also keenly aware of the thrill of listening to the private lives of others: "A great part of my work has been listening to people, in that particular intense privacy of confession, or at least unburdening, and it has been very interesting to me," he admits (44). Yet the privacy of the confessional demands a response that is much more sophisticated, and more compassionate, than lurid curiosity. The interposition of the exclusive addressee serves here as a continuous reminder that we are to listen to Ames with the same compassion and suspension of judgment with which Ames has listened to the confessions of so many in his congregation—and which he finds himself, for complex reasons, unable to extend to Jack Boughton.

Gilead invites readers into a private letter that functions as a figurative confessional, but *Portnoy's Complaint* ([1969] 1994) takes us farther still, interposing us directly between a patient and his therapist. This near-sacrosanct relationship, built on foundations of confidentiality and trust, is one with which Philip Roth was intimately familiar, and one that he took very seriously. Jeffrey Berman (1985; 2007) has convincingly argued that the character of Spielvogel is modeled after Roth's own psychoanalyst, Hans J. Kleinschmidt, who deeply betrayed Roth by publishing a scholarly essay in a special issue of a psychoanalytic journal, "Genius, Psychopathology, and Creativity," which made extensive use of material from their sessions together. Though he recasts his patient as a "successful Southern playwright" in a thinly veiled attempt to preserve Roth's anonymity, Kleinschmidt used the article to treat matters deeply personal to Roth that adumbrate the same set of neurotic traits that reappear in Portnoy: his Oedipal fixation on his mother, his embarrassment regarding his ineffectual and submissive father, and his subsequent hostility toward women, which he "both acted out and channeled into his writing" (Kleinschmidt 1967, 123, 126). So troubled was Roth by the article and the risk it posed to his anonymity that he created a fictionalized account of the violation in his 1974 novel *My Life as a Man*. Here, an outraged writer named Peter Tarnopol discovers an article by Spielvogel—which, like Kleinschmidt's, appears in a special issue of a psychoanalytic journal on the topic of creativity—featuring material from Tarnopol's life that was mined during their private therapy sessions. Like Roth, Tarnopol draws heavily on his own experiences while crafting his fiction; and like Roth, he worries that his therapist's publication will compromise his privacy because of the obvious parallels between the biographical incidents relayed in the article and those relayed in Tarnopol's fiction.

Though Roth never commented publicly on his betrayal by Kleinschmidt, his vivid recreation of the incident for *My Life as a Man* suggests that he recognized its literary potential for modeling the ethics of discretion in matters of personal privacy. The same imperative toward sensitivity and discretion operates in *Portnoy's Complaint*, the novel that most immediately follows the publication of Kleinschmidt's article. Such an approach is not as simple as it may sound; Portnoy is in many ways a remarkably unlikable narrator who does not readily elicit our compassion. The novel did, after all, spark a firestorm of controversy upon its 1969 publication: while many lauded Roth's tour de force for its irreverent humor, others objected strongly to the narrator's antifeminist and, as they saw it, anti-Semitic rhetoric, including Marie Syrkin (1974), who contended that for all of his "hapless[ness]," Portnoy's bold sexual conquests of blond *shikses* promote the familiar stereotype of "the Jew as sexual defiler and malevolent destroyer." Portnoy provokes such a range of critical responses partly because the feelings and events he recounts extend from routine embarrassments to acts of sexual deviance. The early part of the novel, for example, chronicles his compulsive masturbation against the backdrop of an austere Jewish upbringing; to avoid leaving behind any incriminating evidence for his mother to find, Portnoy finds himself masturbating into various fabrics and food items, including his sister's panties, cored apples, and ultimately, a piece of liver that was "rolled round my cock in the bathroom at three-thirty—and then had again at the end of my fork, at five-thirty, along with the other members of that poor innocent family of mine" (134). Once unleashed on the world, his sexuality likewise graduates from wonder to prurience to outright exploitation. Initially marveling at the power of the female genitalia—"Every girl he sees turns out (hold your hats) to be carrying around between her legs—a real cunt. Amazing! Astonishing!" (102)—his desire becomes insatiable, an extension of his narcissism, demonstrated when he articulates his attitude toward love and marriage: "How can I give up what I never even had, for a girl, who delicious and provocative as once she may have been, will inevitably grow as familiar to me as a loaf of bread?" (104). Worse still is his shameless maltreatment of Monkey, "the most recently disappointed (and self-appointed) bride-to-be," who satisfies his every sexual caprice simply because she loves him (105).

In moments like these, we are tempted to judge Portnoy along the lines of the mock entry for the *Diagnostic and Statistical Manual of Mental Disorders*, which opens and consequently frames the novel: "Portnoy's Complaint (pôrt´-noiz kəm-plānt´) *n.* [after Alexander Portnoy (1933–)] A disorder in which strongly-felt ethical and altruistic impulses are perpetually warring with extreme sexual longings, often of a perverse nature." The competing rhetorical frame of the exclusive direct address complicates this reading, however, by serving as a continuous reminder that Portnoy—like Roth—shares these experiences under the guise of complete confidentiality. Here, the exclusive address is a mitigating factor in our assessment of Portnoy, who would not have revealed these aspects of his personality but for their therapeutic importance: "I'm trying to be honest with you, Doctor," he insists (104).

Like the speaker of Olds's collection, Portnoy is aware that his honesty makes him vulnerable to judgment, so he indicts himself in no uncertain terms: "What is he doing to himself, this fool! this idiot! this furtive *boy*! This sex maniac! He simply cannot—*will* not—control the fires in his putz" (101). Yet Portnoy is painfully self-conscious as he continues to anticipate Spielvogel's reactions through a series of leading rhetorical questions: "Do I exaggerate? Am I doing myself in only as a clever way of showing off? Or boasting perhaps? Do I really experience this restlessness, this horniness, as an affliction—or as an accomplishment?" (102). Unlike Olds's speaker, Portnoy seems uncomfortable in his vulnerability. He writhes under the therapist's scrutiny, sensitive to the notion that Spielvogel may slip into the role of judge and jury: "And Doctor, Your Honor, whatever your name is," he remarks flippantly but bitterly (102). He even submits himself, at the novel's conclusion, to a mock trial in which he is sentenced (in all caps) to "A TERRIBLE CASE OF IMPOTENCE" for his sexual degradation of Monkey: "YOU ARE JUSTLY SENTENCED TO A LIMP DICK. GO FIND ANOTHER WAY TO HURT A PERSON" (272).

Portnoy's addresses to Spielvogel may be melodramatic, but they juxtapose these juridical assessments with a yearning for understanding and compassion. "Doctor, do you understand what I was up against?" he asks following a depiction of his mother's meddlesome behavior. "My wang was all I really had that I could call my own" (33). He is also earnest about seeking help: "Doctor, what do you call this sickness I have? . . . Doctor, I can't stand any more being frightened like this over nothing! Bless me with manhood! Make me brave! Make me strong! Make me *whole!*" (37). When he senses Spielvogel's lack of sympathy, however—an assessment validated by the DSM entry—his direct addresses become defensive, aggressive, or mocking. "Doctor, my doctor, what do you say, LET'S PUT THE ID BACK IN YID! Liberate this nice Jewish boy's libido, will you please? Raise the prices if you have to—I'll pay anything!" he declares, playfully imploring Spielvogel to cure him through psychoanalysis (124). Elsewhere, he openly derides the psychoanalytic method: "In language plain and simple, are Alexander Portnoy's sensual feelings fixated to his incestuous fantasies? What do you think, Doc? Has a restriction so pathetic been laid upon my object choice?" (186). The ambivalence of Portnoy's addresses betrays a skepticism toward Freudian psychotherapy that reached its zenith in the United States in the 1960s, but more importantly, it also betrays Portnoy's self-consciousness regarding how his "complaint" will be received. If we read *Portnoy's Complaint* in the context of Roth's oeuvre, Portnoy is right to be concerned: in *My Life as a Man*, Spielvogel dismissively refers to Tarnopol's confessions as "narcissistic melodrama" (168); and after watching Tarnopol weep over his marriage for "fully five minutes," Spielvogel responds by asking simply, "Are you finished?" (204)—a line that echoes his only dialogue in *Portnoy's Complaint*.

In borrowing from the conventions of the lyric, Roth asks that we compensate for Spielvogel's parsimonious response by curtailing our judgment and heightening our sympathy for a troubled character-narrator whose impulses are at war with his cultural heritage. The complaint, after all—like the exclusive direct address—is historically a lyrical mode, not a narrative one.[9] As its generic title suggests, the complaint emerges from a speaker's sense of some cosmic injustice: also classified as "lament," its tone is typically filled with distress, tragedy, and self-pity. Consider the apostrophic Elizabethan lyric "A Lover's Complaint" ([1609] 1986), attributed to Shakespeare, in which a maiden laments her seduction and debauching at the hands of a trusted lover. "Ay me! I fell; and yet do question make / What I should do again for such a sake," she cries, admitting in the poem's final, despairing lines that she would fall for him again if given the chance: "O, that infected moisture of his eye, / O, that false fire which in his cheek so glowed . . . Would yet again betray the fore-betrayed, / And new pervert a reconcilèd maid" (166). Consider too Andrew Marvell's "The Nymph Complaining for the Death of Her Fawn" (1681), in which a nymph grieves her loss by swinging wildly from desperation to self-pity much like Portnoy, though without the ribaldry: "O help, O help! I see it faint / And die as calmly as a saint," the speaker cries as her fawn takes its final breaths, though she quickly sinks into despair following its death: "I in a golden vial will / Keep these two crystal tears, and fill / It till it do o'erflow with mine, / Then place it in Diana's shrine" (1972, 70). A more modern example is Philip Whalen's

"Complaint: To the Muse," in which the speaker issues a distressed entreaty to his muse, who has abandoned him: "Come Back! / or at least answer your telephone / I'm nowhere without you" (1999, 33). Such is the tenor of *Portnoy's Complaint*: hyperbolic, even hysterical, it is filled with lamentations, exclamation marks, and even capital letters that denote shouting. The narrative falls apart under Portnoy's duress, finally dissolving into an unhinged scream that spans five lines of text. Roth infuses the lyrical "complaint" with humor and irreverence, much of which derives from the juxtaposition of Portnoy's residual shame from his conservative Jewish upbringing against the backdrop of the sexual revolution of the 1960s—an irony that is not lost on Portnoy. "Why is the smallest thing I do for pleasure immediately illicit—while the rest of the world rolls laughing in the mud!" he laments with lyrical fervor (272).

Roth correctly wagered that the exclusive direct address would grant him greater license with his narrator and also with the lewd material for which his novel has become so well known. "I did not set out to write a book 'about' an analysis," he claimed in an interview with Martha Saxton, "but utilized the permissive conventions of the patient-analyst situation to get at material that had previously been inaccessible to me, and that in another fictional environment would have struck me as pornographic, exhibitionist, and obscene" (1992, 78). At a time when literature was on trial for its racy content, Roth was wise to buffer his own foray into obscenity through the artifice of the exclusive address. The publication of *Portnoy's Complaint* followed on the heels of some of the most highly publicized obscenity trials of the twentieth century, including the heroic trilogy of courtroom defenses put up by Grove Press following its publication of *Lady Chatterley's Lover* (1960), then *Tropic of Cancer* (1962), and finally *Naked Lunch* (1966). Central to these trials were the court's concerns that the graphic nature of the writing appealed chiefly to "prurient interest" and hence occluded any literary value these texts might otherwise offer.

The situation of the therapy session provides a rhetorical justification not only for the graphic sexuality of this "complaint" but also for the bold and direct manner in which it is presented. Nominally, Spielvogel is the only licensed and intended recipient; we are merely hangers-on whom Roth has graciously allowed to listen in. Portnoy is, after all, remarkably uneasy about his admissions, ribald as they may be: "So. Now you know the worst thing I have ever done," he remarks of the liver incident with a few self-castigating qualifiers: "Unless you share with Monkey her contention that the most heinous crime of my career was abandoning her in Greece. Second most heinous: leading her into that triumvirate in Rome" (134). Portnoy frequently frames his confessions in terms of the rebukes he anticipates from Spielvogel, which in turn are shaped by those he has received from the other people in his life—parents, siblings, love interests. Yet Portnoy is shielded here by the ethic of professional discretion that was denied Roth by his own analyst, which propels us away from the punitive model from which Portnoy shrinks when he mockingly addresses his therapist as "Your Honor." It is easy enough to judge or pathologize Portnoy, but the verbs embedded in his entreaties to Spielvogel demand something different: "Doctor, you can't imagine . . ." begins one anecdote (69); "Listen" begins another (111). Portnoy is asking here for patience and understanding; as reader-overhearers, we are pressed to offer both.

In a recent article on the challenges of teaching *Portnoy's Complaint*, Benjamin Schreier (2013) insists that the novel falls flat with undergraduate students not just because of its failure to "shock" them in the twenty-first century but because its *only* significance seems to lie in its ability to shock audiences in 1969 and, subsequently, as a turning point in Roth's critical reception and career. "Regardless of text, course, level, etc.," he writes, "teaching literature inevitably has to emerge out of, or circle around, a fairly elementary question: how does this text ask to be read? . . . I guess I've come to believe that we are no longer capable of asking this question of *Portnoy's Complaint*" (207). On the contrary, the novel circles around precisely this question because of its strikingly unusual rhetorical scaffolding. How *does* this text ask to be read? In short, with the same disordered mixture of intrigue, discomfort, and compassion that we feel any time we overhear an intimate address that is meant for someone else.

The "overheard novel" certainly has precursors, especially those eighteenth-century epistolary novels—Samuel Richardson's *Pamela* (1740) and *Clarissa* (1748), as well as Pierre Choderlos de Laclos's *Les liaisons dangereuses* (1782)—in which the reader is granted special access to private correspondence. These novels, however, are framed by a fictionalized "editor" who has arranged the material for the edification of the reading public. Richardson's editor offers Pamela's letters as "practical examples, worthy to be followed in the most critical and affecting cases, by the modest virgin, the chaste bride, and the obliging wife" ([1740] 2001, 3). Likewise, the editor of *Les liaisons dangereuses* maintains that the novel "is rendering a service to public morals to reveal the methods employed by those who are wicked in corrupting those who are good" ([1782] 1961, 21). These novels are not similarly framed, and readers must negotiate their own positions at the margins of each text, positions largely motivated by the diplomacy and sensitivity that situations involving discretion tend to demand. Consequently, the overheard novel evokes a combination of distance and sympathy we are not used to seeing in narrative fiction. In her work on narratees in Victorian fiction, Robyn Warhol (1989) distinguishes between "distancing" and "engaging" strategies of narrators who engage in direct address. When the narratee aligns with the reader, she argues, the author seeks to engage with her audience. When it does not align, a narratological and emotional rift emerges between author and reader: "The distancing narrator may evoke laughter, or even annoyance, from an actual reader who cannot identify with the narratee. The task of the engaging narrator, in contrast, is to evoke sympathy and identification from an actual reader who is unknown to the author and therefore infinitely variable and unpredictable" (32). The exclusive address, she argues, functions as a distancing strategy because "the 'you' to whom it speaks . . . is indisputably a literary construct" and not an actual reader (202). It is a special "manipulation of address" that transforms the direct address—"you"—into one that is indirect, even "fictionalized." Hence, the "embarrassment" that the artificiality of this lyrical device causes among its readers, according to Jonathan Culler.

Portnoy may well evoke laughter, annoyance, and even embarrassment, but these reactions derive from the novel's tone and content rather than from its internal structure, which works to temper rather than exacerbate our irritation with the novel's character-narrator. As *Tracks*, *Mama Day*, and *Gilead* have shown, the direct address can be far more sobering and emotionally powerful than Warhol's distancing/engaging dichotomy would suggest. All of these works manage to fuse rhetorical distance with readerly sympathy. Moreover, they uncover important aspects of the exclusive direct address that contribute to the unique dynamic between speaker and addressee in this form: the speaker's attempt to communicate to an addressee, the addressee's inability to hear or respond to the attempt, and the self-discovery that this communication engenders for the lyric speaker.

The exclusive address not only shifts the role of the reader from "hearer" to "overhearer," but alters the very genre of narrative fiction by shifting our attention from plot to the dynamic relationship between narrator and addressee. One would be hard pressed to summarize the events of these novels in a way that is coherently plotted; nor does the narrator necessarily exhibit the kind of character arc we might find in, for example, a bildungsroman or künstlerroman. As in chapter 5, narrative action inheres neither in plot nor in character but in temporal progression, as the relationship between narrator and addressee is gradually revealed over time. Consequently, the suspense that these novels generate tends to also revolve around relationships: we turn the pages to discover why and how Lulu has become estranged from her family, or to watch the rocky evolution of the romance between George and Cocoa unfold.

With the exception of Naylor's *Mama Day*, in which both narrator and addressee are given voices in alternating sections, the relationships in these novels are asymmetrical. Though exclusive direct address transforms each monologue into an act of communication, the addressees of these novels are phantomlike: they are largely nonresponsive, and we learn very little about them. Instead, they provide a mechanism through which wary narrators reveal more about themselves than they would ordinarily venture to share. Portnoy, Nanapush, George and Cocoa, and John Ames all seem to require the presence of a listener to justify their confessions. They are awkward narrators who interrupt their stories to explain or mitigate their telling. Even the typically suave Nanapush, the self-proclaimed "talker . . . who used my brains for a weapon" (Erdrich 1988, 118), falters at points: "I now ask your indulgence," he bashfully pleads with Lulu before relating an anecdote that involves her mother's sexuality (105); "I don't know how to tell this next thing that happened," he laments, prefacing a complicated series of events that leads to an irreparable intratribal feud (109); and preparing Lulu for a story about his own sexual escapades, he begins, "You think I'm going to stop at this point, but I'll go on. You have no one to prepare you for a husband. . . . So I'm going to tell you something about married people. Possibly, you know already. But dear girl, pretend for my sake that you don't?" (183). "Narratives in which explanations and motivations abound," argues Gerald Prince, "are often by narrators who find the dimension of discourse (*discours*) more important than that of narrative (*recit*) or who are acutely aware of the gratuitousness—and even the falseness—of any narrative or of a certain type of narrative and consequently try to exorcise it" ([1973] 1980, 16). These are self-conscious narrators who are uncomfortable, he suggests, not only with their stories but with narrative itself—perhaps the reason they choose to deliver their stories in the confessional mode. Still, the insecurities of Portnoy and Ames are palpable. As Portnoy's "complaint" develops without any input from Spielvogel, his confession becomes hysterical, devolving into one long scream; at the opposite extreme, Ames is so reluctant to engage in the candor required by his epistolary memoir that he endlessly justifies his feelings by couching them in maxims for his young son. A number of other contemporary narrators fall somewhere between. Salinger's Holden Caulfield peppers his confession with sarcasm to mask his discomfort: "If you really want to hear about it," he begins, "the first thing you'll want to know is where I was born, and what my lousy childhood was like, and how my parents were occupied and all before they had me, and all that David Copperfield kind of crap, but I don't feel like going into it, if you want to know the truth" (1951, 1). Like Portnoy, Caulfield appears to direct his narrative to a therapist, though his confession is delivered from the confines of a mental hospital. Consider, too, a novel like William Gass's *The Tunnel* (1995), which begins as Professor William Kohler's introduction to his scholarly magnum opus on Nazi Germany, though it devolves into a personal memoir addressed to his wife, with whom he has an extremely fraught relationship. Kohler becomes so uncomfortable with his confessions and so paranoid that they will be discovered by his wife that he conceals these pages between the covers of his official manuscript.

As hidden extradiegetic listeners, we occupy an uncomfortable moral position when we overhear confessions that are reluctantly made by narrators who clearly cherish their privacy. We are also, however, at an advantage, since we have access to a balanced external perspective that is unavailable to the novel's characters. In *Tracks*, we are witness to the cultural history and decline of the Turtle Mountain Anishinabe, but as objective observers, we are unburdened by the personal animosities that its members bear toward one another—Lulu for Fleur, Nanapush for Pauline, and Pauline for her tribe. As outsiders looking in on domestic scenes in *Mama Day*, we are able to see precisely where George and Cocoa miscommunicate, though they cannot see it for themselves. In *Gilead*, we observe Ames as he displaces his insecurities onto Jack Boughton. *Portnoy's Complaint* grants us access not only to Portnoy's most embarrassing disclosures but also to his therapist's assessment of them. In all four cases, these narrators substantiate and justify their confessions in terms of their exclusive address rather than vice versa; that is, the character-bound addressee provides the exigency for the narrative.

Though exclusive direct address positions readers as unwelcome eavesdroppers who hover somewhere between presence and absence in the rhetorical model of narrative theory, the novels treated here demonstrate that distancing and sympathy may actually go hand in hand. Authors use character-bound addressees not to alienate readers but to solicit sympathetic readings of characters who might otherwise warrant harsher judgment. The exclusive address affords a more objective purview to the reader that is not necessarily available to the novel's characters; because we are discouraged from fully inhabiting the perspective of either narrator or narratee, we are at a remove from their biases, anxieties, and neuroses. Consequently, we are challenged to strike a delicate balance between compassion and impartiality, made sensitive by the fact that we are overhearing confessions meant for someone else.

Of course, the scenario of the "overheard" novel is itself a fiction: we are not violating the privacy of any real person, and authors have deliberately published these texts for a broad readership. Our conflicted position as reader-overhearers is necessarily mitigated by this fact, since we are granted the privilege of eavesdropping without having to face any real-world consequences. This does not necessarily cause the rhetorical frame of the exclusive direct address to lose its potency or utility, however, for the same reasons that narrative theorists argue for fiction's unique ability to exercise the mind and emotions of its readers in an array of make-believe scenarios. Novels function as literary laboratories for the free play of cognitive and emotional states: according to Suzanne Keen, as "safe zones for readers' feeling empathy without experiencing a resultant demand on real-world action" (2010, 4); and according to Lisa Zunshine, as "pretend play" in which "our enjoyment of fiction is predicated—at least in part—upon our awareness of our 'trying on' mental states potentially available to us but at a given moment differing from our own" (2006, 17). Likewise, I venture that the overheard novel provides a forum through which we may satisfy our desire to eavesdrop without the real social risk of violating someone else's privacy. In fact, one could make the case that all literature performs this function, since the literary imagination requires both readers and writers to peer into the lives of others. David Foster Wallace described writers as "oglers" who "tend to lurk and to stare. . . . They are born watchers . . . because human situations are writers' food" (1993, 151). Jeremy Hawthorn's recent study, *The Reader as Peeping Tom*, makes much the same point from the vantage point of the reader: "We respond to the text but the text does not respond to us. The narrators of works of prose fiction and films may address us, but they do not interact with us; as readers and viewers we have a relationship with them that is fundamentally a non-reciprocal one" (2014, 5). By exaggerating the element of surveillance that accompanies all fictional worlds, writers who utilize the exclusive address remind readers of the distance that separates them from both real and fictional others. Perhaps, as these texts suggest, our capacity for sympathy and understanding is not necessarily a function of proximity but may also be found precisely in this distance, the remote position we occupy as reader-overhearers who suspend judgment for the sake of compassion.

Coda

✦

Genre Revisited

This study turns a lyrical lens on narrative fiction, focusing on ways in which the traditional conventions of narrative are altered by, or refracted through, lyrical techniques. Yet a surprisingly large number of the works treated here have delineated their generic alliance with the novel through subtitles that appear on their covers or title pages: Acker's *Blood and Guts in High School*, DeLillo's *Underworld*, Hurston's *Their Eyes Were Watching God*, Ellis's *American Psycho*, Palahniuk's *Fight Club*, Erdrich's *Tracks*, and Robinson's *Gilead* all feature the same subtitle, "A Novel." What are the implications of this study for the form of the novel, which is ultimately reaffirmed by these subtitles, however it might be challenged and tested in these individual works?

As the twentieth century has proven, the novel is an elastic form capable of absorbing many different elements from other genres. The multinarrator novel made popular by Faulkner and his literary descendants relies on elements of drama for its effect, as a single narrator gives way to a fractured narration in which characters speak for themselves like actors on a stage. The novella, a favorite form of Henry James, achieves the compactness and conciseness that was previously the territory of the short story. The nonfiction novel developed by Truman Capote, Norman Mailer, and other postwar writer-journalists fuses reportage with the dramatic artistry of fictional narrative. Howard Weinbrot has argued that Menippean satire is "the genre that ate the world" (2005, 1), but one might more accurately claim this title for the novel, which has even begun, in ways that I have traced here, to accommodate lyrical elements that deliberately work against narrativity.

In fact, the lyrical novel provides a point of access through which we might begin to recuperate the lyric tradition, which currently occupies a benighted position in both commercial and academic industries. Imagine the surprise of my students—allergic as they are to poetry's ambiguity—when they discover that *Fight Club* participates in the same twofold device of the dramatized speaker and the disappearing plot as Robert Browning's verse monologues. This project points to the indebtedness of some of our most celebrated American novels to lyrical strategies ranging from repetition to metaphor to exclusive address. To be sure, the literary lineages constructed in these chapters are more heuristic than historical, but they yield powerful explanatory frameworks for understanding the nonnarrative structure of modern and contemporary novels, which seem to have far more in common with lyric poems than with their novelistic predecessors.

This study also, I hope, helps to crystallize some of the lyric's most salient features, which are often submerged in debates that seek to stake out rigid definitional demarcations, as indicated by my survey of generic criticism in chapter 1: debates over whether, for example, the lyric's temporality represents the realm of the static or dynamic or whether the lyric represents the realm of solitary utterance or social discourse. In this sense, I join Jonathan Culler in his most recent endeavor "to work out a general framework, a theory of lyric, in which attention to these features of lyric is encouraged and not restricted by one of the narrow models of lyric that have in recent years organized most approaches to lyric poetry" (2015, viii). Above all, the lyric is a site of liminality, at once static and dynamic, as evidenced by the role of structural repetition treated in chapter 2; at once solitary and social, as evidenced by the exclusive direct address treated in chapter 6. This liminality is, to my mind, what largely separates the lyric from traditional narrative fiction, which—because of its firm ontological grounding in plot—cannot risk hovering over such thresholds for long. Because the novels examined here do just that, they require that we make special adjustments to our generic expectations for narrative fiction.

Literature involves a dynamic interaction among author, text, and perhaps most importantly, reader. In keeping with the aims of rhetorical narrative theory, I have focused primarily on the reader, who, after all, approaches novels with certain expectations that are frustrated, but also productively challenged, when they are not met.[1] The novels treated in this study, while canonical, have frustrated as many readers as they have won over. By urging readers to consider these novels in terms of lyricality rather than narrativity, I hope to have allayed some of these frustrations so that readers might better appreciate the intricate artistry behind these works. The syntax that drives B. R. Myers to pan contemporary American writers, for instance, aims not for pretension but to deliberately erase those hierarchical distinctions we normally expect from narrative fiction, all the while cultivating a rhythm that turns prose into prosody.

This project showcases the benefits of approaching and conceptualizing American literature outside of historical chronology. The chapters in this study deliberately blur the division between modernist and postmodernist novels formulated by critics such as Brian McHale (1987), Linda Hutcheon (1989), and Frederic Jameson (1991) by arranging novels in terms of lyrical intensity rather than chronology. American literature has long been haunted, perhaps even stymied, by this distinction. Instead, I offer a model that places literary works on a generic continuum running from narrative to lyric, one that better equips us to resolve some of the critical debates surrounding these novels. To some extent, this continuum is modeled within each chapter, which typically ends with the most vivid or dramatic instance of a lyrical trope. Thus, the patterns of repetition in chapter 2 advance in scale from the phrase in Dos Passos to the paragraph in Kathy Acker, and the flattening of hierarchy that begins in Faulkner is carried to an amoral extreme in the dark economy of McCarthy's *Blood Meridian*. This focus on genre enables me to construct groupings of texts that run counter to conventional literary histories in which one would hardly find Toni Morrison aligned with Henry Miller or either writer aligned with the seventeenth-century metaphysical poets. It also highlights the innovation of writers who do not fall neatly into categories such as modernism or postmodernism and, hence, are not typically considered "experimental," including Zora Neale Hurston, Louise Erdrich, Philip Roth, and Gloria Naylor.

The intersection of lyric and narrative extends far beyond the agonistic struggle for literary and cultural dominance depicted by genre critics. This project outlines a cooperative and productive relationship through which narrative fiction paradoxically forgoes narrativity for lyricality. The new millennium promises even greater experimentation with genre in American literature, especially as the line between fiction and nonfiction becomes deliberately blurred in novels such as William T. Vollmann's *Europe Central* (2005) and Junot Díaz's *The Brief, Wondrous Life of Oscar Wao* (2007), both of which contains a dizzying number of informational notes and annotations that disguise themselves as carefully documented secondary texts. Conversely, Percival Everett distorts reality through fiction in his trademark postmodernist fashion: *I Am Not Sidney Poitier* (2009) features real-life celebrities such as Sidney Poitier (sort of), Ted Turner, and Jane Fonda in new and distorted contexts, all in service to Everett's brilliant satire of race and class in the United States. More recently, the breathtakingly transgeneric work of Claudia Rankine represents a true experiment with multiple modalities: her acclaimed collection *Citizen: An American Lyric* (2014) intersperses lyric with narrative vignettes, images, art, and scripts for "situation videos" that appear on her website. These works not only unseat narrativity as the inevitable "Queen of Discourse" (Phelan 2006, 285), but defy readers to decide which modality takes precedence; rather than vying for domination, these genres complement one another in ways that lend depth and dimension to their subjects.

As readers, teachers, and critics of literary texts, we rely on genre all the time. It organizes our bookstores, our course offerings, and our anthologies; it helps us organize our Netflix queues, and it allows Amazon to generate recommendations based on previous orders; it guides our preferences and our distastes; in short, it conditions the way we think about literary texts even before we open their pages. Yet so often we fail to reflect on the purpose and meanings of the categories we use. Twentieth- and twenty-first-century texts demand that we revisit these categories so that we might become better and more flexible readers of works that make use of a variety of generic techniques. We are called to see genres not as tightly sealed containers but as provisional categories with porous boundaries that allow for rich areas of intersection and overlap. The model of genre under which we have been operating, consciously or not, is in need of an update. Our writers have long been exploiting the flexibility of genre for various ends; it is time that we, as critics, begin to catch up.

NOTES

Preface

1. See Wayne Booth ([1961] 1983, esp. 4–6) and Scholes, Phelan, and Kellogg (2006, 263). Robert Caserio locates a strain of modern fiction that rejects plot and story altogether; in rejecting plot, he argues, authors such as Stein, Lawrence, Woolf, and Joyce reject action and meaning in favor of "quietism, purposelessness, inhibition or suspension of will, passive or static states of mind and feeling, and speculation free of connection with deeds" (1979, xiv). Peter Brooks also detects a rebellion against plot in the twentieth-century novel "engendered perhaps by an overelaboration of and overdependence on plots in the nineteenth century" (1984, 7). "Whereas plot continues in our time to be a dominant element in popular fictions of many sorts and to proceed on principles little changed from the nineteenth century," he continues, "in those works that claim to challenge their readers, plot is often something of an embarrassment" (314).

2. For a recent estimation of this problem, see McHale (2009, 11–12).

Chapter 1

1. For more accounts of genres in contest, see Markovits (2012), as well as Kurnick, who understands genres to be "engaged in a kind of Darwinian struggle for survival" (2005, 259).

2. Clearly, there is irony in this argument, as in much of the *Republic*, since all of Plato's dialogues appear in dramatic form.

3. See, for example, Bliss Perry's *Study of Prose Fiction* (1902) and *Study of Poetry* (1920); John Erskine's "The Kinds of Poetry" (1920a); and Gayley and Kurtz's *Lyric, Epic, and Allied Forms of Poetry* (1920).

4. For recent and thoughtful accounts of lyric poetry's potential to contribute productively to a Marxist literary framework, see Nealon (2004; 2007). See also the New Formalist responses to Marxist assertions about the lyric's social irresponsibility, such as Levine (2006) and Tucker's rejoinder to Levine (2006).

5. Gertrude Stein and her experiments with lyric and prose forms were very influential for the Language poets, who often cite Stein as a revered ancestor and who insist, as does Stein, that "prose is not necessarily not poetry" (Hejinian 2000, 323). See Bernstein (1992), Hejinian (2000), and Retallack (2003). In the same vein, Pound and Williams are reclaimed by the objectivist poets such as Charles Olson; see "This Is Yeats Speaking" and "Paterson, Book V" in his *Collected Prose* (1997).

6. James Phelan has defined *lyricality* through "two main modes: (1) somebody telling somebody else (or even himself or herself) on some occasion for some purpose that something is—a situation, an emotion, a perception, an attitude, a belief; (2) somebody telling somebody else (or even himself or herself) on some

occasion about his or her meditations on something; to put it another way, in this mode, the poem records the speaker's thoughts" (2007a, 22). Rather than staking out any definitional claims, my study characterizes lyricality through a cluster of key tropes, each of which serves as the focal point for individual chapters.

7. For more on the metaphysical groundwork that underpins genre, see Owens-Murphy (2013).

Chapter 2

1. See, for instance, the entry for "repetition" in the *Encyclopedia of Poetry and Poetics*, ed. Alex Preminger and T. V. F. Brogan (1993): "Repetition is a basic unifying device in all poetry" (1035). See also Helen Vendler's *Poems, Poets, Poetry: An Introduction and Anthology* (2002), which argues that a repeated word serves as the "linch-pin" of a poem (166).

2. For a related, though not equivalent, discussion of repetition's potential for signaling difference rather than sameness, see also Gates's account of "Signifyin(g)" in *The Signifying Monkey* (1988): "Free of the white person's gaze, black people created their own unique vernacular structures and relished in the double play that these forms bore to white forms. Repetition and revision are fundamental to black artistic forms, from painting and sculpture to music and language use. I decided to analyze the nature and function of Signifyin(g) precisely because it *is* repetition and revision, or repetition with a signal difference. Whatever is black about black American literature is to be found in this identifiable black Signifyin(g) difference" (xxiv).

3. An exception here is Porter Abbott, who argues for a much broader definition of narrative as the representation of a single event (2002, 13). Yet even his illustrative examples belie causal and sequential chains of action. The nonnarrative description "My dog has fleas," for example—juxtaposed to his narrative account, "My dog was bitten by a flea"—already implies that a flea first bites his dog and the dog, in turn, becomes the parasite's host.

4. Some theorists, including Brian Richardson, maintain that causality—even more so than time—is an essential part of narrative fiction: "Every narrative includes (along with space and time) some system of causation as part of its setting" (1997, 15).

5. Boris Tomashevsky (1965) also makes this argument in his essay "Thematics." For a more recent look at repetition as building theme within narrative fiction, see J. Hillis Miller (1982).

6. For an in-depth discussion of the importance of sequence, succession for the intelligibility of plot, see Caserio (1979, 5–6).

7. Usually, this speaker is identified as Dos Passos himself, since these sections are heavily autobiographical and correlate with events and impressions from Dos Passos's life.

8. Mac joins up with the I.W.W. and the Anarchist Union of Industry and Agriculture in his narrative sections. Big Bill Haywood, founding member and leader of the I.W.W. and member of the Western Federation of Miners, appears both as a character in Mac's narrative and in a separate historical biography.

9. For an extensive treatment of traditional narrative and its link to heteronormativity, see Judith Roof: "Interwound with one another," she writes, "narrative and sexuality operate within the reproductive and/or productive, metaphorically

heterosexual ideology that also underwrites the naturalized understanding of the shape and meaning of life" (1996, xxvii).

10. Lisa Ruddick sees this split in epistemological terms, arguing that "Melanctha" hinges on these "two 'ways of knowing.' One is linear and progressive; the other is circular and rhythmic and has something in common with the wandering quality of Melanctha's mind" (1990, 33).

11. For a compatible critique of narrative sequence as inherently male-centered and heteronormative, see Susan Winnett's critique of Peter Brooks's *Reading for the Plot* in her article, "Coming Unstrung" (1990).

12. The link between repetition and trauma, termed "repetition compulsion" in psychoanalysis, was developed by Sigmund Freud in his essay *Beyond the Pleasure Principle* ([1920] 1990).

13. For an alternative reading of the dream maps, see Kate R. Muth. Muth argues that one can in fact construct relatively coherent narratives around portions of these maps, paying special attention to what she calls the "worm nightmare," though she ultimately argues that such narratives "both invite and subvert narratological or allegorical interpretation" (2011, 94).

Chapter 3

1. An expanded version of the argument appeared in Myers's book of the same title, published in the following year (2002). The article version sparked a number of responses from other periodicals: favorable responses appeared in the *Washington Post* and the *Observer of London* while the *New York Times* and the *Los Angeles Times* featured negative appraisals of Myers's piece.

2. Myers (2001) twice accuses McCarthy of hijacking a syntax that is better suited to the Bible than to contemporary novels. In addition to identifying the "stern biblical tone that runs through all of McCarthy's recent novels," Myers also responds to critical praise for *All the Pretty Horses* by remarking, "What a difference a pseudo-biblical style makes."

3. Parataxis is a similar construction that omits conjunctions, often replacing them with punctuation. The result is a series of short, staccato phrases in contrast to the smooth cadence created by polysyndeton.

4. The original collection does not contain pagination; the poem is simply listed as number 10.

5. This irony is continuously highlighted in studies of Faulkner and humor. See Campbell and Foster (1951, 98), R. Cross (1967, 210–11), and Cox (1986, 2). For a serious close reading of the erotic scenes between Ike and the cow, see Godden (2003, 609–11).

6. Michael Reynolds also experiments with breaking Hemingway's prose into verse lines in his study *Hemingway's First War* (1976), 56.

7. Philip Nel (2008, 20–21) briefly touches on Hemingway's stylistic influence on DeLillo. See also Cowart's discussion of Hemingway's imprint on *End Zone* and *Mao II* (2002a, 21–22 and 115).

8. For a reading of the juxtaposition of these two plots and what they might reveal about the relationship between plot and motive, see Bérubé (2006).

9. In fact, DeLillo maintains that this juxtaposition on the front page of the October 4, 1951, edition of the *New York Times* inspired *Underworld*. See his essay "The Power of History" (1997).

10. For an extended treatment of the motif of "recycling" and its connection to the novel's "vision of art," see Cowart (2002a, 197).

11. Mark Osteen argues that "what unites these disparate events and strands is capitalism" (2000, 243), but the passages I have quoted at length in this chapter reveal other, emotional dimensions of connectivity that are not easily explained by capitalism.

12. For "paranoid" readings of interconnection in *Underworld*, see Knight (1999), Kellman (2002), Ostrowski (2002), and Apter (2006).

13. Albert Erskine served as Faulkner's editor from 1958 until Faulkner's death in 1962 (Williamson 1993, 322); he served as McCarthy's editor from 1965 until his retirement in the mid-1980s, *Blood Meridian* marking their final collaboration. Faulkner published all of his novels beginning with *Absalom, Absalom!* with Random House; McCarthy has published all of his work to date with Random House, confessing that he sent his first manuscript there because "it was the only publisher I had heard of" (Woodward 1992).

14. See especially Caryn James's 1985 review in the *New York Times*, which concludes: "There are, of course, no answers to the life-and-death issues Mr. McCarthy raises, but there are more rigorous, coherent ways to frame the questions."

15. See, for example, V. Bell (1988), Shaviro (1999), and Winchell (1990).

16. According to Nick Monk, *Blood Meridian* critiques "a version of modernity that owes its existence to the European Enlightenment" and that is used to justify colonialism (2002, 83). Likewise, Mark Eaton argues that "the violence in *Blood Meridian* clearly occurs . . . as one consequence of a larger conflict over land and cultural dominance" (2003, 157).

Chapter 4

1. According to Hrushovski, metaphors establish two "frames of reference": "The first frame of reference (*fr1*) is presented as *existing* in the world of the poem (it is further enriched from what we know about the external world indicated by the real geographical names). The second frame of reference (*fr2*) . . . is introduced as *non-existing* in the fictional world of the poem . . . it is presented to the imagination of the reader for the sake of metaphorical transfers" (1984, 8).

2. For a discussion of the opalescence of metaphor in postmodernist fiction, which prolongs metaphor's hesitation between the realms of style and ontology, see McHale (1987, 134–37).

3. For accounts of Eliot's literary anti-Semitism, see Strauss (2007), Cheyette (2009), and Julius (1995).

4. Two exceptions are Barbara Johnson (1993) and Phillip Novak (1999). Johnson argues that Morrison "aestheticizes" violence—rape, war, murder, slavery—in order to display, with irony, the deeply political dimension of aesthetics. In positioning aesthetics as "the domain of the contemplation of forms, implying detachment and distance" (170), however, Johnson reads into Morrison's fiction an emotional distance between narrator and character that, I argue, is closed by her reliance on the conceit.

5. This passage is also cited in Novak and Thompson as microcosmic of the novel's preoccupation with violence and decapitation, respectively.

6. For more on the difficulty of moral judgment in *Sula*, see Yung-Hsing Wu (2003).

7. For example, Samuels and Hudson-Weems (1990, 43) argue that Sula "seems to lack interest in assuming any responsibility for her fellow human beings." La Vinia Delois Jennings (2008, 27) even argues that Sula is "evil" in a way that she claims is consistent with the African Ndoki paradigm. Similarly, Christopher Okonkwo (2004) likens her to the "malevolent ogbanjeabiku" of West African folklore.

8. After Miller was charged with obscenity by five state courts (Connecticut, Florida, Illinois, Pennsylvania, and New York), a landmark 1964 Supreme Court decision overturned these verdicts and vindicated *Tropic of Cancer*, declaring that "material dealing with sex in a manner that advocates ideas, or that has literary or scientific or artistic value or any other form of social importance, may not be branded as obscenity and denied the constitutional protection" (Karolides, Bald, and Sova 1999, 325–27).

9. "The Last Book" was Miller's original title for *Tropic of Cancer*.

10. According to James Phelan, the dynamic progression we experience as we read narratives from beginning to end actively engages our ethical judgment; indeed, Phelan argues that readerly judgment is essential to "our experience—and understanding—of narrative form" in marked contrast to the lyric, which places readers "less in the position of the observer and judge and more in the position of participant" (2007b, 3, 22). Martha Nussbaum's Aristotelian-inspired study of the intersection of ethics and literature in *Love's Knowledge* (1990) likewise privileges the novel as a model for ethical judgment based on its richness of detail and context; consequently, her case studies consist of lengthy novels by Marcel Proust and Henry James. For a broader discussion of judgment versus compassion, see chapter 6.

11. For a critique of this claim and an argument for plot's dynamic relationship to our psychological needs, see Peter Brooks (1984).

Chapter 5

1. An exception is Dorrit Cohn (1978, 257), who makes a similar observation from the other direction, arguing that all dramatic monologue is first-person narration: "The presence of a fictive speaker relates the dramatic monology not only to soliloquy in drama, but also to ficional narrative in the first person—a relationship that has been largely disregarded in discussions of the dramatic monologue, perhaps because of the 'dramatic' emphasis of the English term. Viewed from this vantage point, all dramatic monologues are first-person narratives in verse form."

2. Several critics have also suggested that the text's ambiguities cannot be resolved. See especially Perry and Sternberg's discussion of "gap-filling" in biblical and literary texts: "The main compositional principle in *The Turn of the Screw* is the impossibility of choosing between the alternative hypotheses," they write (1986, 317). The essay does not, however, detail the evidence for each reading that precludes readers from adopting a single hypothesis. For a more thorough analysis of the text's dueling, "mutually exclusive" interpretations, see Shlomith Rimmon, who carefully traces the "linguistic ambiguities" that lead readers toward different readings (1977, 116, 154). In contrast, I locate the plot's obscurity within our dramatized narrator, who becomes incrementally unreliable as the novella unfolds. Christine Brooke-Rose argues for an ambiguous reading that is structured around the "long glasses" or mirrors at Bly that supply "the

sudden expansion of a previously restricted consciousness" (1981, 161). She also argues that the mirror lends the story a "poetic structure" by analogy since, "with all the play of vision-variation it affords, [it] functions around this same system of repetition and reversal at work in the projection of these images" (165). I argue that the relationship between *The Turn of the Screw* and the lyric tradition is more direct than this, and that it inheres in the persona of its character-narrator.

3. See Phelan's extended treatment of this problem in "Estranging Unreliability" (2007) and *Living to Tell about It* (2004). For an evaluation of Nabokov's careful balance between "human warmth" and a gritty rendering of sexual obsession in Humbert's first-person narrative, see Toker (1989, 207–11).

4. As Brian Richardson (2011, 87) notes of Vivian Darkbloom and her corollaries in Nabokov's other works, "The primary (if not sole) function of these names is to inject the alphabetical presence of the author into the text of the fiction, in the way that most of Hitchcock's films include an image of the director unconvincingly portraying a supernumerary character or a most unlikely 'man on the street.'"

5. Again, Appel (1991) provides an exhaustive list: see 31n9.

6. These same issues arise with a vengeance in Nabokov's experimental *Pale Fire*, which hovers somewhere between novel, poem, and secondary criticism. For a discussion of critical debates surrounding its unstable plot, see Rabinowitz (1977, 121–22).

7. Critics who focus on the novel's consumerism also tend to read the plot in terms of allegory. Thomas Heise (2011, 135), for instance, describes the novel as "a terrifyingly intimate experience of violence by a psychotic subject who embodies neoliberal theory and performs it through his repeated acts of disembowelment." Richard Godden (2011, 420) reads the torturing of the homeless by Bateman and his fellow financiers, who offer money to beggars and then quickly withdraw it, as analogous to the "structural adjustment programs used by the International Monetary Fund and the World Bank during the 1980s and 1990s, in which loans and debt rescheduling were made dependent on market reorganization by the recipient nation." Leigh Claire La Berge (2010) has argued that, in part, *American Psycho* is a literal rendering of the violent language—e.g., "the men who make the killings"—that was used in news media to depict financiers in the 1980s.

8. For a compelling reading that bridges these critical responses via ethics, see Serpell (2010). I am also indebted to her articulation of the critical debate surrounding Patrick Bateman and his ontological status as a character and murderer.

9. Ellis's choice to set the novel in the 1980s has a deliberate distancing effect between narrator and reader. Many of the styles, consumer products, technology, musical artists, etc., that Bateman mentions in order to gain stature in the eyes of the reader would already seem outdated to the novel's 1991 audience. More importantly, the crash of 1987 effectively ended the yuppie lifestyle Bateman depicts here. This chronological gap will only continue to widen for future generations of readers.

10. For a fuller discussion of pacing and violence in both the novel and film version, see Abel (2007, 29–59).

11. The killings do become less patterned and meaningful toward the end of the novel, which Bateman himself acknowledges. After killing a child, he waxes

philosophical about his victim: "I'm suddenly jolted with a mournful despair at how useless, how extraordinarily painless, it is to take a child's life," he reflects with disappointment (299). He goes on to kill a saxophone player, a cab driver, a cashier, a cop, a watchman, and a janitor in a senseless and fast-paced killing rampage (348–49).

12. Bateman is also mistaken for Ebersol (55), McDonald (111), Williams (127), Taylor (137), Simpson (141), Kinsley (151), Baxter (195), Ted Owen (262), and Saul Steinberg (262). There are many other cases of mistaken identity, as well: Bateman mistakes Madison for Turnball (55); Preston and Price mistake Paul Owen for Morrison (36); Price mistakes a stranger for Victor Powell (7–8); Evelyn mistakes a Christmas elf for Laurence Tisch (183); and Stephen Hughes mistakes Hubert Ainsworth for Paul Owen (273). These characters seem to be incapable of distinguishing themselves from one another.

13. There is, after all, the possibility that Carnes has again misidentified a different yet identical Wall Street colleague just as does he with Bateman.

14. Gerald Prince's often-cited *Dictionary of Narratology* defines character as "an existent endowed with anthropomorphic traits and engaged in anthropomorphic actions; an actor with anthropomorphic attributes" (2003, 1956); Uri Margolin (1996, 205) likewise understands character as "designating a human or human-like individual, existing in some possible world." Current cognitive-based approaches to narrative are also invested in reading characters as real people: in *Why We Read Fiction*, Lisa Zunshine famously argues that characters are possible people upon whom we can exercise what cognitive scientists call our "theory of mind" (2006). Other critics, however, caution against our tendency to automatically imbue characters with human traits. Mieke Bal (1997, 115) argues that fictional characters walk a precarious line between artifice and reality: "The character is not a human being, but it resembles one. It has no real psyche, personality, ideology, or competence to act, but it does possess characteristics which make psychological and ideological descriptions possible." Therefore, she continues, "we must restrict our investigation to only those facts that are presented to us in the actual words of the text" (116). Details may be said to "create," "map out," or "build up" a fictional person, but to mistake a character for a human being is to be guilty of "anthropomorphism," a narratological faux-pas in Bal's view (116). For more on the distinctions among "thematic," "synthetic," and "mimetic" dimensions of character, see Phelan 1989.

15. For an examination of the "double-construction" of Bateman as serial killer and Wall Street yuppie with regard to both the film and the novel, see Kooijman and Laine (2003).

16. M. Cross (1993, 3) writes that James's sentences in *Turn of the Screw* are "qualifying to the point of seeming surreal." James R. Giles (2006, 160) writes that Ellis's characters "live in a narrative mode that falls somewhere between literary naturalism and surrealism." Peter Rabinowitz (2004, 325) points to the "almost surrealistic shootout" that serves as *Lolita*'s climax. Jesse Kavadlo (2005, 4) highlights the "violent surrealism" that characterizes *Fight Club*.

Chapter 6

1. David Gooblar (2011) argues that psychoanalysis acts as a platform for the novel's humor whereas David Brauner (2000) argues that humor is a platform

for psychoanalysis. Essentially, Brauner locates an underlying seriousness in Portnoy's "complaint," which he characterizes as Alex Portnoy's "attempt to free himself from the confines of his comical identity" (87).

2. Phelan amends this account in his preface by stating that he ultimately moves toward a model in which "the lines between author, reader, and text become blurred" and in which "rhetoric is the synergy occurring between authorial agency, textual phenomena, and reader response" (1996, xii). Either way, his conception of "narrative as rhetoric" is one in which readers are expected to engage actively with the text.

3. This problem was first pointed out by Gerald Prince ([1973] 1980). The concept of the narratee has since been treated by Robyn Warhol (1989) as well as in several studies that appeared in a 1994 special issue of *Style* on the topic of second-person narration: for example, Irene Kacandes's "Narrative Apostrophe: Reading Rhetoric, Resistance in Michel Butor's 'La modification' and Julio Cortazar's 'Graffiti,'" which uses communication theory (addresser, message, addressee) to understand the narrative apostrophe's emotional impact on audience; and James Phelan's "Self-Help for Narratee and Narrative Audience: How 'I'—and 'You'—Read 'How,'" which explores the distinction between Prince's concept of the narratee and Rabinowitz's concept of narrative audience. Much work remains to be done on this concept, especially on uses and applications of the fictional addressee.

4. In keeping with Nanapush's preferred appellation, I will henceforth refer to the Chippewa as the Anishinabe.

5. These policies are not referenced in the novel itself but, as Nancy J. Peterson convincingly argues in her excellent article on *Tracks* and history (1994), they are certainly within the novel's historical backdrop, since the novel's events begin in 1912 and end in 1924.

6. For more on the orality of Nanapush's narrative, see also Hughes (2000, 96–97).

7. Robinson does not provide many dates in this novel, but Ames's grandfather was an acquaintance of John Brown's, an "old issue" of *Ladies' Home Journal* magazine article is dated 1948, and television is a new addition to the Ames household, which would place this novel somewhere in the 1950s.

8. See, for example, Leise (2009), Douglas (2011), Latz (2011), and R. Williams (2011). See also *Christianity and Literature*'s 2010 special issue featuring religious readings of the novel.

9. For an analysis of "aggressive" narrative complaints in contemporary American fiction that "make readers feel attacked" (41)—including *Portnoy's Complaint*—see Kathryn Hume (2011, 40–76).

Coda

1. For an analysis of the expectations readers typically bring to narrative fiction and the ways in which these expectations shape the act of interpretation, see Rabinowitz (1998).

BIBLIOGRAPHY

Poetry

Blake, William. 2002. *Collected Poems*. Edited by W. B. Yeats. London: Routledge.

Brown, Sterling. (1939) 1980. *Collected Poems*. Edited by Michael S. Harper. Evanston, Ill.: Northwestern University Press.

Browning, Robert. 1981. *The Poems: Volume One*. Edited by John Pettigrew. New Haven, Conn.: Yale University Press.

Clifton, Lucille. 1970. *Good Times: Poems by Lucille Clifton*. New York: Random House.

Collins, Billy. 1998. *The Apple That Astonished Paris: Poems*. Fayetteville: University of Arkansas Press.

Dickinson, Emily. 1992. *Emily Dickinson: Selected Poems*. Edited by Ian Hamilton. New York: St. Martin's.

Donne, John. 1985. *The Complete English Poems*. Edited by C. A. Patrides. London: Dent.

Eliot, T. S. 1963. *Collected Poems 1909–1962*. Orlando, FL: Harcourt Brace.

Graves, Robert. 1977. *New Collected Poems*. New York: Doubleday.

Hughes, Langston. 1994. *Collected Poems*. Edited by Arnold Rampersad. New York: Random House.

Lawrence, D. H. 1964. *Complete Poems*. Edited by David Herbert Lawrence, Vivian de Sola Pinto, and Warren Roberts. New York: Penguin.

Lee, Li-Young. 1986. *Rose: Poems by Li-Young Lee*. Rochester: BOA Editions.

Lowell, Amy. 2002. *Selected Poems*. Edited by Melissa Bradshaw and Adrienne Munich. New Brunswick, N.J.: Rutgers University Press.

Marvell, Andrew. 1972. *The Complete Poems*. New York: Penguin Classics.

Olds, Sharon. (1984) 2009. *The Dead and the Living*. New York: Alfred A. Knopf.

Poe, Edgar Allan. 1984. *Complete Stories and Poems*. New York: Doubleday.

Rankine, Claudia. 2014. *Citizen: An American Lyric*. Minneapolis: Graywolf P.

Shakespeare, William. (1609) 1986. *The Sonnets and A Lover's Complaint*. Edited by John Kerrigan. New York: Viking.

Szirtes, George. 2008. *New & Collected Poems*. Northumberland, England: Bloodaxe Books.

Weinbrot, Howard. 2005. *Menippean Satire Reconsidered: From Antiquity to the 18th Century*. Baltimore: Johns Hopkins University Press.

Whalen, Philip. 1999. *Overtime: Selected Poems*. Edited by Michael Rothenberg. New York: Penguin Books.

Whitman, Walt. 1855. *Leaves of Grass*. In the Walt Whitman Archive, edited by Ed Folsom and Kenneth M. Price. http://whitmanarchive.org/published/LG/1855/whole.html.

Fiction

Acker, Kathy. 1978. *Blood and Guts in High School*. New York: Grove Press.
Banks, Russell. 1985. *Continental Drift*. New York: Harper Perennial.
Cheever, John. 1979. *The Stories of John Cheever*. New York: Alfred Knopf.
DeLillo, Don. 1997. *Underworld: A Novel*. New York: Scribner.
Díaz, Junot. 2007. *The Brief Wondrous Life of Oscar Wao*. New York: Riverhead.
Dos Passos, John. (1930) 2000. *The 42nd Parallel*. Boston: Houghton Mifflin.
———. (1932) 2000. *1919*. Boston: Houghton Mifflin.
———. (1933) 2000. *The Big Money*. Boston: Houghton Mifflin.
Ellis, Bret Easton. 1991. *American Psycho*. New York: Vintage.
Erdrich, Louise. 1988. *Tracks*. New York: Harper Perennial.
Everett, Percival. 2009. *I Am Not Sidney Poitier*. Minneapolis: Graywolf Press.
Faulkner, William. (1942) 1990. *Go Down, Moses*. New York: Random House.
Gass, William H. 1995. *The Tunnel*. New York: Alfred A. Knopf.
Hemingway, Ernest. (1929) 1957. *A Farewell to Arms*. New York: Charles Scribner's Sons.
Hurston, Zora Neale. (1937) 2006. *Their Eyes Were Watching God*. New York: Harper Perennial Modern Classics.
James, Henry. (1898) 1999. *Turn of the Screw*. Norton Critical Edition. Edited by Deborah Esch and Jonathan Warren. New York: W. W. Norton.
Laclos, Pierre Choderlos de. (1782) 1961. *Les liaisons dangereuses*. London: Penguin Books.
McCarthy, Cormac. 1985. *Blood Meridian: Or the Evening Redness in the West*. New York: Random House.
———. *The Crossing*. 1994. New York: Random House.
Miller, Henry. (1934) 1961. *Tropic of Cancer*. New York: Grove Press.
Morrison, Toni. 1973. *Sula*. New York: Penguin.
———. *Beloved*. (1987) 2004. New York: Vintage.
———. *The Bluest Eye*. (1970) 2007. New York: Vintage.
———. *Song of Solomon*. (1977) 2004. New York: Vintage.
Nabokov, Vladimir. *Lolita*. (1955) 1997. New York: Vintage International.
Naylor, Gloria. *Mama Day*. (1988) 1993. New York: Vintage Contemporaries, 1993.
Palahniuk, Chuck. *Fight Club*. 1996. New York: W. W. Norton.
Richardson, Samuel. (1740) 2001. *Pamela; Or, Virtue Rewarded*. Edited by Thomas Keymer and Alice Wakely. Oxford: Oxford University Press.
Robinson, Marilynne. 2004. *Gilead*. New York: Farrar, Straus and Giroux.
Roth, Philip. (1969) 1994. *Portnoy's Complaint*. New York: Vintage Contemporaries.
Salinger, J. D. 1951. *The Catcher in the Rye*. New York: Little Brown.
Stein, Gertrude. (1909) 2006. *Three Lives* and *Q.E.D.* Edited by Marianne DeKoven. New York: W. W. Norton.
Toomer, Jean. (1923) 1975. *Cane*. New York: Liveright.
Vollman, William T. 2005. *Europe Central*. New York: Penguin.

Secondary Works

Abbott, H. Porter. 2002. *Cambridge Introduction to Narrative*. Cambridge: Cambridge University Press.

Abel, Marco. 2007. *Violent Affect: Literature, Cinema, and Critique after Representation*. Lincoln: University of Nebraska Press.

Alber, Jan. 2016. *Unnatural Narrative: Impossible Worlds in Fiction and Drama*. Lincoln: University of Nebraska Press.

Appel, Alfred, Jr., ed. 1991. *The Annotated Lolita: Revised and Updated*. New York: Vintage.

Apter, Emily. 2006. "On Oneworldedness: Or Paranoia as a World System." *American Literary History* 18, no. 2: 365–89.

Aristotle. 1984. *Rhetoric and Poetics*. Translated by W. Rhys Roberts and Ingram Bywater. New York: Modern Library.

Avishai, Bernard. 2012. *Promiscuous:* Portnoy's Complaint *and Our Doomed Pursuit of Happiness*. New Haven, Conn.: Yale University Press.

Bailey, Lisa M. Siefker. 2010. "Fraught with Fire: Race and Theology in Marilynne Robinson's *Gilead*." *Christianity and Literature* 59, no. 2: 265–80.

Baker, Carlos, ed. 1981. *Ernest Hemingway: Selected Letters 1917–1961*. New York: Charles Scribner's Sons.

Bakhtin, M. M. 1981. *The Dialogic Imagination: Four Essays*. Edited and translated by Michael Holquist. Austin: University of Texas Press.

Bal, Mieke. 1997. *Narratology: Introduction to the Theory of the Study of Narrative*. 2d ed. Toronto: University of Toronto Press.

———. 2006. "Over-writing as Un-writing: Descriptions, World-Making, and Novelistic Time." In *The Novel: Volume 2, Forms and Themes*, edited by Franco Moretti, 571–610. Princeton, N.J.: Princeton University Press.

Begley, Adam. 1993. "Don DeLillo, The Art of Fiction No. 135." *Paris Review* 128 (Fall). http://www.theparisreview.org/interviews/1887/the-art-of-fiction-no-135-don-delillo.

Bell, Bernard. 1989. *The Afro-American Novel and Its Tradition*. Amherst: University of Massachusetts Press.

Bell, Vereen M. 1988. *The Achievement of Cormac McCarthy*. Baton Rouge: Louisiana State University Press.

Berman, Jeffrey. 1985. *The Talking Cure: Literary Representations of Psychoanalysis*. New York: NYU Press.

———. 2007. "Revisiting Roth's Psychoanalysts." In *The Cambridge Companion to Philip Roth*, edited by Timothy Parrish, 94–110. Cambridge: Cambridge University Press.

Bernstein, Charles. 1992. "Professing Stein/Stein Professing." In *A Poetics*. Cambridge: Harvard University Press.

Bérubé, Michael. 2006. "Plot Summary: Motives and Narrative Mechanics in *Underworld* and *White Noise*." In *Approaches to Teaching DeLillo's* White Noise, edited by Tim Engles and John N. Duvall, 135–43. New York: MLA.

Black, Max. 1979. "More about Metaphor." In *Metaphor and Thought*, edited by Andrew Ortnoy. Cambridge University Press.

Blasing, Mutlu Konuk. 2006. *Lyric Poetry: The Pain and Pleasure of Words*. Princeton, N.J.: Princeton University Press.

Bloom, Harold. 2001. "Introduction." In Cormac McCarthy, *Blood Meridian*. New York: Modern Library.

Booth, Wayne C. [1961] 1983. *The Rhetoric of Fiction*. Chicago: University of Chicago Press.

Brauner, David. 2000. "Masturbation and Its Discontents: Or, Serious Relief: Freudian Comedy in *Portnoy's Complaint*." *Critical Review* 40: 75–90.

Bromwich, David. 1998. *Disowned by Memory: Wordsworth's Poetry of the 1790s*. Chicago: University of Chicago Press.

Brooke-Rose, Christine. 1981. *A Rhetoric of the Unreal: Studies in Narrative Structure, Especially of the Fantastic*. Cambridge: Cambridge University Press.

Brooks, Cleanth. 1947. *The Well Wrought Urn: Studies in the Structure of Poetry*. New York: Harcourt, Brace, and World.

Brooks, Peter. 1984. *Reading for the Plot: Design and Intention in Narrative*. New York: Knopf.

Campbell, Harry, and Ruel Foster. 1951. *William Faulkner: A Critical Appraisal*. Norman: University of Oklahoma Press.

Caserio, Robert L. 1979. *Plot, Story, and the Novel: From Dickens and Poe to the Modern Period*. Princeton, N.J.: Princeton University Press.

Chatman, Seymour. 1978. *Story and Discourse: Narrative Structure in Fiction and Film*. Ithaca, N.Y.: Cornell University Press.

Cheyette, Bryan. 2009. "Eliot and 'Race': Jews, Irish, and Blacks." In *A Companion to T. S. Eliot*, edited by David Chinitz, 335–49. Hoboken, N.J.: Wiley-Blackwell.

Chu, Seo-Young. 2011. *Do Metaphors Dream of Literal Sleep? A Science-Fictional Theory of Representation*. Cambridge, Mass.: Harvard University Press.

Clarke, Deborah. 2001. "'The porch couldn't talk for looking': Voice and Vision in *Their Eyes Were Watching God*." *African American Review* 35, no. 4: 599–613.

Cohn, Dorrit. 1978. *Transparent Minds: Narrative Modes for Presenting Consciousness in Fiction*. Princton, N.J.: Princeton University Press.

Cowart, David. 2002a. *Don DeLillo: The Physics of Language*. Athens: University of Georgia Press.

———. 2002b. "Shall These Bones Live?" In *Underwords: Perspectives on Don DeLillo's* Underworld, edited by Joseph Dewey, Steven G. Kellman, and Irving Malin, 50–67. Newark, Del.: University of Delaware Press.

Cox, James M. 1986. "Humor as Vision in Faulkner." In *Faulkner and Humor*, edited by Doreen Fowler and Ann J. Abadie, 1–20. Jackson: University Press of Mississippi.

Cross, Mary. 1993. *Henry James: The Contingencies of Style*. New York: St. Martin's Press, 1993.

Cross, Richard K. 1967. "The Humor of *The Hamlet*." *Twentieth Century Literature* 12, no. 4: 203–15.

Culler, Jonathan. 1981. *The Pursuit of Signs: Semiotics, Literature, Deconstruction*. Ithaca, N.Y.: Cornell University Press, 1981.

———. 2008. "Why Lyric?" *PMLA* 123, no. 1 (January): 201–6.

———. 2015. *Theory of the Lyric*. Cambridge, Mass.: Harvard University Press, 2015.

DeLillo, Don. 1997. "The Power of History." *New York Times Magazine*, September 7, 60–61.

De Man, Paul. 1986. *The Resistance to Theory*. Minneapolis: University of Minnesota Press.

Dimock, Wai Chee. 2006. "Genre as World System: Epic and Novel on Four Continents." *Narrative* 14, no. 1: 85–101.

Douglas, Christopher. 2011. "Christian Multiculturalism and Unlearned History in Marilynne Robinson's *Gilead*." *Novel: A Forum on Fiction* 44, no. 3: 333–53.

Dubrow, Heather. 2006. "The Interplay of Narrative and Lyric: Competition, Cooperation, and the Case of the Anticipatory Amalgam." *Narrative* 14, no. 3: 254–71.

———. 2008. *The Challenges of Orpheus: Lyric Poetry and Early Modern England*. Baltimore: Johns Hopkins University Press.

DuPlessis, Rachel Blau. 1996. "Manifests." *Diacritics* 26, nos. 3/4: 31–53.

Eagleton, Terry. 2013. *How to Read Literature*. New Haven, Conn.: Yale University Press.

Eaton, Mark. 2003. "Dis(re)emembered Bodies: Cormac McCarthy's Border Fiction." *Modern Fiction Studies* 49, no. 1: 155–80.

Edmunds, Susan. 2003. "The Race Question and the 'Question of Home': Revisiting the Lynching Plot in Jean Toomer's *Cane*." *American Literature* 75, no. 1: 141–68.

Eliot, T. S. (1921) 1975. "The Metaphysical Poets." In *Selected Prose*, edited by Frank Kermode, 59–67. Orlando: Harcourt.

Erskine, John. 1920a. "The Kinds of Poetry." In *The Kinds of Poetry & Other Essays*, 3–42. Indianapolis: Bobbs-Merrill.

———. 1920b. "The New Poetry." In *The Kinds of Poetry & Other Essays*, 99–142. Indianapolis: Bobbs-Merrill .

Falk, Eugene. 1971. *The Poetics of Roman Ingarden*. Chapel Hill: University of North Carolina Press.

Faulkner, William. 1977. *Selected Letters*. Edited by Joseph Blotner. New York: Random House.

Ferry, Anne. 1996. *The Title to the Poem*. Stanford, Calif.: Stanford University Press.

Fludernik, Monika. 1999. "Defining (In)sanity: The Narrator of *The Yellow Wallpaper* and the Question of Unreliability. In *Grenzüberschreitungen: Narratologie im Kontext/ Transcending Boundaries: Narratology in Context*, edited by Walter Grünzweig and Andreas Solbach, 75–95. Tübingen: Gunter Narr Verlag.

Forster, E. M. (1927) 2005. "Flat and Round Characters." In *Essentials of the Theory of Fiction*, edited by Michael J. Hoffman and Patrick D. Murphy, 35–43. Durham, N.C.: Duke University Press.

Fowler, Alasdair. 1982. *Kinds of Literature: An Introduction to the Theory of Genres and Modes*. Cambridge, Mass.: Harvard University Press.

Frank, Joseph. 2005. "Spatial Form in Modern Literature." In *Essentials of the Theory of Fiction*, edited by Michael J. Hoffman and Patrick D. Murphy, 61–74. Durham, N.C.: Duke University Press.

Freccero, Carla. 1997. "Historical Violence, Censorship, and the Serial Killer: The Case of *American Psycho*." *Diacritics* 27: 44–58.

Fredman, Stephen. 1983. *Poet's Prose: The Crisis in American Verse*. Cambridge: Cambridge University Press.

Freud, Sigmund. (1920) 1990. *Beyond the Pleasure Principle*. New York: W. W. Norton.

Friedman, Ellen G. 1989. "A Conversation with Kathy Acker." *Review of Contemporary Fiction* 9, no. 3: 12–22.

Friedman, Susan Stanford. 1989. "Lyric Subversions of Narrative in Women's Writing: Virginia Woolf and the Tyranny of Plot." In *Reading Narrative: Form, Ethics Ideology*, edited by James Phelan, 162–85. Columbus: Ohio State University Press.

———. 2005. "Spatial Poetics and Arundhati Roy's *The God of Small Things*." In *Companion to Narrative Theory*, edited by James Phelan and Peter J. Rabinowitz. Malden, Mass.: Blackwell.

Frye, Northrop. 1957. *Anatomy of Criticism: Four Essays*. Princeton, N.J.: Princeton University Press.

Fussell, Paul. 1979. *Poetic Meter and Poetic Form*. New York: McGraw-Hill.

Gates, Henry Louis, Jr. 1988. *The Signifying Monkey: A Theory of African-American Literary Criticism*. Oxford University Press.

Gayley, Charles Mills, and Benjamin Putnam Kurtz. 1920. *Lyric, Epic, and Allied Forms of Poetry*. Boston: Athenæum.

Genette, Gérard. 1983. *Narrative Discourse: An Essay in Method*. 1980. Translated by Jane E. Lewin. Ithaca, N.Y.: Cornell University Press.

Giles, James. R. 2006. *The Spaces of Violence*. Tuscaloosa: University of Alabama Press, 2006.

Gilman, Richard. 1997. "Dos Passos and the Many Lives of 'U.S.A.'" *New York Times*, March 16. www.nytimes.com/books/97/03/16/bookend/bookend.html.

Gingrich, Arnold. 1936. Editor's Note to "The Camera Eye." *Esquire* 51 (April): 112.

Godden, Richard. 2003. "Comparative Cows: Or, Reading 'The Hamlet' for Its Residues." *ELH* 70, no. 2: 597–623.

———. 2011. "Labor, Language, and Finance Capital." *PMLA* 126, no. 2: 412–21.

Goffman, Erving. 1981. *Forms of Talk*. Philadelphia: University of Pennsylvania Press.

Gooblar, David. 2011. *The Major Phases of Philip Roth*. New York: Continuum.

Haas, Robert Bartlett. 1971. "A Transatlantic Interview, 1946." In *A Primer for Gradual Understanding of Gertrude Stein*, edited by Robert Bartlett Haas, 15–35. Los Angeles: Black Sparrow.

Hanson, Ellis. 2003. "Screwing with Children in Henry James." *GLQ: A Journal of Gay and Lesbian Studies* 9, no. 3: 367–91.

Hawkins, Susan E. 2004. "All in the Family: Kathy Acker's *Blood and Guts in High School*." *Contemporary Literature* 45, no. 4: 637–58.

Hawthorn, Jeremy. 2014. *The Reader as Peeping Tom: Nonreciprocal Gazing in Narrative Fiction and Film*. Columbus: Ohio State University Press.

Heise, Thomas. 2011. "*American Psycho*: Neoliberal Fantasies and the Death of Downtown." *Arizona Quarterly* 67, no. 1: 135–60.

Hejinian, Lyn. 2000. *The Language of Inquiry*. Berkeley: University of California Press.

Hemingway, Ernest. (1932) 1960. *Death in the Afternoon*. New York: Scribner.

Henke, Suzette. 2008. "Oedipus Meets Sacher-Masoch: Kathy Acker's Pornographic (Anti)Ethical Aesthetic." *Contemporary Women's Writing* 2, no. 2: 91–110.

Hobbs, June Hadden. 2010. "Burial, Baptism, and Baseball: Typology and Memorialization in Marilynne Robinson's *Gilead*." *Christianity and Literature* 59, no. 2: 241–62.

Hoberek, Andrew. 2011. "Cormac McCarthy and the Aesthetics of Exhaustion." *American Literary History* 23, no. 2: 483–99.

Hollander, John. 2000. *Rhyme's Reason: A Guide to English Verse*. New Haven, Conn.: Yale University Press.

Howe, Elisabeth. 1996. *The Dramatic Monologue*. New York: Twayne.

Hrushovski, Benjamin. 1984. "Poetic Metaphor and Frame of Reference." *Poetics Today* 5, no. 1: 5–43.

Hughes, Sheila Hassell. 2000. "Tongue-Tied: Rhetoric and Relation in Louise Erdrich's *Tracks*." *MELUS* 25, nos. 3/4: 87–116.

Hume, Kathryn. 2007. "Diffused Satire in Contemporary American Fiction." *Modern Philology* 105, no. 2: 300–325.

———. 2011. *Aggressive Fictions: Reading the Contemporary American Novel*. Ithaca, N.Y.: Cornell University Press.

Hutcheon, Linda. 1989. *The Politics of Postmodernism*. London: Routledge.

Innes, Catherine L. 1972. "The Unity of Jean Toomer's *Cane*." *CLA Journal* 15, no. 3: 306–22.

Irr, Caren. 1998. *The Suburb of Dissent: Cultural Politics in the United States and Canada during the 1930s*. Durham, N.C.: Duke University Press.

Ivey, Adriane L. 2005. "Beyond Sacrifice: Gloria Naylor Rewrites the Passion." *MELUS* 30, no. 1: 85–108.

Jackson, Virginia. 2008. "Who Reads Poetry?" *PMLA* 123, no. 1: 181–87.

Jakobson, Roman. 1987. "Grammatical Parallelism and Its Russian Facet." In *Language in Literature*, edited by Krystyna Pomorska and Stephen Rudy, 145–79. Cambridge, Mass.: Harvard University Press.

James, Caryn. 1985. Review of *Blood Meridian*. *New York Times Book Review*, April 28. http://www.nytimes.com/1985/04/28/books/mccarthy-meridian.html.

James, Henry. 1914. *Notes on Novelists with Some Other Notes*. New York: Charles Scribner's Sons.

Jameson, Fredric. 1981. *The Political Unconscious: Narrative as a Socially Symbolic Act*. Ithaca, N.Y.: Cornell University Press.

———. 1991. *Postmodernism, or the Cultural Logic of Late Capitalism*. Durham, N.C.: Duke University Press.

Jeffreys, Mark. 1994. "Brevity and the Idea of Lyric." *Texas Studies in Literature and Language* 36, no. 2: 117–34.

Jennings, La Vinia Delois. 2008. *Toni Morrison and the Idea of Africa*. Cambridge: Cambridge University Press.

Johnson, Barbara. 1993. "'Aesthetic' and 'Rapport' in Toni Morrison's *Sula*." *Textual Practice* 7, no. 2: 165–72.

Johnson, Samuel. 1971. *Lives of the Poets: A Selection*. Edited by J. P. Hardy. Oxford: Clarendon Press.

Johnson, W. R. 1982. *The Idea of Lyric: Lyric Modes in Ancient and Modern Poetry*. Berkeley: University of California Press.

Jones, Alexander E. 1959. "Point of View in *The Turn of the Screw*." *PMLA* 74, no. 1: 112–22.

Julius, Anthony. 1995. *T. S. Eliot, Anti-Semitism, and Literary Form*. Cambridge: Cambridge University Press.

Kacandes, Irene. 1994. "Narrative Apostrophe: Reading, Rhetoric, Resistance in Michel Butor's 'La modification' and Julio Cortazar's 'Graffiti.'" *Style* 28, no. 3: 329–49.

Karolides, Nicholas J., Margaret Bald, and Dawn B. Sova. 1999. *100 Banned Books: Censorship Histories of World Literature*. New York: Checkmark Books.

Kavadlo, Jesse. 2005. "The Fiction of Self-Destruction: Chuck Palahniuk, Closet Moralist." *Stirrings Stirrings Still: The International Journal of Existential Literature* 2, no. 2: 3–24.

Keen, Suzanne. 2010. *Empathy and the Novel*. Oxford: Oxford University Press.

Kellman, Steven G. 2002. "Don DeLillo's Logogenetic *Underworld*." In *Underwords: Perspectives on Don DeLillo's* Underworld, edited by Joseph Dewey, Steven G. Kellman, and Irving Malin, 68–78. Newark, Del.: University of Delaware Press.

Kennett, Paul. 2005. "*Fight Club* and the Dangers of Oedipal Obsession." *Stirrings Still: The International Journal of Existential Literature* 2, no. 2: 57.

Kittay, Eva Feder. 1987. *Metaphor: Its Cognitive Force and Linguistic Structure*. Oxford: Clarendon Press.

Kleinschmidt, Hans J. 1967. "The Angry Act: The Role of Aggression in Creativity." *American Imago* 24, no. 1: 98–128.

Knight, Peter. 1999. "Everything Is Connected: *Underworld*'s Secret History of Paranoia." *Modern Fiction Studies* 45, no. 3: 811–36.

Kooijman, Jaap, and Tarja Laine. 2003. "American Psycho: A Double Portrait of Serial Yuppie Patrick Bateman." *Post Script* 22, no. 3: 46–56.

Kurnick, David. 2005. "Empty Houses: Thackeray's Theater of Interiority." *Victorian Studies* 48, no. 2: 257–67.

La Berge, Leigh Claire. 2010. "The Men Who Make the Killings: American Psycho, Financial Masculinity, and 1980s Financial Print Culture." *Studies in American Fiction* 37, no. 2: 273–97.

Lakoff, George, and Mark Johnson. 1980. *Metaphors We Live By*. Chicago: University of Chicago Press.

Lakoff, George, and Mark Turner. 1989. *More Than Cool Reason*. Chicago: University of Chicago Press.

Lamothe, Daphne. 2005. "Gloria Naylor's *Mama Day*: Bridging Roots and Routes." *African American Review* 39, nos. 1/2: 155–69.

Langbaum, Robert. 1957. *The Poetry of Experience: The Dramatic Monologue in Modern Literary Tradition*. New York: W.W. Norton.

Latz, Andrew Brower. 2011. "Creation in the Fiction of Marilynne Robinson." *Literature & Theology: An International Journal of Religion, Theory, and Culture* 25, no. 3: 283–96.

Leise, Christopher. 2009. "'That Little Incandescence': Reading the Fragmentary and John Calvin in Marilynne Robinson's *Gilead*." *Studies in the Novel* 41, no. 3: 348–67.

Levine, Caroline. 2006. "Strategic Formalism: Towards a New Method in Cultural Studies." *Victorian Studies* 48: 625–57.

Levinson, Marjorie. 1986. *Wordsworth's Great Period Poems: Four Essays*. Cambridge: Cambridge University Press.

Locke, John L. 2010. *Eavesdropping: An Intimate History*. Oxford: Oxford University Press.

Lukács, György. (1938) 2001. "Realism in the Balance." In *The Norton Anthology of Theory and Criticism*, edited by Vincent B. Leitch, 1033–58. New York: W. W. Norton.

———. 1971. *The Theory of the Novel: A Historico-Philosophical Essay on the Forms of Great Epic Literature*. Translated by Anna Bostock. Cambridge, Mass.: MIT Press.

Margolin, Uri. 1996. "The Doer and the Deed: Action as a Basis for Characterization in Narrative." *Poetics Today* 7, no. 2: 205–25.

Markovits, Stefanie. 2012. "The Impact of Lyric, Drama, and Verse Narrative on the Novel Form." In *The Cambridge History of the English Novel*, edited by Robert Caserio and Clement Hawes, 549–64. Cambridge: Cambridge University Press.

Martin, Jay. 1977. "'The King of Smut': Henry Miller's Tragical History." *Antioch Review* 35, no. 4: 342–67.

Mayes, Frances. 2001. *The Discovery of Poetry: A Field Guide to Reading and Writing Poems*. Orlando: Harcourt.

McGurl, Mark. 2009. *The Program Era: Postwar Fiction and the Rise of Creative Writing*. Cambridge, Mass.: Harvard University Press.

McHale, Brian. 1987. *Postmodernist Fiction*. London: Methuen.

———. 2001. "Weak Narrativity: The Case of Avant-Garde Narrative Poetry." *Narrative* 9, no. 2: 161–67.

———. 2009. "Beginning to Think about Narrative in Poetry." *Narrative* 17, no. 1: 11–27.

Mill, John Stuart. (1833) 1996. *Autobiography and Literary Essays*. Edited by John M. Robson and Jack Stillinger. Oxford: Routledge.

Miller, J. Hillis. 1982. *Fiction and Repetition: Seven English Novels*. Cambridge, Mass.: Harvard University Press.

Miller, Shawn E. 2004. "'Some Other Way to Try': From Defiance to Creative Submission in 'Their Eyes Were Watching God.'" *Southern Literary Journal* 37, no. 1: 74–95.

Monk, Nick. 2002. "Modernity, Flight, and Crisis in the Border Trilogy and *Blood Meridian*." In *Sacred Violence Volume 2: Cormac McCarthy's Western Novels*, edited by Wade Hall and Rick Wallach, 83–104. El Paso: Texas Western Press.

Morgan, Monique R. 2009. *Narrative Means, Lyric Ends: Temporality in the Nineteenth-Century British Long Poem*. Columbus: Ohio State University Press.

Morrison, Toni. 1992. *Playing in the Dark: Whiteness and the Literary Imagination*. Cambridge, Mass.: Harvard University Press.

Müller, Wolfgang G. 2005. "The Lyric Insertion in Fiction and Drama: Theory and Practice." In *Theory into Poetry: New Approaches to the Lyric*, edited by Eva Müller-Zettelman and Margarete Rubik, 173–88. Amsterdam: Rodopi.

Muth, Kate R. 2011. "Postmodern Fiction as Poststructuralist Theory: Kathy Acker's *Blood and Guts in High School*." *Narrative* 19, no. 1: 86–110.

Myers, B. R. 2001. "A Reader's Manifesto: The Growing Pretentiousness of American Literary Prose." *Atlantic*, July/Aug .

Nafisi, Azar. 2003. *Reading Lolita in Tehran: A Memoir in Books*. New York: Random House.

Nealon, Christopher. 2004. "Camp Messianism, or, the Hopes of Poetry in Late-Late Capitalism." *American Literature* 76, no. 3: 579–602.

———. 2007. "The Poetic Case." *Critical Inquiry* 33, no. 4: 865–86.

Nel, Philip. 2008. "Delillo and Modernism." In *Cambridge Companion to Don DeLillo*, edited by John Duvall, 13–26. Cambridge University Press.

Nelson, Deborah. 2002. *Pursuing Privacy in Cold War America*. New York: Columbia University Press.

Nissen, Axel. 1999. "Form Matters: Toni Morrison's *Sula* and the Ethics of Narrative." *Contemporary Literature* 40, no. 2: 263–85.

Novak, Phillip. 1999. "Circles and Circles of Sorrow: In the Wake of Morrison's *Sula*." *PMLA* 114, no. 2: 184–93.

Nünning, Ansgar. 2008. "Reconceptualizing the Theory, History and Generic Scope of Unreliable Narration: Towards a Synthesis of Cognitive and Rhetorical Approaches." In *Narrative Unreliability in the Twentieth-Century Novel*, edited by Elke D'hoker and Gunther Martens, 29–76. Berlin: Walter de Gruyter.

Nussbaum, Martha. 1990. *Love's Knowledge: Essays on Philosophy and Literature*. New York: Oxford University Press.

O'Brien, Maureen. 1991. "American Gothic: The 'American Psycho' Controversy." *Entertainment Weekly*, March 8. http://www.ew.com/ew/article/0,,313573,00.html.

O'Donnell, Patrick. 2008. "Underworld." In *Cambridge Companion to Don DeLillo*, edited by John Duvall, 108–22. Cambridge University Press.

Okonkwo, Christopher. 2004. "A Critical Divination: Reading *Sula* as Ogbanje-Abiku." *African American Review* 38, no. 4: 651–68.

Olson, Charles. 1969. *Letters for Origin, 1950–1956*. Edited by Albert Glover. London: Cape Golliard Press.

———. 1997. *Collected Prose*. Edited by Donald Allen and Benjamin Friedlander. Berkeley: University of California Press.

Olson, Elder. 1964. *American Lyric Poems: From Colonial Times to the Present*. New York: Meredith.

Olson, Greta. 2003. "Reconsidering Unreliability." *Narrative* 11, no. 1: 93–109.

Osteen, Mark. 2000. *American Magic and Dread: Don DeLillo's Dialogue with Culture*. Philadelphia: University of Pennsylvania Press.

Ostrowski, Carl. 2002. "Conspiratorial Jesuits in the Postmodern Novel: *Mason and Dixon* and *Underworld*." In *Underwords: Perspectives on Don DeLillo's* Underworld, edited by Joseph Dewey, Steven G. Kellman, and Irving Malin, 93–102. Newark, Del.: University of Delaware Press.

Owens-Murphy, Katie. 2011. "The Frontier Ethic behind Cormac McCarthy's Southern Fiction." *Arizona Quarterly* 67, no. 2: 155–78.

———. 2013. Trope Theory, *Cane*, and the Metaphysical Case for Genre." *Genre* 46, no. 3: 239–63.

Perry, Bliss. 1902. *A Study of Prose Fiction*. Boston: Houghton Mifflin.

———. 1920. *A Study of Poetry*. Boston: Houghton Mifflin.

Perry, Menahem, and Meir Sternberg. 1986. "The King through Ironic Eyes: Biblical Narrative and the Literary Reading Process." *Poetics Today* 7, no. 2: 275–322.

Peterson, Nancy J. 1994. "History, Postmodernism, and Louise Erdrich's *Tracks*." *PMLA* 109, no. 5: 982–94.

Petit, Susan. 2010. "Finding Flannery O'Connor's 'Good Man' in Marilynne Robinson's *Gilead* and *Home*." *Christianity and Literature* 59, no. 2: 301–18.

Phelan, James. 1989. *Reading People, Reading Plots: Character, Progression, and the Interpretation of Narrative.* Chicago: University of Chicago Press.

———. 1990. "Distance, Voice, and Temporal Perspective in Frederic Henry's Narration: Successes, Problems, and Paradox." In *New Essays on* A Farewell to Arms, edited by Scott Donaldson, 53–74. Cambridge: Cambridge University Press.

———. 1994. "*Self-Help* for Narratee and Narrative Audience: How 'I'—and 'You'—Read 'How.'" *Style* 28, no. 3: 350–65.

———. 1996. *Narrative as Rhetoric: Technique, Audiences, Ethics, Ideology.* Columbus: Ohio State University Press.

———. 2004. *Living to Tell about It: A Rhetoric and Ethics of Character.* Ithaca, N.Y.: Cornell University Press.

______. 2006. Preface to the Second Edition. In *The Nature of Narrative*, by Robert Scholes, James Phelan, and Robert Kellogg, xiii–xv. Oxford: Oxford University Press.

———. 2007a. "Estranging Unreliability, Bonding Unreliability, and the Ethics of 'Lolita.'" *Narrative* 15, no. 2: 222–38.

———. 2007b. *Experiencing Fiction: Judgments, Progressions, and the Rhetorical Theory of Narrative.* Columbus: Ohio State University Press.

Phelan, James, and Mary Patricia Martin. 1999. "The Lessons of 'Weymouth': Homodiegesis, Unreliability, Ethics, and *The Remains of the Day*." *Narratologies: New Perspectives on Narrative Analysis*, edited by David Herman. Columbus: Ohio State University Press.

Phillips, Dana. 1996. "History and the Ugly Facts of Cormac McCarthy's *Blood Meridian*." *American Literature* 68, no. 2: 433–60.

Pinsky, Robert. 1998. *The Sounds of Poetry: A Brief Guide.* New York: Farrar, Straus and Giroux.

Plato. *Complete Works.* 1997. Edited by John M. Cooper. Indianapolis: Hackett.

Pound, Ezra. 2005. "The Serious Artist." In *Early Writings: Poems and Prose*, edited by Ira B. Nadel, 41–57. New York: Penguin, 2005.

Preminger, Alex, and T. V. F. Brogan. 1993. *The New Princeton Encyclopedia of Poetry and Poetics.* Princeton, N.J.: Princeton University Press.

Prescott, Orville. 1965. "Still Another Disciple of William Faulkner," *New York Times*, May 12.

Prince, Gerald. (1973) 1980. "Introduction to the Study of the Narratee." In *Reader-Response Criticism: From Formalism to Post-Structuralism*, edited by Jane P. Tompkins, 7–25. Baltimore: Johns Hopkins University Press.

———. 1982. *Narratology: The Form and Function of Narrative.* Berlin: Mouton.

———. 1999. "Revisiting Narrativity." In *Grenzüberschreitungen: Narratologie im Kontext / Transcending Boundaries: Narratology in Context*, edited by W. Grünzweig & A. Solbach, 43–51. Tübingen: Gunter Narr.

———. 2003. *Dictionary of Narratology.* Rev. ed. Lincoln: University of Nebraska Press, 2003.

Rabinowitz, Peter J. 1977. "Truth in Fiction: A Reexamination of Audiences." *Critical Inquiry* 4, no. 1 (Autumn): 121–41.

———. 1998. *Before Reading: Narrative Conventions and the Politics of Interpretation.* Columbus: Ohio State University Press.

———. 2004. "Lolita: Solipsized or Sodomized? or, Against Abstraction—in General." In *A Companion to Rhetoric and Rhetorical Criticism*, edited by Walter Jost and Wendy Olmsted, 325–39. Oxford: Blackwell.

Rader, Ralph W. 1976. "The Dramatic Monologue and Related Lyric Forms." *Critical Inquiry* 3, no. 1: 131–51.

Reilly, John M. 1970. "The Search for Black Redemption: Jean Toomer's *Cane*." *Studies in the Novel* 2, no. 3: 312–24.

Retallack, Joan. 2003. *The Poethetical Wager*. Berkeley: University of California Press.

Reynolds, Michael S. 1976. *Hemingway's First War: The Making of* A Farewell to Arms. Princton, N.J.: Princeton University Press.

Richardson, Brian. 1997. *Unlikely Stories: Causality and the Nature of Modern Narrative.* Newark, Del.: University of Delaware Press.

———. 2011. Nabokov's Experiments and the Nature of Fictionality." *Storyworlds: A Journal of Narrative Studies* 3: 73–92.

Richter, David. 2001. "Late Reconfiguration, or Who is Keyser Söze? and Who Cares?" Paper presented at the International Society for the Study of Narrative Conference, Rice University, Houston, Texas. http://people.qc.cuny.edu/Faculty/david.Richter/Documents/Late.html.

Ricoeur, Paul. 1977. *The Rule of Metaphor: Multi-Disciplinary Studies of the Creation of Meaning in Language.* Translated by Robert Czerny. Toronto: University of Toronto Press.

Riggan, William F. 1981. *Picaros, Madmen, Naifs, and Clowns: The Unreliable First-Person Narrator.* Norman: University of Oklahoma Press.

Rimmon, Shlomith. 1977. *The Concept of Ambiguity—the Example of James.* Chicago: University of Chicago Press.

Robbins, Bruce. 1986. *The Servant's Hand: English Fiction from Below*. New York: Columbia University Press.

Rogers, William Elford. 1983. *The Three Genres and the Interpretation of Lyric.* Princeton, N.J.: Princeton University Press.

Roof, Judith. 1996. *Come as You Are: Sexuality and Narrative*. New York: Columbia University Press.

Ruddick, Lisa. 1990. *Reading Gertrude Stein: Body, Text, Gnosis*. Ithaca, N.Y.: Cornell University Press.

Sanders, David. 1969. "John Dos Passos, The Art of Fiction No. 44." *Paris Review*. http://www.theparisreview.org/interviews/4202/the-art-of-fiction-no-44-john-dos-passos.

Samuels, Wilfred D., and Clenora Hudson-Weems. 1990. *Toni Morrison*. Boston: Twayne.

Saxton, Martha. 1992. "Philip Roth Talks about His Own Literary Work." In *Conversations with Philip Roth*, edited by George J. Searles. Jackson: University Press of Mississippi.

Scholes, Robert, James Phelan, and Robert Kellogg. 2006. *The Nature of Narrative*. Oxford: Oxford University Press.

Schreier, Benjamin. 2013. "Why It's Impossible to Teach *Portnoy's Complaint*." *Studies in Jewish American Literature* 32, no. 2: 205–7.

Serpell, C. Namwali. 2010. "Repetition and the Ethics of Suspended Reading in *American Psycho*." *Critique: Studies in Contemporary Fiction* 51, no. 1: 47–73.

Shaviro, Steven. 1999. "'The Very Life of the Darkness': A Reading of *Blood Meridian*." *Perspectives on Cormac McCarthy*, edited by Edwin T. Arnold and Diane Luce, 145–58. Jackson: University Press of Mississippi.

Siskin, Clifford. 1996. "The Rise of Novelism." In *Cultural Institutions of the Novel*, edited by Deidre Lynch and William Beatty Warner, 423–40. Durham, N.C.: Duke University Press.

Sivils, Matthew Wynn. 2006. "Reading Trees in Southern Literature." *Southern Quarterly* 44, no. 1: 88–102.

Sommer, Doris. 1999. *Proceed with Caution, when Engaged by Minority Writing in the Americas*. Cambridge, Mass.: Harvard University Press.

Stein, Gertrude. 1998. *Writings 1932–1946*. Edited by Catharine R. Stimpson and Harriet Chessman. New York: Library of America.

Stein, Jean. (1956) 2007. "William Faulkner, the Art of Fiction No. 12." In *The Paris Review Interviews, vol. II*, edited by Philip Gourevitch, 34–57. New York: Picador.

Sternlieb, Lisa. 2008. "Vivian Darkbloom: Floral Border or Moral Order?" In *Approaches to Teaching Nabokov's* Lolita, edited by Zoran Kuzmanovich and Galya Diment, 158–62. New York: Modern Language Association.

Stewart, Garrett. 1996. *Dear Reader: The Conscripted Audience in Nineteenth-Century British Fiction*. Baltimore: Johns Hopkins University Press.

Storey, Mark. 2005. "'And as Things Fell Apart': The Crisis of Postmodern Masculinity in Bret Easton Ellis's *American Psycho* and Dennis Cooper's *Frisk*." *Critique* 47, no. 1: 57–72.

Strauss, Walter A. 2007. "The Merchant of Venom? T. S. Eliot and Anti-Semitism." *South Central Review* 14, nos. 3/4: 31–44.

Sturgess, Philip J. M. 1992. *Narrativity: Theory and Practice*. Oxford: Clarendon Press.

Syrkin, Marie (with Philip Roth). 1974. "Philip Roth and the Jews: An Exchange." *New York Review of Books*, November 14. http://www.nybooks.com/articles/1974/11/14/philip-roth-and-the-jews-an-exchange/.

Tekiner, Christina. 1979. "Time in *Lolita*." *Modern Fiction Studies* 25: 463–69.

Thompson, Carlyle V. 2003. "'Circles and Circles of Sorrow': Decapitation in Toni Morrison's *Sula*." *CLA Journal* 47, no. 2: 137–74.

Thorel-Cailleteau, Sylvie. 2006. "The Poetry of Mediocrity." In *The Novel, Volume 2: Forms and Themes*, edited by Franco Moretti, 64–94. Princeton, N.J.: Princeton University Press.

Todorov, Tzvetan. 1975. *The Fantastic: A Structural Approach to a Literary Genre*. Translated by Richard Howard. Ithaca, N.Y.: Cornell University Press.

Toker, Leona. 1989. *Nabokov: The Mystery of Literary Structures*. Ithaca, N.Y.: Cornell University Press.

Tomashevsky, Boris. 1965. "Thematics." In *Russian Formalist Criticism: Four Essays*, translated by Lee T. Lemon and Marion J. Reis, 61–98. Lincoln: University of Nebraska Press.

Trilling, Lionel. 1958. "The Last Lover: Vladimir Nabokov's 'Lolita.'" *Encounter*: 9–19.

Tucker, Herbert F. 2006. "Tactical Formalism: A Response to Caroline Levine." *Victorian Studies* 49, no. 1: 85–93.

Turner, Frederick. 2012. *Renegade: Henry Miller and the Making of* Tropic of Cancer. New Haven, Conn.: Yale University Press.

Vander Weele, Michael. 2010. "Marilynne Robinson's *Gilead* and the Difficult Gift of Human Exchange." *Christianity and Literature* 59, no. 2: 217–39.

Vendler, Helen. 2002. *Poems, Poets, Poetry: An Introduction and Anthology*. 2d ed. Boston: Bedford/St. Martin's.

Wagner-Martin, Linda. 1995. "Toomer's *Cane* as Narrative Sequence." In *Modern American Short Story Sequences*, edited by J. Gerald Kennedy, 19–34. Cambridge: Cambridge University Press.

Walker, Jeffrey. 1989. "Aristotle's Lyric: Re-imagining the Rhetoric of Epideictic Song." *College English* 51, no. 1: 5–28.

Wallace, David Foster. 1993. "E Unibus Pluram: Television and U.S. Fiction." *Review of Contemporary Fiction* 13, no. 2: 151–94.

Warhol, Robyn. 1989. *Gendered Interventions*. New Brunswick, N.J.: Rutgers University Press.

Washington, Mary Helen. 1979. "Zora Neale Hurston: A Woman Half in Shadow." In *I Love Myself when I am Laughing . . . and Then Again when I am Looking Mean and Impressive: A Zora Neale Hurston Reader*, edited by Alice Walker, 7–25. New York: Feminist Press.

Waters, William. 2003. *Poetry's Touch: On Lyric Address*. Ithaca, N.Y.: Cornell University Press.

Watkins, Patricia. 1972. "Is There a Unifying Theme in *Cane*?" *CLA Journal* 15: 303–5.

Weathers, Glenda B. 2005. "Biblical Trees, Biblical Deliverance: Literary Landscapes of Zora Neale Hurston." *African American Review* 39, nos. 1/2: 201–12.

Weinbrot, Howard D. 2005. *Menippean Satire Reconsidered: From Antiquity to the Eighteenth Century*. Baltimore: Johns Hopkins University Press.

Westerhoven, James N. 1976. "Autobiographical Elements in the Camera Eye." *American Literature* 48, no. 3: 340–64.

Whalan, Mark, ed. 2006. *The Letters of Jean Toomer 1919–1924*. Knoxville: University of Tennessee Press.

Williams, Rowan. 2011. "Native Speakers: Identity, Grace, and Homecoming." *Christianity and Literature* 61, no. 1: 7–18.

Williams, William Carlos. 1984. *Selected Letters*. Edited by John Thirlwall. New York: New Directions.

Williamson, Joel. 1993. *William Faulkner and Southern History*. New York: Oxford University Press.

Wilson, Edmund. (1938) 2007. "The Ambiguity of Henry James." In *Literary Essays and Reviews of the 1930s & 40s*, 90–133. New York: Library of America.

Winchell, Mark Royden. 1990. "Inner Dark; or, The Place of Cormac McCarthy." *Southern Review* 26, no. 2: 293–309.

Winnett, Susan. 1990. "Coming Unstrung: Women, Men, Narrative, and Principles of Pleasure." *PMLA* 103, no. 3: 505–18.

Wood, James. 2005. "Red Planet: The Sanguinary Sublime of Cormac McCarthy." *New Yorker*, July 25. http://www.newyorker.com/archive/2005/07/25/050725crbo_books.

Woodward, Richard B. 1992. "Cormac McCarthy's Venomous Fiction." *New York Times*, April 19. http://www.nytimes.com/books/98/05/17/specials/mccarthy-venom.html.

Wordsworth, William. [1805] 2007. "Preface." In *Lyrical Ballads*, edited by Michael Mason. 62. Harlow, England: Pearson.

Wu, Yung-Hsing. 2003. "Doing Things with Ethics: *Beloved*, *Sula*, and the Reading of Judgment." *Modern Fiction Studies* 49, no. 4: 780–805.

Yardley, Jonathan. 1974. "Alone, Alone, All, All Alone . . ." *Washington Post Book World* 13: 1.

Young, Elizabeth. 1992. "The Beast in the Jungle, the Figure in the Carpet." In *Shopping in Space: Essays on America's Blank Generation Fiction*, edited by Elizabeth Young and Graham Caveney, 85–122. London: Serpent's Tail.

Young, Philip. 1966. *Ernest Hemingway: A Reconsideration*. University Park: Penn State University Press.

Zunshine, Lisa. 2006. *Why We Read Fiction: Theory of Mind and the Novel.* Columbus: Ohio State University Press.

INDEX